Bound to Sin

This book tests the explanatory and descriptive power of the doctrine of sin in relation to two concrete situations: sexual abuse of children and the holocaust. Taking seriously the explanatory power of secular discourses for analysing and regulating therapeutic action in relation to such situations, the book asks whether the theological language of sin can offer further illumination by speaking of God and the world together. Through its discussion of abuse and the holocaust, an engagement with Augustine, original sin and feminism, a fresh and sometimes surprising perspective is offered, both on the theology of sin and on the pathologies under consideration. The understanding of sin that emerges is centred on joyful worship of the trinitarian God. This essay is more systematic and more theological than most practical, pastoral or applied theology and more practical and concrete than most systematic or constructive theology. It is a genuinely concrete, systematic theology.

ALISTAIR MCFADYEN is Senior Lecturer in Theology at the University of Leeds. Author of *The Call to Personhood* (Cambridge, 1990) and a number of journal articles, he is a former Samaritan counsellor and member of the Leeds Ritual Abuse Study Group. He is currently a member of the Church of England's Doctrine Commission, and Secretary to the Society for the Study of Theology.

Cambridge Studies in Christian Doctrine

Edited by
Professor COLIN GUNTON, *King's College London*
Professor DANIEL W. HARDY, *University of Cambridge*

Cambridge Studies in Christian Doctrine is an important series
which aims to engage critically with the traditional doctrines of
Christianity, and at the same time to locate and make sense of
them within a secular context. Without losing sight of the
authority of scripture and the traditions of the Church, the books
in this series will subject pertinent dogmas and credal statements
to careful scrutiny, analysing them in light of the insights of both
church and society, and will thereby practise theology in the
fullest sense of the word.

Titles published in the series

1. Self and Salvation: Being Transformed
   DAVID F. FORD

2. Realist Christian Theology in a Postmodern Age
   SUE PATTERSON

3. Trinity and Truth
   BRUCE D. MARSHALL

4. Theology, Music and Time
   JEREMY S. BEGBIE

5. The Bible, Theology, and Faith: A Study of Abraham and Jesus
   R. W. L. MOBERLY

6. Bound to Sin: Abuse, Holocaust and the Christian Doctrine
   of Sin
   ALISTAIR MCFADYEN

Forthcoming titles in the series

Church, World and the Christian Life: Practical–Prophetic
Ecclesiology
NICHOLAS M. HEALY

Church, Narrativity and Transcendence
ROBERT JENSON

A Political Theology of Nature
PETER SCOTT

Remythologizing Theology: Divine Action and Authorship
KEVIN J. VANHOOZER

Bound to Sin

Abuse, Holocaust and the Christian Doctrine of Sin

ALISTAIR McFADYEN

University of Leeds

CAMBRIDGE
UNIVERSITY PRESS

PUBLISHED BY THE PRESS SYNDICATE OF THE UNIVERSITY OF CAMBRIDGE
The Pitt Building, Trumpington Street, Cambridge, United Kingdom

CAMBRIDGE UNIVERSITY PRESS
The Edinburgh Building, Cambridge CB2 2RU, UK   www.cup.cam.ac.uk
40 West 20th Street, New York, NY 10011–4211, USA   www.cup.org
10 Stamford Road, Oakleigh, Melbourne 3166, Australia
Ruiz de Alarcón 13, 28014 Madrid, Spain

First published 2000

Printed in the United Kingdom at the University Press, Cambridge

Typeface TEFFLexicon 9/13 pt   *System* QuarkXPress® [SE]

A catalogue record for this book is available from the British Library

Library of Congress Cataloguing in Publication data
McFadyen, Alistair I.
    Bound to sin: abuse, Holocaust, and the Christian doctrine of sin / Alistair McFadyen.
        p.   cm. – (Cambridge studies in Christian doctrine; 6)
    Includes bibliographical references and index.
    ISBN 0-521-43286-3 – ISBN 0-521-43868-3 (pbk.)
        1. Sin.   2. Child sexual abuse – Religious aspects – Church of England.   3. Holocaust
    (Christian theology)   I. Title.   II. Series.
    BT715.M376 2000
    241'.3–dc21   99-058733

ISBN 0 521 43286 3 hardback
ISBN 0 521 43868 3 paperback

In joy:

To Catherine, with whom I have found so much;
And to George and Tom, Helen and Catriona, who deserve and give us so much;
And to Mike, a different Helen, Kim and Steve, who offered so much;
And to Peter, David and Dan, who helped me weave together so much;
And to Haddon, who has taught me so much about sin (who first suggested I write this book, and who might enjoy the ambiguities of having a book on sin dedicated to him).

Contents

Acknowledgments

This book has been almost seven years in preparation, the course of which has run far from smooth and has brought me into closer proximity to some of its general themes than I could ever have anticipated or would ever have wished. I have therefore accumulated, in this time, a deep vein of gratitude to many for much that goes far beyond the normal range of professional or personal courtesies. It is a measure of the spirit in which so much was given me, that I have accumulated gratitude, not debts. Appropriate to the way in which the argument of this book develops, the theme of these acknowledgments is very much, therefore, joyous acknowledgment of gracious generosity in overwhelming abundance.

I am grateful to the Department of Theology and Religious Studies at the University of Leeds for granting me two short periods of leave to allow me to complete a good deal of the research and writing of this book. But more than that, I am grateful to members of the Department for their unfailing support and understanding of an at times less than fully functional colleague. The friendship and community of the Department has sustained me, stimulating, disciplining and otherwise shaping my thinking, probably more than colleagues realise and often in surprising – if not downright off-the-wall – ways. It has never ceased to amaze me how widespread and constant are the sources of illumination from others' thinking in a Department that spans the spectrum of religious traditions and approaches to religious phenomena. I should like especially to record my thanks to Kim Knott, and also to Linda Hogan, Jim Ginther, Adrian Hastings, Alistair Mason, Phil Mellor, Hugh Pyper, Jacqui Stewart and Kevin Ward for all that they have given me in working towards completion of this text, either directly or indirectly. I am especially fortunate in having Haddon Willmer as a (now allegedly retired) colleague, whose wisdom in

relation to the topic of this book (hard-won through many years of thinking about forgiveness in its personal and political dimensions) I have
eagerly and constantly tapped. I am not least grateful for the time and
care he took in reading and commenting on early drafts of virtually the
whole of the book as they were being written.

The two sabbaticals granted by the Department, I spent at the Center
of Theological Inquiry in Princeton. I should like to record my thanks to
them for their generous, practical support for two immensely productive
and fruitful periods. But mostly, I wish to thank them for the vibrant aca-
demic community which their hospitality institutionalised. I was especially fortunate in that the then director, Dan Hardy, was editor of this
series and that David Ford, already a good friend writing the companion
book on salvation, was resident throughout my first stay. That afforded
the opportunity of many two- and three-way conversations through
which the early thinking and writing developed – indeed, flourished.
Dan has read and commented on the whole text; David, virtually the
whole of it. The result is a book, not only greatly enriched by their
contributions, but bearing very close affinities with the line developed in
David's book on salvation.[1] In it, he constructs an understanding of salvation related to joy in God which, in many respects, has prefigured and
shaped my account of sin.

Colin Gunton, co-editor of this Series, also read an initial draft. Whilst
nobody else has been subjected to the whole, the final text has benefited
from comments made on various parts by Adrian Hastings, Peter Scott,
Tony Thiselton, Chris Hobbs, Helga Hanks and Jane Wynne; from comments made on presentations given in various seminars at the Center of
Theological Inquiry, in the Department, at the Society for the Study of
Theology, at Nottingham Theological Society, and for Worcester Diocese;
and in discussions at meetings of the Archbishop's Urban Theology
Group and the Church of England's Doctrine Commission. In relation to
these latter, discursive contexts, and in addition to those I have already
thanked above, I am particularly grateful for the comments and support
of Peter Selby, Michael Northcott, Peter Sedgwick, Jeremy Begbie, Steven
Sykes and Alan Torrance.

An especially sensitive word of gratitude is reserved for those who,
over the last sixteen years, in various contexts and for quite other purposes, have shared with me their stories of childhood sexual abuse. I

---

1. *Self and Salvation: Being Transformed* (Cambridge University Press, 1999).

hope, more than anything, that they might feel that this work has not done them a disservice and that they may recognise the profound ways in which their stories have affected me theologically, as well as personally.

Given the length of time I have taken to deliver this text, a special word in thanks for the patience of publishers is due, and duly given to Alex Wright (now with SCM), who commissioned the book, and Kevin Taylor, who has seen it through at the end.

Finally, I want to convey a very inadequate word of thanks to the many friends who have offered support in practical and other ways through the period of writing this book: in particular, Steve Jarratt, Mike and Helen Sutcliffe; Phil Spence and Dave Miles; and to members of my family: Patsy, Angus, Jane, Jim and Jenny McFadyen and Catherine Falconer.

Part I

Drawing into Conversation

1

The loss of God: pragmatic atheism and the language of sin

This book on sin – why bother?

'Why?!'

That cry – simultaneously one of exasperated disbelief, plain bemusement and gently derisory humour[1] – has been the most frequent response to the news that I am currently working on the doctrine of sin. It expresses good-humoured doubt that sin is worth taking seriously as a means for speaking about reality. In part, the humour reflects a now-conventional association (especially in sensationalist reporting) between the language of sin and what are seen to be trivial (though often as titillating) peccadilloes and temptations. But such trivialisation itself reflects the fact that the language of 'sin' has fallen largely into disuse in general public (but also in much Christian and theological) discourse as a language for talking about the pathological in human affairs. In part, that reflects the general secularisation of our culture (discussed in this chapter); in part, the suspicion that Christian understanding of sin might be counter-moral and/or counter-scientific (discussed in the following chapter); in part, the suspicion that sin is a language of blame and condemnation (encouraged by its flourishing in religious enclaves where it is used to whip up artificial and disproportionate senses of personal guilt and shame – addressed implicitly throughout Part III). For all these reasons, sin-talk may be thought anachronistic or dangerous, and it is easy to see how the idea that it yet holds descriptive, explanatory and interpretive power in relation to the discernment and understanding of pathologies in human affairs might appear bemusing, exasperating or just plain laughable.

1. I have lost count of the times I have been asked whether I need help with the practical research, and admit to not being above such silly jokes myself.

Given all that, should not the disappearance of sin from serious public discourse be passed over in silence, for fear of resurrecting a source of considerable potential embarrassment for Christian faith in the modern world?[2] Is the marginalisation of sin-talk to the privatised sphere of (trivialised and titillating) personal morality, not to be greeted by Christians as relief and liberation from public anachronism and irrelevance? Such a response to the implicit challenge issued by the cry of exasperated bemusement with which I began is tempting, given the existential situation of Christians in a highly secularised culture (discussed below), but would quite misjudge both its force and its scope.

For that challenge pertains, not only to specific, substantive issues related to the doctrine of sin, but to more general difficulties concerning the possibilities of speaking of God in relation to the world. The cry of exasperation, then, cuts to the very heart of the difficulties faced by Christian faith and theology in the modern world. For that reason alone, the general absence of sin-talk from serious public discussion of human pathologies is not something that may either be passed over in silence or enthusiastically embraced by Christians without colluding with the more general retreat of God-talk from public life and discourse. Losing our ability to speak of the world's pathologies in relation to God represents a serious, concrete form of the loss of God that is a general characteristic of contemporary, Western culture. The doctrine of sin is not so much an isolated case of Christian embarrassment concerning anachronistic aspects of Christian faith, as a crucial test of our ability to speak of God in relation to the world at all.

Appreciating the range of this challenge and its potency beyond the doctrine of sin helps towards an understanding of its force and significance in relation to sin-talk itself. For, since the challenge reflects suspicions concerning the possibilities of speaking of God and the world together, it threatens to incapacitate sin-talk in its essential, functional core. Speaking of God and world (in its pathological aspects) together is the core function of the language of sin. For sin is an essentially relational language, speaking of pathology with an inbuilt and at least implicit reference to our relation to God. To speak of what damages human beings as

2. I have no wish to become embroiled in debates about whether our contemporary situation is best characterised as post-modern rather than modern, or whether the post-modern is really only a form of late modernity. By 'modern', I merely wish to designate a cultural stream which runs back to the agenda and consequences of the Enlightenment, and which continues to shape our cultural situation, albeit through a complex history of modification.

sin is to claim that the essential character and defining characteristic of such pathology, however else it may be described and identified in non-theological languages, is theological: disruption of our proper relation to God. It is of the essence of sin-talk, therefore, that it should function as a *theological* language, and this is the source of its distinctiveness from and irreducibility to other languages through which the pathological may be discerned and described.

Therefore, anything less than facing head-on the implicit challenge of both the specific and the more general suspicions raised concerning sin-talk in our culture is heading for trouble in at least one of two ways (outlined in more detail in the following section). One potential response effectively colludes with the public meaninglessness of sin-talk by restricting either its use (to a religious enclave) or its referential range (to the private and personal). Hence, talk of God is carried on, but without any meaningful connection being made between sin as a functioning theological language and the world of public meaning and living. Alternatively, its public meaning and reference might be secured by evaporating it of any distinctively theological referent and function. Yet, eclipsing any functioning reference to God shears sin-talk of its essential, functional characteristic and mark of distinctiveness, eliding the difference between speaking of sin in theological and in any other terms. Why use the empty terminology of sin if, stripped of its essential and distinctive theological frame of reference, it conforms itself precisely and without remainder to the contours offered by, say, secular psychology, psychiatry, sociology or ethics?

It is against the backdrop of these considerations that this book is written. In it, I seek to test whether sin holds, not just public meaning, but explanatory and descriptive power in relation to concrete pathologies. Beginning with this challenge is not only a device for making clear the nature of the contemporary problematisation of sin-talk, against which it must be tested. Since the challenge to sin-talk is to its very essence, it helps clarify its nature in the very act of objecting to it and finding it so problematic. That, in turn, helps clarify a significant aspect of what it is that is being tested: the meaningfulness and explanatory power of a functioning, *theological* language. Sin-talk cannot survive testing unless it continues to function as a distinctive theological language, speaking of concrete pathologies in relation to God. The challenge implied by the exasperated bemusement with which it is frequently greeted cannot be met by turning sin into a form of non-theological discourse, collapsing it into the categories and frame of reference offered by, say, secular ethics, philosophy, psychology or sociology. If sin-talk attempts to meet the challenge by evacuating itself of all functioning reference to God, conforming itself to the standards or reference afforded by non-theological discourses, then it defeats itself in the process.

That is why it is right – even, perhaps, necessary – for a discussion of sin to begin with the exasperated bemusement with which sin-talk is frequently greeted and to take it seriously by meeting it head-on. That is why it is necessary, as a means for appreciating the essence of sin-talk, to be clear about the nature and sources of the difficulties it faces in our cultural situation. For that will help clarify what sin-talk must be if it is to hold explanatory and descriptive power in relation to concrete pathologies, and what must be tested in the course of the book.

In the following chapter, I shall turn to consider two substantive reasons for resistance to the language of sin (especially in the form of the doctrine of original sin). But first, I want to characterise the more generalised difficulty we face in speaking about God in relation to the world, the better to understand what might be involved in deploying a theological language, such as 'sin'.

Pragmatic atheism

We live in a culture which is basically secular, which affirms the world's integrity and independence from any external, non-worldly reality so that it may be understood in its own terms, without immediate or explicit reference to God.[3] Such secularity is neither necessarily nor intrinsically atheist, but it does issue a special challenge to faith and theology: if the world may be understood and lived in without transcendent reference, what place is there for God, and what point is there in speaking of God? If speaking of the world (e.g., its pathologies) in theological terms (as sin) makes no difference to secular ways of speaking, which are entirely adequate on their own, then why bother to speak of God at all? Would it not be better, less confusing and more honest, openly to abandon talk of God in these respects, if not to give up on God altogether?

Perhaps the most common religious response to secularity is for God

---

3. For two markedly different studies of the impact of secularisation on sin, see Richard K. Fenn, *The Secularization of Sin: An Investigation of the Daedalus Complex* (Louisville: Westminster/John Knox, 1991) and Marsha Witten, *All is Forgiven: The Secular Message in American Protestantism* (Princeton: Princeton University Press, 1993).

to be withdrawn to the margins of the public world, but allowed free reign in the world of personal values, morality and spirituality. (This strategy also effectively withdraws theology from interaction with secular discourses, the spiritual/religious from the material and the private from the public). Thus, God is admitted into the 'gaps' left where the explanatory power of secular discourses gives out.[4] Hence, for example, the doctrine of creation ceases to function as a means for affirming the presence and activity of God in and through the very integrity of the world's *natural* order and processes as these may be described by the natural sciences. Instead, creation is evaporated to the point of God's initial responsibility for the natural world. After which, ceasing to have any 'natural' function, God is irrelevant to the task of understanding the natural order and processes of the world. For 'natural' is here understood as that which has its own integrity in *separation* from God, which functions without God's involvement, and so may now be understood through disciplines which exclude God from their frames of reference.

Whether creaturely integrity (of the world, human beings or non-theological discourses) separates from and excludes God is a question that constantly resurfaces throughout this book. For reasons that should become clear in what follows, I consider it to be the main challenge posed in our culture to theology and faith. Is God-talk only possible by distancing God from the world, by making God utterly transcendent and 'other' to it,[5] whilst permitting a compensatory proximity in the subjective dimension of moral and spiritual values? If so, then God-talk is redundant to the task of understanding and living in the world. For, if it is no longer possible to think of God as related to, present and active in the world, to speak of God and world together, then God has ceased to hold any explanatory power for understanding the world in its own integrity. The world, at least in its public and material aspects, does not need God in order to understand itself in its own terms. So, why bother to speak of God at all in these contexts?

This is, indeed, very much the situation in which we find ourselves, in a secular culture that operates an effective exclusion of God-talk from the

---

4. Thus, Dietrich Bonhoeffer, *Letters and Papers from Prison*, enlarged edn (London: SCM, 1971), pp. 325f., 360f. (letters to Bethge, 8 June and 16 July, 1944), whose recognition of the chief issue as our understanding of God's transcendence and immanence cries out for development in a more explicitly trinitarian direction than he was able to achieve himself.
5. Here Paul Ricoeur's rhetorical question, 'Does not sin make God the Wholly Other?' (*The Symbolism of Evil* (Boston: Beacon Press, 1969), p. 58), achieves an added significance and poignancy.

discourses and practices through which we understand, live and work in the public and material world. Reference to God is effectively absent from every discipline of interpretation, analysis, explanation and action, from the natural and social sciences to public, political discourse, community development work, management, administration and social action. God is operationally excluded from those social and cultural processes which structure and shape our basic intentionality in desire, thought, action; reference to God is taken in practice to make no difference to the interpretation, explanation and understanding of the world; no difference to acting and living in it.

And so it is not easy to see how (or, indeed, why one might wish) to draw a specifically theological world-view and language (such as sin) into relation to ways of speaking about the world (in its pathological aspects) in its own terms (sociology, criminology, psychology, psychiatry, etc.). Reference to God is functionally redundant where we have developed effective and powerful disciplines for understanding and living in the world which, assuming God's irrelevance to analysis and interpretation, bracket God out of the picture. The prevailing assumption is that God is a private decision concerning personal values and motives, which would make no difference to the frameworks through which we understand the world by disciplined attentiveness to it in its phenomenal integrity. Therefore, the exclusion of God from the frames of reference through which we interpret reality is supposedly neutral in relation to beliefs. Habitual use of and reliance on the exclusion of God as the means for discerning objective truth about reality is reckoned to have as little impact on beliefs about God as they may allowedly have on our understanding and interpretation of the world.

Yet, as we utilise frameworks of understanding which exclude and assume the irrelevance of God, is this not a performance of atheism? It is not a straightforward atheism, to be sure, since it does not necessarily involve specific or conscious beliefs or disbeliefs. But it is an operational or pragmatic mode of atheism, in that it assumes the *practical* irrelevance of God's existence to the disciplines of reflection and practice we all use as we interpret and act in the world.[6] This is, indeed, the character of our culture's mode of secularity: an atheism mediated, not so much by argued or reasoned conviction, as by basic and habitual *practice*. Atheism is something that we all *live out and enact* in the public world, even if we refuse to

---

6. This anticipates the understanding of idolatry which emerges through the course of the book and is discussed explicitly in chapters 9 and 10.

give it consent in the form of explicit beliefs. For what characterises the basic secularity of our society is not so much that there are publicly accepted arguments against the existence of God, positive reasons for disbelieving in God, but that there is a *de facto* exclusion of God from public rationality, reference and discussion. Arguments against God are not needed where mentioning or invoking God makes no perceptible difference to the way in which we understand and explain the world. For then talk of God becomes meaningless. Our common and collective habits of mind, spirit and agency exclude God from consciousness. We live in our world *as if there were no God* – or at least a God who makes some actual difference to the way in which the world is to be interpreted, spoken about, acted in and upon – no matter what personal beliefs or faith we may have.

Hence, we live in a culture that shapes us all, in our most basic ways of making sense of and intending ourselves and our world, as practical atheists. That goes equally for those who live from a strong sense of faith in God as for those who do not. For faith in God makes no practical difference to the way in which we understand and live in the world; the ways in which we think, speak, act and make judgments – except possibly at the level of internal, personal motivation. We manage our lives, understand and interpret reality in the public domain, for all intents and purposes, as if we were atheists, as if there were no God actively and dynamically present in and related to the world. Because our secular culture is a form of *practical* atheism, rather than one of explicitly argued or acknowledged conviction, then, we may all be performatively incorporated into its atheism without any apparent contradiction with or loss of theistic conviction.[7] It does not lead Christians into open and conscious conflict with the ideas and beliefs we explicitly assent to and affirm concerning God, since we have colluded with the removal of such beliefs from the public sphere of ordinary life. For the atheism of which I speak concerns our *operational* beliefs; those which we hold *in practice*.

It is our incorporation into this practical atheism which explains how it is that many will be bemused by the claim that the doctrine of sin holds, not just meaning, but explanatory power for us today. Our pragmatic atheism seems to me to offer the most viable explanation of the impotence and public irrelevance of the language of sin. Other ways of accounting for

---

7. I might also point out here the further implication that secularity which takes the form of a *pragmatic* atheism is unlikely successfully to be countered by theological (or philosophically theistic) arguments which show the existence of God to be a useful or even necessary metaphysical (and therefore purely ideational) assumption.

the public meaninglessness of Christian talk of sin fail, in the end, to take the *secularity* of our culture as a form of pragmatic atheism at all seriously as a source of resistance to it. Consequently, they fail also to give sufficient weight to the essentially *theological* nature of the language of sin.[8] Merely changing the categories through which it is presented so that it accords with the psychological or moral consciousness of the age cannot rehabilitate the doctrine of sin. The real problem is the loss of God's active and dynamic relation to the world as the necessary correlate without which any form of human experience or consciousness may become a form of sin-consciousness. The task facing theology is consequently more radical than correlating the traditional forms of doctrinal expression with culturally predominant ways in which the pathological is understood. The theological task cannot then be reduced to the changing of its language and pattern of basic conceptuality, in order to render it more meaningful to the supposed psychological and cultural forms of consciousness prevailing in contemporary, Western culture. The meaninglessness of the language of sin in our secular culture issues a challenge to Christian faith and theology: to show that reference to God holds explanatory and descriptive power; that it invokes and enables a more truthful relation to reality in both theory and practice. It is that claim which this book, in a small way, sets out to test.

Let me be clear what my own position is before proceeding, since I have now expressed the most basic premiss of this book: I take the language of sin to be fundamentally a theological language. It functions by building relation to God into its way of speaking of the pathological, by speaking of God and the pathological together. So, in a culture that has effected a pragmatic eclipse of God from its basic frames of public reference, which systematically explains reality, including the pathological, without such reference, the language of sin is rendered problematic. If it is deployed at all, it will prove difficult to retain its integrity as a function-

8. In two very dissimilar books, Karl Menninger (*Whatever Happened to Sin?* (London: Hodder & Stoughton, 1973)) and Henri Rondet (*The Theology of Sin* (Notre Dame: Fides, 1960), pp. 103ff.) effect a reductive analysis in moral (non-theological) terms, despite the latter's frequent avowal of the view that relation to God is a necessary constituent of the notion of sin. For both, the lack of sin-consciousness is related to the reduction of *moral* consciousness, and so recovery of sin-consciousness is achieved through the revivification of the moral, which then captivates their comprehension of sin in retrieval. Donald Capps, on the other hand, suggests, not that we have lost our ability to experience ourselves as 'in the wrong', but that there has been a cultural shift in the categories through which we so experience ourselves, from guilt to shame. See *The Depleted Self: Sin in a Narcissistic Age* (Minneapolis: Fortress Press, 1993). The resultant retrieval of sin, however, is conducted in overwhelmingly secularised, psychological terms.

ing *theological* language. And so we are likely to find the language of sin retained, if at all, without its intrinsic and active theological reference, as reduced to a rhetorical flourish added to secular discourses. Where the terminology of sin remains in public use, it tends either to be trivialised or deployed as an emotive device for passing judgment and attaching blame.

Beyond Post-It™ label theology[9]

In such a secular context as our own, it is perfectly understandable that people might initially be bemused by the prospect of drawing the doctrine of sin back into public discourse, in conversation with secular thought and practice. For, properly deployed, the language of sin carries an inbuilt reference to God, naming the pathological as the denial of and opposition to God. But if God has no explanatory power in relation to reality, including its pathological aspects, and if our secular ways of speaking of and addressing the pathological (criminology, medicine, sociology, social science, psychology, philosophy, etc.) appear to be sufficient, why stick God on to secular analyses, descriptions, therapies, and so on?

It must be admitted from the outset that, if God-talk merely appends itself to an analysis already in place, then renaming as sin that which secular thought identifies as pathological is no more than a rhetorical flourish. It adds precisely nothing at the level of explanation and understanding to baptise and bless conclusions arrived at by secular means for secular reasons. Only if Christian faith possesses a specifically theological understanding of what sin is and how it functions might it have something to offer secular diagnosis and therapy. Only then will it have its own basis for recognition and interpretation of the pathological and for engaging secular analyses in a mutually enriching and correcting conversation.

I hope it is clear by now why I consider the question of the meaningfulness and explanatory power of the doctrine of sin to be *in essence the same question* as that of God as an active and dynamic presence in the world. To

---

9. I have used the image of a Post-It™ label, since it neither makes any difference to that to which it is appended nor leaves any sign of its presence when removed. Significantly here, Paul Tillich construes sin as the separation of the holy and the secular, in which God becomes merely '"in addition to" all other things'. (*Systematic Theology*, I (London: SCM, 1978), p. 218.) Cf. here Friedrich Schleiermacher's characterisation of 'God-forgetfulness' as 'an absence of facility for introducing the God-consciousness into our actual lives and retaining it there' (*The Christian Faith* (Edinburgh: T. & T. Clark, 1928), p. 55).

ask whether the language of sin can have anything significant to say in addition to secular ways of speaking of the human condition which are pragmatically atheist is to ask whether God, and therefore talk of God, makes any difference. It is to ask whether, in fact, God-talk has any real referent in the world incapable of being adequately referred to in secular, pragmatically atheist ways. Can God-talk be different enough from our secular ways of speaking to be irreducible to them, to make a difference, to be worth bothering with? Yet, can it at the same time show that it really is speaking about and enriching our lived understanding of the world (including its pathologies), achieved and secured through secular discourses and disciplines? If God is the most basic reality and explanation of the world, then it must be the case that the world cannot *adequately* be explained, understood, lived in, without reference to God in our fundamental means both of discernment and of action. That is a far cry from suggesting that secular disciplines of discernment, interpretation and action are worthless and may comprehensively be replaced by theology. But it is to suggest the inadequacy of merely sticking God on to secular talk at the last or the first moments, but disallowing it to function in between, an effective bracketing-out of God from the secular picture of the world, which fails in the end to relate the world to God.[10]

This book represents one small attempt to test the claim that consciously relating the world to God (specifically, its pathologies through the language of sin) holds explanatory and symbolic power in relation to reality. This means constructing a conversation between theology and secular analyses in which the Christian theological tradition (in this case, its understanding of sin) participates on the basis of its own integrity. That does not imply disabusing the capacity of secular disciplines to discern and speak the truth, a blind resistance to secular accounts of reality, matched only by the blind affirmation of Christian tradition in the face of the contradictions and resistance offered by secular disciplines, or even by reality itself. For the kind of integrity proper to Christian tradition is (and, historically, always has been) conversational: that which is maintained in and through conversation, including that with non-Christian forms of understanding and life. Truth, including the truthfulness of Christian doctrine, is something to be discovered and decided in

---

10. Think of all those church reports on social issues, which begin with ten biblical reasons why Christians should be concerned about poverty, and then proceed in the bulk of the report to present an analysis conducted entirely in secular terms – as if God is irrelevant to our understanding of what, say, poverty really is – without any theological intrusion into the language, conceptuality or frame of reference of the basic analytical tools.

the conversation.[11] That clearly requires a mutual openness in encounter that a conception of theology as mere repetition of tradition would undermine. Yet theological integrity is also needed, a minimum requirement of which is refusing to give up on an effective reference to God; resisting the urge to translation of theological into secular and pragmatically atheist categories.

A discussion of the broader methodological implications of the conversation I am attempting to construct in this book can be found in chapter 3. In the next chapter, I shall turn to a somewhat more substantive invitation to give up on the theological integrity of the tradition in our culture: the turn to 'natural' morality.

11. See further my article, 'Truth as Mission: The Christian Claim to Universal Truth in a Pluralist Public World', *Scottish Journal of Theology*, 46 (1993), 437–56.

2

_____

Speaking morally? The case of original sin

In the previous chapter, I discussed a major source of formal resistance to sin-talk, which applies to theological discourse more generally, as a means for clarifying both the nature of sin-talk itself and what might be involved in testing its explanatory and descriptive power. In this chapter, I continue the process of elucidating the intrinsic nature of sin-talk by exploring some of the points of resistance to it. Here I am concerned with substantive objections to the conceptual content of the language of sin, beyond the more general problematisation of God-talk in a secularised culture discussed in the previous chapter. These come into sharpest focus (and so may be more clearly identified) in relation to the understanding of sin found most abhorrent when judged by non-theological standards: the doctrine of original sin in its traditional formulation. Modern critique and resistance is not only strong and sustained, but widespread (shared by Christians and non-Christians alike) and often so 'taken for granted' as to be beyond the need for explication. That suggests that it emanates from something innate in or foundational to our culture; that it represents the background understanding of a whole culture, not just the specialised, technical concerns of an elite, intellectual sub-culture. Constructing an engagement between modern culture and a mode of Christian discourse that chafes against it as its antithesis should, therefore, throw into sharp relief the basic beliefs and assumptions concerning human beings and the human situation that shape the way we habitually construe and deal with the pathological in human affairs.

Thus may be identified the dominant cultural mode of discourse about the pathological. (As it happens, that turns out to be founded on similar assumptions concerning the nature of freedom which problematise God-talk in general.) It is in relation to this (moral) language that original sin is found to be offensive and against which any understanding of sin will have to prove itself as a viable alternative or supplement. The explanatory power of that language is taken for granted and problematises at least one way of deploying the language of sin. In subsequent chapters, I shall endeavour to test that claim in the course of exploring the potential explanatory and descriptive power of the language of sin.

I have already explained why it makes sense to engage with the doctrine of original sin at this juncture, from the point of view of identifying the dominant language through which our culture speaks of those human pathologies of which sin also speaks. But does it make sense in relation to the theological tradition? Am I not in danger of selecting an easy and unrepresentative target, one that has already been kicked so hard and so often that it lies prostrate at the feet of post-Enlightenment and post-evolutionary culture already? To assuage such suspicions, it might help if I state clearly now why and how I am using original sin. First, I am not using original sin as representative, in the sense of standing in for other theologies of sin, so that what may be found in relation to this doctrinal formulation may be applied by extension to other doctrinal formulations and constructive possibilities. Notwithstanding that, however, this particular formulation does occupy a specially significant position in the history of Christian doctrine in the West, in which it has secured dominance.[1] Original sin permeates all discussions of sin in the Western traditions of Christianity. Those that advocate different constructive possibilities generally do so as self-conscious counters and alternatives to original sin, which therefore continues to shape their formulation as negations of it. More significant than that, however, the resistance of such alternative conceptions to original sin tends to echo the substantive objections of the wider culture. Limiting engagement to the alternatives to original sin would not, therefore, be a good means of highlighting and questioning the general background understanding of human pathology which they themselves share. Furthermore, in engaging with original sin we may entertain the possibility that its objectionable aspects, those

---

1. Whilst it achieved hegemony in Western Christianity, the doctrine has always met with resistance and may be found in varied forms, attempting to meet some of the concerns of its various detractors. Those who reject the traditional understanding of original sin find support in its implied or explicit rejection by many of the early Fathers (e.g., Clement of Alexandria, *Stromata*, I, 83.5, IV, 153.2; Irenaeus, *Adversus Haereses*, 4.37; Justin, *Dialogue with Trypho*, 88, 141; *Second Apology*, 7; Origen, *De Principiis*, 1.3, 5, 2.1, 2.9.6, 3.1; Cyril of Jerusalem, *Catech.* 4.18–21; John Chrysostom, Homily 10 in *Romans*), as well as in the traditions of Eastern Orthodoxy. (See here the helpful orientation in Henri Rondet, *Original Sin: The Patristic and Theological Background* (Shannon: Ecclesia, 1972).)

points resistant to cultural assimilation, may yet represent sin's distinctiveness as a *theological* language. Thus, the resistance of secular culture to original sin may throw the distinctively theological aspects of understanding pathology as sin into sharp relief. We may therefore ask whether alternative conceptions remain functionally theological, as well as whether they hold as much or more explanatory power than original sin or the secular, moral discourse with which they are allied.

Beginning with original sin, then, maximises the possibilities of testing the explanatory and descriptive power of sin as a theological language.

Basic co-ordinates

The doctrine of original sin consists of two constitutive components, which are analytically separable. First, it expresses a view as to the *source* of sin which relies on the account of the Fall of Adam and Eve in Genesis 3: sin enters the world through a particular human being's free decision to turn away from God. This is *the* original sin. Second, all subsequent generations of human beings inherit the consequences of this first sin. This inheritance, according to the most prominent strand of the tradition, is not adequately construed merely in terms of a universally inherited incapacity to do the good. We inherit more than the accumulated consequences of Adam's sin, compounded by that of subsequent generations, more than a *tendency* to choose sin above goodness. That would leave inherited sin as nothing more than a latent capacity awaiting activation through our own individual or collective acts. The doctrine of original sin, however, claims that what is communicated to us from Adam is not merely a *tendency* towards our own sinning, but accountability for inherited sin – we inherit, that is, the sin itself in the form of guilt. We inherit Adam's sin, not just its consequences, and we do so (according at least to the Augustinian version) through the biological mechanism of reproduction – before we achieve anything approaching full personhood; indeed, before we are born. And so we stand before God guilty for Adam's sin even before we get around to doing any sinning of our own.

The doctrine of original sin carries four crucial, interrelated corollaries: sin is **contingent, radical, communicable** and **universal**.

First, sin is a contingent (not necessary) consequence of human freedom; its origin, if not its present reality, was constituted in a free act of the human creature through which was lost the creaturely and unaided possibility of perfection and of goodness. Sin was neither inevitable nor an aspect of our proper nature, but a distortion of it. It is not an inevitable concomitant or consequence of our creaturely finitude.

Second, sin's reality and hold on people is radical. One way of expressing this would be to say that original sin refers primarily to a *situation*,[2] which we are in, or a condition we have, and only secondarily to individual *acts* of sin. Consequently, sin's reality is not taken to be momentary or episodic, arising and falling with particular sinful acts. Rather, it subsists and endures as a distortion of our fundamental ways of being in the world. There is an underlying, systemic and structural distortion of the conditions of human sociality, of the most basic patterns of disposition which constitute our personal identities, and which underlie our actions.

Third, sin is said to effect a fundamental distortion of the conditions of sociality through which we are called into personhood (even of its biological basis). Its reality is held to be communicated to us pre-personally, in the basic material out of which we construct our personhood. It therefore infects us *prior* to our achievement of personhood, before we are constituted as centres of personal experience, action and intention, and so before we are capable of performing morally culpable (personal) acts. This communication of a pre-personal distortion, which then underlies all our personal acts, is itself named as sin. And it is so named, not just because it is in itself a form of alienation from God, but because inheriting that alienation incurs guilt. Hence the tradition, when pressed, asserts that even a newly born baby may be said to be in the situation of original sin with the rest of us – in a distorted relation to God which is characterised by guilt.

Finally, it follows from the radical nature of sin in the basic structures of our humanity that sin must be universally extensive, both as a condition and as an actualised possibility: because we are all in a situation of sin, we all commit individual acts of sin. Since the universality of sinning has its root in the universal conditioning effect of the Fall, it represents rather more than the claim that, *as it happens,* no-one so far has avoided actually committing sin. The form of the traditional doctrine of original sin implies a universal solidarity in sin which is certainly exhibited in, but is neither simply the product of nor reducible to, the fact that all do, in fact, perform sinful acts. The solidarity that is claimed here is therefore not merely axiological, accidental and empirical.

2. The term 'state', which is often used in opposition to 'act', is better avoided since it suggests a static, non-dynamic human situation before God and others.

When these four corollaries are held together a basic tension emerges in the doctrine. The latter three together begin to imply that sin – at least in its current reality, if not in its origin – has rather more of the character of nature, destiny or fate; of a substance; of being, rather than doing.[3] That some aspects of the doctrine are capable of interpretation in a direction that appears to suppress the personal dimensions of human life (freedom, responsibility and will) is sufficient to render it entirely unusable for some. To them, the doctrine appears to ontologise sin, to render it an inescapable structure of existence. Original sin may therefore be suspected of breaching the most fundamental Christian conviction about sin: that it has no ontological basis in reality, but is the contingent product of human willing; not (quasi-)matter, but personal decision and will.

If sin is radical and universal, communicable pre-personally, what then is the place of personal willing and responsibility? That is a question that has achieved a heightened significance in the context of modern (and which has not been eclipsed in so-called post-modern) culture, though it is of more than simply modern significance. The nature of freedom, will, responsibility and guilt; their interrelation with determining and limiting factors in the historical, interpersonal, societal and natural environments is a matter of central and enduring significance – in discussions of original sin as of concrete pathology, as we shall discover in Parts II and III.

The scandal of a doctrine

The two points at which this traditional doctrine of original sin chafes against modern assumptions and inbuilt ways of thinking are immediately obvious: one scientific; the other, moral. First, it appears to require assent to the literal facticity of the Biblical myth of the Fall, and therefore to the creation narratives related to it, with their non-evolutionary view of human origins.[4] Second, the traditional formulation of the doctrine of

---

3. The contrast is expressed in this last way by Paul Ricoeur in 'Original Sin: A Study in Meaning', in *The Conflict of Interpretations: Essays in Hermeneutics* (Evanston: Northwestern University Press, 1974), p. 273.

4. The Fall story is non-evolutionary first in supposing monogenism (descent from a single (pair of) ancestor[s]); second, in ignoring the evolution of moral consciousness, that the first human beings would not yet have evolved the conditions of free, personal action necessary for moral deliberation. On the question of monogenism, see further Karl Rahner, 'Theology and Monogenism', in *Theological Investigations*, I (London: Darton, Longman & Todd, 1961), pp. 229–96; 'Evolution and Original Sin', *Concilium*, 26 (1967), 61–73;

original sin promulgates a notion of responsibility which is judged counter-moral in holding us accountable for: what others have done; what we have done through inherited and unavoidable predisposition; and the general situation in which we find ourselves. It is this moral source of offence at the doctrine of original sin that (as I shall suggest more fully below) is both the most powerful in contemporary culture and the most enduring.[5] The various points of conflict between the traditionally expressed doctrinal corpus of the Christian faith and the natural sciences assuredly raise a series of pressing issues concerning the relationship between science and Christian doctrine; issues which have yet adequately to be addressed either at the methodological or the substantive level. But, at least in relation to the doctrine of sin, the conflict is more significant in the way in which it has encouraged an uncritical flight into the moral and away from the material. It is the reductive reading of the language of sin in moral categories, the migration of theology to ethics (accompanied by that from the ontological to the social), which constitutes the most pressing challenge to sin as a theological language – indeed, to God-talk in general – in contemporary culture.[6]

The assumptions underlying the moral challenge to original sin will surface in a number of guises at several points in the book. Before proceeding any further, it will be helpful to bring these underlying assumptions to somewhat clearer expression.

The conditions of the moral

Part of the function of moral discourse is the location and tracking of responsibility for the performance of acts that may be subject to moral evaluation. It is a language of responsibility, in the sense that it holds and calls people to account for their actions. That accountability concerns a particular form of relation between an individual, an action and its consequences. Merely tracing a line of sufficient causation back from a given circumstance to behaviour is insufficient. The moral is concerned with a

'Erbsünde und Monogenismus', in Karl Weger, *Theologie der Erbsünde* (Freiburg: Herder, 1970), pp. 176–223; John J. O'Rourke, 'Some Considerations about Polygenism', *Theological Studies*, 26 (1965), 407–16; Maurice Flick, 'Original Sin and Evolution: I, The Problem', *The Tablet*, 9/10/66, [?]1088–10; 'Original Sin: II, 'Towards a Possible Solution', *The Tablet*, 17/9/66, [?]1039–1041.

5. For a useful orientation here, see H. D. Lewis, *Morals and the New Theology* (London: Victor Gollancz, 1947); *Morals and Revelation* (London: George Allen & Unwin, 1951).

6. H. Richard Niebuhr makes a different and powerful case for the independence of sin as a religious category over against the hegemony of the moral in our culture in 'Man the Sinner', *Journal of Religion*, 15 (1935), 272–80.

special form of causality, such that it is a necessary but insufficient condition for the attribution of moral responsibility to trace the cause of an effect back to an individual's action. In itself, that could involve little more than a mechanical association. Beyond that, moral judgment requires the relationship between the act and the individual to be *personal*.[7] That means tracing the line of causation back to that which is considered the constitutive element of personhood: freedom in the sense of self-determination. What makes for a *personal* relationship to action, what makes acts *our* acts, acts of our *person*, is that, in their commission, we are acting freely: *we* are their self-determining cause. Hence, moral evaluation concerns itself with action that is freely willed, and we escape moral responsibility where our acts may be shown to be compelled, determined or otherwise unavoidable.[8] Where we are subject to irresistible force or impulse, our action is not a product of our person; we are not its cause; it is not ours. We may be neither morally praised nor blamed for that which we have not freely chosen or could not avoid.[9]

7. Although the referential scope of moral judgment is not restricted to the *acts* of moral agents (since moral evaluation may be made of internal dispositions), it is the *behaviour* of *persons* – rather than the nature of situations – which is its primary concern. Judgments concerning the morality of a *situation* (say, unjust social structures) in fact work by making an indirect judgmental reference to the behaviour of persons: those who may be accounted responsible for creating or sustaining the situation through their free will. Moral language effects judgments concerning *personal* (although not necessarily individual) behaviour. For moral judgments are ultimately made, and can only be made, through the tracking of responsibility in the sense of will-contingent causation. That causation is personal, in the sense that it requires the additional supposition of freedom of will, such that the cause has free agency in relation to the effect. That is to say, one could have acted or may now act otherwise in a way which would change the situation. Situations may only be judged immoral or moral if there are people who have brought them about or sustain them in being through their action or inaction where there is a possibility of doing otherwise.

8. Furthermore, if the consequences of action were unpredictable or if greater harm has been avoided, then we may yet escape moral blame, even though we stand in a relation of personal causation to the action. On the conditions for the attribution of responsibility, see further H. L. A. Hart, *Punishment and Responsibility: Essays in the Philosophy of Law*, reprinted edn with revisions (Oxford: Clarendon Press, 1992); Joel Feinberg, *Doing & Deserving: Essays in the Theory of Responsibility* (Princeton: Princeton University Press, 1970); John M. Fischer, ed., *Moral Responsibility* (Ithaca: Cornell University Press, 1986); Anthony Kenny, *Will, Freedom and Power* (Oxford: Blackwell, 1975) and *Freewill and Responsibility* (London: Routledge & Kegan Paul, 1978). See also William S. Babcock, 'Augustine on Sin and Moral Agency', *Journal of Religious Ethics*, 16 (1988), 28f.

9. Immanuel Kant, for instance, makes it clear that even the fundamental dispositions of the moral agent must be said to have been adopted by a free choice of the will (which he held must have taken place pre-temporally) if one is to be culpable both directly for these dispositions themselves and for the acts they incline us towards. See *Religion Within the Limits of Reason Alone* (New York: Harper & Row, 1960), pp. 16f., 20, 24, 26f., 33. See also Julius Müller's rather different development of the idea of a pre-temporal fall in The …tian *Doctrine of Sin* II (Edinburgh: T. & T. Clark, 1853), pp. 50, 90–6, 165–8, 409ff. On the …eral point, see Roger Trigg, 'Sin and Freedom', *Religious Studies*, 20, 191–202. Whilst …ding any metaphysical assumption such as pre-temporal choices, Sharon Lamb

There has been a long and complex history of ethical discussion concerning the essential role of freedom, of willing and of knowledge in moral behaviour. The bottom line is that freedom is a prerequisite for there to be a moral accounting of behaviour, at least in the sense that it would have been possible to have willed or done otherwise. Determination and moral evaluation are usually considered antithetical. In that sense at least moral behaviour involves free willing and intentionality, coupled with freedom in action sufficient to enact the will. That need not necessarily imply, however, that moral agents are only held to account for the intended or foreseen consequences of their behaviour. Whether moral praise and blame are considered appropriate in relation to the unintended and unforeseen consequences of behaviour often depends on whether it is considered that the agent *should* have been able to foresee those consequences. Ignorance is not usually deemed a moral defence if it arises out of a lack of proper attention, foresight, deliberation or application (so weakness of will is not necessarily a defence).

A cluster of interrelated assumptions is embedded here. First, that I may only be held responsible for that which I am the cause of; which I could have willed to do otherwise; which is a product of my own freedom in action and not an outcome of determining conditions. In other words moral culpability works where there is a non-necessary relation between person and action, where the action therefore embeds a deliberate or implied choice. The guiding assumption here is that the moral subject is free and neutral in relation to the possible objects of moral choice, so that her moral choices may be deemed to be freely made – that is, decisions of pure internality or subjectivity, unfettered and uninfluenced by external factors and relationships. To this might also be added the Kantian axiom that I must be capable of performing any good, the non-performance of which could rationally (justly) attract moral censure (ought implies can).

Original sin therefore offends against the most fundamental, twin tenets of natural, rational and just moral order: that we are held to account only for our own free acts, what *we* have done (which are acts of our person) and that which we could have avoided doing. The doctrine of original sin posits that we inherit sin in the form of guilt for others' actions; that there has been a total and universal moral collapse which

nonetheless seems to me implicitly to maintain that we are responsible for our characters because they are to some degree always freely chosen: see *The Trouble with Blame: Victims, Perpetrators and Responsibility* (Cambridge, MA: Harvard University Press, 1996), pp. 11, 85f. Throughout the book she works with a notion of responsibility defined by freedom of will and of choice (see also pp. 8, 23).

makes avoidance of sin impossible; and that we are yet accountable for this situation and for our individual acts of sin which this situation pre-conditions us to commit.

Doubling the offence? Science and the moral

In chafing against the 'natural', rational assumptions of morality, the doctrine of original sin is set against an absolutely fundamental (indeed, constitutive) aspect of modernity. The moral objections are not, however, a peculiar feature of modern consciousness. They represent instead a comprehension of the basis of morality and of moral order which is 'natural' to views of the human which take the individual and her autonomy as primary. That may justly be termed *the* defining characteristic of modernity. For, in the characteristically modern 'turn to the subject', it has achieved the status of a basic axiom, the foundation of a whole culture's moral, political and philosophical discourse. It is so operationally basic, one of the rules of the game, that it appears to us to be self-evidently true and beyond question, to be 'natural' – that which cannot be questioned without stopping the game, the basic standard and criterion of rationality.

Whilst this assumption is deeply characteristic of modernity, however, it is not an absolutely peculiar characteristic. Indeed, the earliest formulations of the doctrine of original sin were accompanied by similar objections and resistance, based both on this understanding of the moral and the insistence that the moral is a basic criterion of truth and reasonableness to which God and God's dealings with human beings must conform.[10] But in the culture of modernity, this understanding of moral rationality, based on a conception of the individual person as a free, willing subject, has achieved a significantly different status.

When, more recently, the basis of the doctrine (the existence of a first couple) is rendered dubious on scientific grounds, moral resistance to it is given additional force and impetus. For, in modernity, if there is any stronger criterion of truth than a naturally obvious basis for morality, it is the natural sciences. Natural science and 'natural' morality in amalgamation present the odiousness of the doctrine as so obvious as to require no further argument. Time should not be wasted defending the indefen-

---

10. Or one could put the matter the other way about and say that Augustine first developed the doctrine precisely in order to counter the implications of a framework of 'natural' moral reasoning as it was deployed by Pelagius. For Pelagius' position, see his *Epistle to Demetrius*, 16; *On the Possibility of not Sinning*, 2, 4 and Augustine, *On Nature and Grace*, 34; *On Man's Perfection in Righteousness*, 2.

sible, one might understandably say in relation to original sin. This impression has been further reinforced by the more general, modern migration (scientifically induced) of religious and theological frames of reference from the public, objective and material world to that of inner, spiritual and moral values. Increasingly, it has been accepted that science tells us about material, objective reality; religion, if it tells us anything, is confined to the moral and spiritual. And so there is a great pressure for doctrine to conform to the rules and criteria of an independently constituted and structured sphere of morality (which carries a quite particular anthropology with it), since there is no other place where Christian doctrine may gain a purchase in modern culture.

Even in those modern discussions in which primacy *appears* to be given to the scientific critique of the Adam and Eve story, it most often *actually* serves a preparatory function for a *moral* critique or evaluation (whether implicitly or explicitly made). The argument from science often appears as a supporting device for an argument and reinterpretation that actually proceeds by moral criteria. Science, it is supposed, shows us that the traditional basis of the doctrine cannot be true. It then affords the opportunity for doctrinal revision which represents a more fundamental root of uneasiness with the doctrine – its contradiction of fundamental tenets of 'natural' morality. And so, in a cultural situation in which science achieved an elevated intellectual authority in deciding matters of public truth, science became the impetus for moral critique and reinterpretation which have more ancient origins, but which have achieved a particular significance for us by virtue of their consonance with the undergirding assumptions of modernity: the individually autonomous subject.[11]

It may be science that is adduced as the expert witness to establish that the Fall story (and so the doctrine of original sin built on that edifice) is a mythological construct. But it is the criteria established by a moral rationality taken to be 'natural' (and related to the foundational presuppositions of modernity) which establish the direction in which the myth is to

11. Science achieved intellectual authority in the West by furnishing what was supposed to be a convincing explanatory framework for the whole of reality, and one which bore many hopes for human progress through technology. It is true that the hegemony of science and of its associated technologies has come under increasing suspicion and attack as its social and cultural determinacy and its relation to structures of power have been recognised, and its capacity to meet material human aspirations without attendant ecological or political disaster has been radically questioned. Notwithstanding all that, however, the intellectual and moral authority of science, especially in relation to traditional Christian belief, seems to be remarkably robust in the face of recent intellectual and spiritual critiques (which might themselves be critical of Christianity and not above using science itself as a tool in that argument), especially in popular, non-intellectual culture.

be interpreted and which appear as the real motivation for reinterpretation. One aspect of the modern situation is new: that the 'naturally obvious' morality through which the doctrine is reinterpreted now contains not even an implicit reference to God as its ultimate legitimator and guarantor (consequently, in a culture which is pragmatically atheist, God cannot stand over against 'natural morality' as its criterion and judge). Therefore, when the doctrine of original sin is reinterpreted in this situation in the direction of a moral language, its functioning theological reference is imperilled as it turns itself into a pragmatically atheist language, which relates God to moral codes (if at all) externally and historically – as legislative origin.

This helps, I think, to explain how and why it is that many theologians who have worked on the doctrine of original sin in the twentieth century have so eagerly greeted the requirement to restate or more radically reinterpret it in the light of the natural sciences. The display of a sense of liberation is common. For now one does not have to make a case based on a preference for 'natural' moral reasoning over tradition. Arguing on that basis was always prone to the charge that one was making theological judgments on the basis of that which it is easier ('naturally') to believe. A deal of pressure is taken off those engaged in the theological task of reconstruction and reinterpretation if there is some clear, 'objective' reason for contesting the factual basis of a doctrine which one might have wished to reject (at least in its traditional terms) for quite other reasons. For, naturally, if there was no first couple, then there can have been no original sin, no Fall, and therefore no inherited guilt. Therefore, so it is assumed, when we free ourselves from the mythological construct of Eden, we free ourselves also from the burden of ideas of inherited guilt; from the burden of having to treat sin as a condition, passively received. Science is the agent of liberation that frees Christian theology and faith from precisely those aspects of the doctrine that have been found so offensive to 'natural' morality.[12]

Aside from the work of those setting out to defend tradition against any constructive, theological endeavour through dogmatic restatement,

12. Modern science also permits a sharp distinction to be made between medical and moral taxonomy. Disease may be presented and experienced in impersonal categories, as that which one passively receives, which one is the victim of and for which one therefore bears no guilt. Moral failing, in contradistinction, is then presented as a matter of individual free choice, construed as the essential condition for the allocation of blame. There are a number of works discussing the effects of this distinction in the context of the language of sin in the experience and treatment of addiction. See Patrick McCormick, *Sin as Addiction* (New York: Paulist, 1989); Linda A. Mercadante, *Victims and Sinners: Spiritual Roots of Addiction and Recovery* (Louisville: Westminster/John Knox, 1996).

come what may, modern treatments of original sin typically begin with a sense of liberation from having to articulate sin in terms of the historical Fall of Adam and Eve, and therefore of the universal inheritance of sin in the form of guilt. If science shows us that the Fall story and the doctrine of original sin are mythological constructs, then they are either to be dispensed with or reinterpreted. For the purposes of the present work, the interesting question to ask about these attempts at reinterpretation, prompted by science, is: what operatively controls the reinterpretation? Against which aspects of, or ways of understanding, reality is tradition to be tested – and is this a one-way process? By what criteria are elements of the tradition deemed to be mythological or non-mythological, dispensable, recoverable, interpretable or otherwise? By what criteria do strategies of reinterpretation – which claim to retain the kernel, the core idea, of the doctrine of original sin – identify and then interpret that core? How is a judgment made as to what is the kernel and what the mythological husk of metaphysical, cosmological and ontological accretions from which it is to be stripped?[13]

Sin in modern theology

Freedom as a basic structure of humanity

When these questions are put to discussions of original sin which criticise it as non-evolutionary, we find that the doctrine tends to be rejected or reinterpreted against operative norms and criteria which are not, in the end, scientific, but moral.[14] When sin is interpreted according to the

13. These questions may be asked of deconstructive as well as reconstructive treatments, since there is no firm dividing-line between some of the more radical reinterpretations, which arrive at a moralistic conception of sin claiming to represent the true meaning of original sin, and those finding such moralistic notions so radical a departure from the doctrine's traditional meaning that it is disingenuous to retain its nomenclature.

14. Exceptions are rare, but the following examples deserve to be noted of theologies in which evolution is not only the initial motivation, but also the vehicle, criterion for and mode of reinterpretation: Karl Schmitz-Moorman, *Die Erbsünde: Ueberholte Vorstellung, bleibender Glaube* (Olten-Freiburg i Br.: Walter Verlag, 1969) and Juan Luis Segundo, *Evolution and Guilt* (Dublin: Gill & Macmillan, 1980). In both accounts, sin is resistance to the evolution of higher forms of order, whether biological-social (Schmitz-Moorman) or social-political (Segundo). Schmitz-Moorman, following Teilhard de Chardin, is clear that sin and evil are necessary consequences and correlates of an evolving order (pp. 80ff., 102, 155f., 198, 228); whilst Segundo runs perilously close to collapsing salvation into the dynamic structures of the natural social and biological order (pp. 83f., 111f.). Friedrich Schleiermacher prefigured something of this in speaking of sin as the resistance of a prior developmental stage in culture, mirrored in each individual's maturation (sensible self-consciousness), to the emergence of God-consciousness; or of flesh to spirit (*The Christian Faith* (Edinburgh: T. & T. Clark, 1928), §§66–8). On this, cf. Ernst Troeltsch, *Glaubenslehre* (Aalen: Scientia, 1981), §22.7. More generally, see also Pieter Smulders, *Theologie und Evolution: Versuch über Teilhard de Chardin* (Essen: Driewer, 1963); 'Evolution and Original Sin', in Michael J. Taylor, *The Mystery of Sin and Forgiveness* (Staten Island: Alba House, 1971).

criteria of 'natural' morality, it is construed in terms of *acts* for which one is *personally* responsible in the terms already delineated.[15] The undergirding definition of sin which operates as a criterion for modern reinterpretation, then, is a construal of sin primarily in axiological terms which raises the freedom of the subject (construed as the freedom to have done otherwise) to prominence as the basis of personal attribution of guilt and responsibility. Sin thence refers to *acts* of *free* moral agents; to *sins* rather than to *sin* as some conditioning substratum of action; to culpable breaches of moral law.[16] In modernity, then, sin becomes formally a moral language, and the principal criterion of culpability is shifted to the structure of independent and autonomous subjectivity.[17]

And so the real point of resistance is to an understanding of sin that extends its range of reference beyond that of moral evaluation, especially where it appears to depersonalise sin and guilt,[18] turning both into non-moral categories. In particular, it is the attribution – indeed, the transference – of guilt by natural or metaphysical means, rather than by free, personal action, which is a major sticking point. The traditional construction of original sin seems to include a reference to that which people inherit or otherwise passively receive and are not responsible for *as persons* – that is, as free moral agents. It attributes guilt, holds people accountable, for that which was not their *personal* act in the sense defined above. It

15. For a clear example, see the definition offered by F. R. Tennant in *The Origin and Propagation of Sin*, 2nd edn (Cambridge: Cambridge University Press, 1906), pp.xxiii–xxvi, 20f., 104f., 163ff., 167ff. and the general understanding which operates throughout his discussion (see also *The Sources of the Doctrines of the Fall and Original Sin* (Cambridge: Cambridge University Press, 1903) and *The Concept of Sin* (Cambridge: Cambridge University Press, 1912)). So also Richard Swinburne, *Responsibility and Atonement* (Oxford: Clarendon Press, 1989), pp. 34–8, 43, 51, 52; Bernard Ramm, *Offense to Reason: A Theology of Sin* (San Francisco: Harper & Row, 1985), pp. 90ff.; Cornelius Plantinga, 'Not the Way It's S'posed to Be', *Theology Today*, L/2, 184, 186, 187, 189f.

16. So, e.g., David G. Attfield, 'The Morality of Sins', *Religious Studies*, 20, 227–37, following Tennant. Attfield is clear that he is being true to Tennant in proclaiming that morality is prior to a concept of sin: 'sin is a concept which is parasitic on morality' (p. 227). Such is also the implication of Swinburne's entire approach in *Responsibility and Atonement*.

17. Significantly, this is a structure capable of explication without reference to God, since its integrity is supposed to consist in autonomy and independence from external relations. It stands in its own space, independent of and neutral in relation to the (supposedly) external influence of God or any other possible object of choice. Free choices are made on the basis of a relationally pure internality, a pure point of (at least limited) transcendence of any and all relationships.

18. Emil Brunner, for instance, holds that sin is depersonalised in the traditional interpretation of original sin through its elision of personal responsibility into nature and fate. Even though he explicitly accepts that sin is partly nature and fate (and so therefore irreducible to moral categories), it is clear that he can only countenance talk of the latter if they are somehow yet confined within the sphere of personal responsibility (*Man in Revolt: A Christian Anthropology* (Philadelphia: Westminster, 1939), pp. 117–21, 128).

appears to work with an entirely objective notion of legal or moral offence, paying no regard to the subjective nature of action which 'natural' morality takes to be an essential correlate of guilt.[19]

But worse than this, the traditional doctrine of original sin does not stop at holding people accountable for that which is not a consequence of their own free action. It goes far beyond that in suggesting that people do not, in any case, enjoy the sort of freedom which enables personal action and moral accountability. For it characterises the human situation in terms of bondage to sin, not of freedom. Consequently, the traditional reading of the doctrine of original sin appears to run counter to the most fundamental affirmations of modernity's turn to the subject: that the individual is autonomous, and that autonomy is the sole basis for establishing responsibility and guilt. The standard supposition of modernity has been that freedom (construed as a freedom *from* determination, the capacity for transcendence of determining conditions and hence as the capacity for unforced and undetermined choice) is an innate and inalienable property of the individual, since freedom – and hence personal-moral responsibility – belongs to the basic structure of

---

19. For a clear statement, see Tennant, *The Origin and Propagation of Sin*, pp. 93, 164, where there is an explicit reduction of sin to the breach of that legislated or apprehended by conscience. Hence, this position reflects Tennant's evolutionary optimism that the only limitations to conscience as an accurate and sufficient indicator of God's will merely reflect the stage of development so far achieved. There is thus little consciousness that individual, social or societal conscience may themselves be fundamentally prone to distortion (on this point, see the remarks of Ricoeur, 'Original Sin', p. 282). Such could not be said of Troeltsch, who insisted that sin is 'conscious resistance to the ideal' (*Glaubenslehre*, §22.2). Cf. Rudolf Bultmann's distinction between ethical (personal, subjective) and legal (objective) guilt in *Theology of the New Testament* I (London: SCM, 1952), pp. 250ff. See also Alfred Vanneste, *The Dogma of Original Sin* (Louvain: Nauwelaerts, 1975), p. 89; Swinburne, *Responsibility and Atonement*, pp. 35–8, 43, 48. For Brunner, it is the eclipse of the role of decision which marks the false naturalisation of sin in the traditional formulation of the doctrine (*Man in Revolt*, pp. 267f., 276, 401); cf. the role of deliberation in Segundo, *Evolution and Guilt*, p. 25. Ricoeur argues that the turn (even in Biblical religion itself) to individual consciousness of guilt represents a migration of viewpoint in the discernment of sin, from that of God to that of the individual person (*The Symbolism of Evil* (Boston: Beacon Press, 1969), pp. 108, 143f., 147). (Elsewhere he explicitly defends the objective realism of original sin's understanding of sin against subjectivising interpretations: 'The consciousness of sin is not its measure. Sin is my true situation before God. The "before God" and not my consciousness of it is the measure of sin ... No becoming aware of myself on my part is sufficient, all the more so because consciousness is itself included in the situation and is guilty of both lies and bad faith' ["Original Sin", p. 282].) In the OT, we can also find a primary concern with the objective, legal nature of offence against God (usually God's command) which makes one (and sometimes others) guilty and requires ritual atonement (e.g., Lev. 4:2f., 13; 5:2–6, 17; Num. 15:22–31). Cf. here also Julius Müller's criticism of Schleiermacher's reduction of guilt to a subjective category of consciousness: *The Christian Doctrine of Sin* (Edinburgh: T. & T. Clark, 1852), I, p. 222. (I am grateful to Stanley Russell for his careful, concise exposition of Müller in 'Two Nineteenth Century Theologies of Sin: Julius Müller and Søren Kierkegaard', *Scottish Journal of Theology*, 40 (1987), 249–58.)

human being.[20] In modernity, then, freedom is not merely considered an essential condition for the passing of moral judgment. Freedom enjoys an ontological and metaphysical status as a basic and enduring structure of human existence. It is therefore inalienable; it cannot be destroyed or lost within existence.[21] It is an assumption shared by diverse modern theologies that we retain sufficient freedom to be personally responsible for what we do in at least some domains of life.[22] Characteristically in modern theology, it is freedom rather than sin which is a received structure of being which we cannot avoid.[23] This involves an at least implicit rejection of the view that we are subject to a profound, pre-personal distortion at the very heart of our beings, which destroys our freedom to avoid sinning; that sin encompasses us, determining our situation before God *already* as one of guilt, prior to and independently of anything we do or will.

Modernity's core premiss concerning human nature clashes immediately, then, with the traditional doctrine of original sin, which holds that sin (at least since the Fall) is not in any simple way a *phenomenon* of, but is *prior to* individual freedom. Sin *pre-conditions* freedom. It is a structural co-determinant of human being and action. Sin lies *behind* action, in the basic intentionality of the agent (indeed, in the biological and social processes which lie behind that), and not only in the acts themselves. But how then may, not merely moral acts, but the human condition itself, be said to be characterised by freedom? In its traditional form, the doctrine of original sin appears to modern sensibilities to propose a metaphysics of sin (to ontologise sin in the form of bondage and non-personal attribution of guilt) which runs directly counter to the metaphysics of freedom characteristic of modernity. In so doing, the traditional doctrine also appears to

20. This optimistic assessment of the inherent, natural properties and capacities of a sphere of freedom untainted by sin – whether of the reason, the spirit or the will – which became characteristic of Enlightenment thinking was roundly attacked by Jonathan Edwards as early as 1758 in his *Original Sin* (New Haven: Yale University Press, 1970) and four years later in *Freedom of the Will* (New Haven: Yale University Press, 1957).

21. So, e.g., Søren Kierkegaard, *The Concept of Dread* (Princeton: Princeton University Press, 1957), p. 39.

22. For example, cf. here the positions of Tennant, *The Origin and Propagation of Sin*, pp. 163–9, 173; Piet Schoonenberg, *Man and Sin: A Theological View* (London: Sheed & Ward, 1965), pp. 104f., 112–18, 138ff; Paul Tillich, *Systematic Theology* II (London: SCM, 1978), p. 57; Trigg, 'Sin and Freedom', 197.

23. That freedom is the common constitutive element of both sin and humanity (or, more properly, the realm of the personal) has enabled Vanneste (*The Dogma of Original Sin*, pp. 99f., 102) to suggest that their origin might be coincident. See also Sebastian Moore, 'Original Sin, Sex, Resurrection and Trinity', *Lonergan Workshop*, 4 (1983), 85f.

the modern (just as much as it frequently did to the pre-modern) mind to undermine the possibilities of deploying sin as a moral language; to undermine the very conditions for making moral judgments.

For those reasons, the traditional understanding of original sin cannot stand alongside the base assumptions of modern culture. Of course, conservative theologies which operate on the basis of a positivism of the tradition, simply sweeping modern cultural assumptions aside to reassert the tradition, are still to be found within the modern period. Aside from those confident repetitions of tradition which refuse to grant modernity any purchase on doctrinal interpretation, modern theology has been characterised on the whole by an attempt to assimilate or to restate the tradition in relation to modernity's base assumptions. In relation to the doctrine of original sin, modern constructive theology moves in one of two directions. In one, the doctrine is judged to be irretrievable in any form and an alternative interpretation of sin is advanced which meets the requirements of modern assumptions concerning freedom. In the other, there is an attempt at retrieval of those aspects of the doctrine which might be compatible with modern cultural understanding through a strategy of reinterpretation. In the following sections, I shall examine each of these strategies in turn. Before that, however, I want to continue to take note of what they share in common.

Both strategies reject the idea of a guilt-inducing, fundamental, structural distortion inflicting the whole of humanity. Despite appearances, both assume that the freedom which enables personal, responsible action implies that it is *possible*, but not necessary, to sin. In such a view, every particular instance of sin is a free act in the sense that it does not arise 'naturally' out of the ontological structure of human existence. If sin is removed from the domain of necessity in order to preserve its moral character as free, personal act, its contingency is evidently preserved. But can it at the same time be held to be strictly universal, or is that correlate of original sin to be lost equally in counter-interpretation and reinterpretation? A number of modern positions argue that, whilst any particular sin is a free, responsible act which might have been avoided; empirically, it is not possible for anyone to avoid sinning altogether. For the structure of free (self-, relation- and situation-transcending) subjectivity is always in tension with the limiting conditions of finitude, and hence marked by fragility and ambiguity in concrete existence so that sinning at some time is an unavoidable consequence of taking on the responsibilities of freedom in existence.[24] Human nature is not therefore to be considered corrupted in its essence or fallen from some primordial perfection; it is rather fragile and ambiguous in the conditions of existence.[25]

Some modern interpretations may seem, then, to retain the notion that, in sinning, I find myself in solidarity with universal humanity. Yet this is not so much a solidarity *in sin*, but in the substructure of freedom and finitude which makes sin (and, indeed, all free, responsible action) possible. Insofar as this may be termed solidarity, it is not one which names either a common history or any real bondedness one to another; it is there as sin's anterior possibility and is unaffected by our actual sinning. Indeed, it now begins to look less and less like what the tradition means by *solidarity* in sin. 'Solidarity' here indicates merely the substructure of self-transcending finitude which is the hallmark of the human condition. We share in this condition as *individuals* and, in so doing, we exhibit the characteristics of our species. Insofar as we may speak here of solidarity, then, we do so in a way analogous to that sharing of common physiological characteristics which mark us as members of a common species.

Beyond this affirmation of a common structure of humanity prior to, independent of or 'behind' sin, modern theology may yet attempt to speak of a solidarity which is a consequence of sin. Whereas the traditional imagery is of a metaphysical solidarity in sin which is biologically conditioned and mediated, here we have a solidarity which is axiological and empirical. That traditional imagery then becomes a symbolic and mythological expression of a reality which does not precede, but is rather a *consequence* of, personal decision and action, albeit arising out of the structure of finite freedom held in common by all. In modern interpretation, my membership of a universal community of sinners does not come to me through some form of biological or metaphysical mediation prior to my own conscious decision and action. It is rather my free decision and action which graft me into whatever corporate reality sinful humanity,

---

24. See Schleiermacher, *The Christian Faith*, §§67.2, 71.1; Reinhold Niebuhr's critique of locating sin in the 'inertia of nature' in *The Nature and Destiny of Man* I (New York: Charles Scribner's Sons, 1941), chs. VI–VIII); Søren Kierkegaard, *The Sickness Unto Death* (Princeton: Princeton University Press, 1941); *The Concept of Dread*; Langdon Gilkey, *Message and Existence* (New York: Seabury, 1979), pp. 138–42; Edward Farley, *Good and Evil: Interpreting a Human Condition* (Minneapolis: Fortress Press, 1990). Tillich is able to affirm the uncorrupted goodness of creation only as idealised essence. Adam then becomes the symbolic representation of the human passage from essence to existence (*Systematic Theology*, II, pp. 44, 56). See further the remarks of David H. Kelsey, 'Whatever Happened to the Doctrine of Sin?', *Theology Today*, L/2 (1993), pp. 172ff. and cf. Ernst Troeltsch, *Glaubenslehre*, §22.7 (who in the end explicitly affirms that sin is 'given with nature' and so involves neither freedom nor guilt (pp. 315f.)).   25. See also here Schleiermacher, *The Christian Faith*, §§ 57.1, 59f.

qua sinful, may be admitted to have. For here solidarity is not a metaphysical reality, passively received with existence; it is something created and realised only through free personal agency. And so a modern affirmation of universal solidarity in sin boils down to the affirmation that, empirically, all in fact sin and, in so doing, join themselves into the global ecology of human affairs distorted by sin.[26]

It is hard to see how the proclaimed universality of sin, and therefore of human community in sin, may be sustained if they are removed from the realm of necessity and made reliant on free personal agency. Is it really possible for modern interpretation to affirm any more than the *near* inevitability and *probable* universality of sin?[27] The most which modern interpretation may make of the traditional understanding of original sin transmitted at birth (and sometimes it is far less than this) is to consider it a piece of mythological symbolism, a way of speaking about the universality of sinning in practice.[28] It may be affirmed, then, only as a technique for mythologically securing the fundamental Christian affirmation that the need for God's grace is universal whilst refusing its corollary, that freedom is itself subject to radical distortion – and that is why sin is universal.

Counter-interpretation

In the traditional formulation of original sin, there is a dialectical tension between the active and passive: between sin as a fundamental distortion received with one's basic humanity and the way in which one actively enacts and personally joins oneself to it.[29] In one strand of

26. Ibid., §71; Albrecht Ritschl, *The Christian Doctrine of Justification and Reconciliation: The Positive Development of the Doctrine* (Clifton, NJ: Reference Book Publishers, 1966), pp. 335, 350. See also G. Vandervelde's discussion of Vanneste's position in *Original Sin: Two Major Trends in Contemporary Roman Catholic Reinterpretation* (Amsterdam: Rodopii N.V., 1975), pp. 268, 273. Although Vanneste declares that universality is not simply contingent, it is hard to see how his (or any) view may affirm the absolute and necessary universality of sinning without asserting a trans-empirical and trans-historical 'law' which both falls prone to Hume's critique of causality as an empirically derived conception, and breaks his own strictures against transcendental explanation.
27. By way of illustration, cf. Ritschl, *The Christian Doctrine of Justification and Reconciliation*, p. 380 with 'Instruction in the Christian Religion', in *Albrecht Ritschl: Three Essays* (Philadelphia: Fortress Press, 1972), p. 28.
28. For a clear example, see Vanneste, *The Dogma of Original Sin*, pp. 26, 30, 82–90, 102, 104.
29. The point is well grasped by Tillich, in his discussion of the relationship between the tragic and the moral in *Systematic Theology*, II, pp. 41ff., 46, 56; as by Sally Alsford in her unpublished Ph.D. thesis, 'Sin as a Problem of Twentieth Century Systematic Theology' (University of Durham, 1987), pp. 7ff., 284f., 291f., 303ff., who argues that, if the tensions are ironed out of the doctrine of sin, they reappear elsewhere in the systematic corpus. Whilst 'realists' such as W. G. J. Shedd affirmed the dynamic interrelation of active and passively received sin, G. C. Berkouwer is correct in his observation that this has no more substance than a merely logical affirmation (*Sin* (Grand Rapids: Eerdmans, 1971), ch.13).

This is too simplistic of an account.

modern interpretation, however, the emphasis on the active and the personal eclipses any sense of sin's trans-personal reality, much less holds them in dialectical tension. Here the freedom understood to characterise human being and action is supposed to be not only inalienable but unqualified by anything external to the person. Here sin shifts from metaphysical power to an atomic decision of an asocial, individual self. For the autonomous core of the individual subject is assumed to remain untouched and unaffected by the concrete history of its own action, just as the person is supposedly unaffected by external influences in any significant way. Freedom as a formal capacity for unconstrained choice has no preconditions but itself; is contingent on nothing but the free decision of the subject. Neither anything in the social, nor in one's own personal, inheritance effects a distortion of one's inner, personal core of freedom. That inner, personal core always stands in an external relationship to both one's own history of action and to social and other realities external to the self. So, one's acts have no significant after-life in relation to one's freedom. There is no accretion of the consequences of action which might diminish the freedom constitutive of one's status as an autonomous subject. One returns to neutral, so to speak, after each action. Each and every act is consequently the free act of the autonomous subject, isolated from and purified of any personal, social or material influence.

In this somewhat simplistic and asocial view, each and every sin becomes a new fall from a regained state of innocent freedom – a freedom not predisposed towards sin, but suspended in neutrality between sinful and good choices.[30] Adam's sin, if it is taken seriously at all – even as myth – can be admitted as having introduced nothing more than sin as *possible* object of choice for the rest of us.[31] Similarly, the trans-personal history of sin through the generations presents us with nothing more than the pressure of a bad example, even where institutionalised in social conventions and mores. It might make choosing against sin harder; it does not eradicate our inalienable freedom to avoid sin. In an individualistic interpretation, sin remains primarily an individual reality. Even where the distortion of

---

30. Despite his avowal of radical evil as an innate propensity of the will, Kant could speak in this way (*Religion Within the Limits of Reason Alone*, p. 36), by maintaining that this is a pre-temporal choice made by each individual (pp. 16f., 26f., 33, 36f. – such is his basis for marking a distinction between this and a predisposition (p. 26)). See also Kierkegaard, *The Concept of Dread*, p. 26 and, on pre-temporal choice, Julius Müller, *The Christian Doctrine of Sin* II (Edinburgh: T. & T. Clark, 1853), p. 402.

31. Bultmann, *Theology of the New Testament*, I, pp. 252f.

the social and historical context in which the person is set might be admitted, this distortion may neither be termed sin (since sin is personal act, not social structure or process), nor does it eradicate the conditions (freedom of choice) in which sin is possible.[32]

In this strand of interpretation, sin is contingent on nothing other than my own, free choice. Here it is freedom which is proclaimed as radical. Sin no longer appears as a radical and trans-personal distortion at the heart of each and every human being. And yet in one way this is a radical view of sin. For if the causation of one's sins ultimately rests with one's own free decision alone, then one cannot advert to other individual, supra-individual or natural factors which condition and constrain decision. One is isolated with total and undivided responsibility for what one has done. And, since these acts were free, one could have done otherwise. We are all, then, in the position of Adam, having fallen of our own free choice. Each human life replicates the Biblical story.[33] Consequently, a view which on some grounds might be termed liberal, often turns into a rather severe moralism in its entire elimination of excusing conditions and the correlate intensification of blame.[34]

Radical decision of the self

Not all modern interpretations of sin which disavow the traditional metaphysics of sin's transmission in favour of the free and personal character of action opt for an atomised view of action in relation to the self, however. The (initially free) acts of sin are in some positions taken to be self-involving decisions – that is, acts which decide the self as much as acts decided by the self. Where a narrative or existentialist position is taken, for instance, sin may be construed, not so much as a series of free acts which bear no intrinsic relation either to one another or to the self, but as a life-in-act. This term indicates the unitary nature of a life-trajectory, charted through all of one's action, as a character built up out of a story of

---

32. Ibid., p. 253; Swinburne, *Responsibility and Atonement*, pp. 142f. N. P. Williams (*The Ideas of the Fall and of Original Sin: A Historical and Critical Study* (London: Longmans, Green & Co., 1927), pp. 453–63) is able to speak of a weakening of freedom through history. The first sin merely led human beings on to a lower evolutionary path than that intended, weakening us morally and spiritually – though not in a way which eradicates our freedom from and to sin. See also here the argument of Albert C. Knudsen, *The Principles of Christian Ethics* (New Haven: Yale University Press, 1943), pp. 83–101.

33. Kierkegaard, *The Concept of Dread*, pp. 29f., 54f.

34. Such did, in fact, characterise the position of Pelagius. See Augustine, *On Nature and Grace*, 1, 56f., 59; *On the Proceedings of Pelagius*, 54 and cf. Vanneste's comments in *The Dogma of Original Sin*, p. 89.

multiple actions and interactions.[35] Then the history of sinning may be described as a kind of decision about the self; or, better, as a life in which the self is decided and through which freedom not to sin is progressively lost. Here freely chosen acts gradually bind the self in an orientation on sin which can no longer adequately be spoken of in purely axiological terms. For sin pertains now not just to the bad acts performed by the free self, but to the enduring structure of decision-making, of selfhood. Sin begins therefore to achieve here a more substantial (and yet not metaphysical) quality, as an enduring distortion of the self which lies behind its action – although itself the *consequence* of the self's history of personal agency. This is an internal, *self*-binding in sin, not the impersonal inheritance and transmission of an external distortion, bondage and guilt. It is decisive, self-involving life-in-act.

Reinterpretation

Alongside the individualistic strand of counter-interpretation, however, there stands another, which attempts to take more seriously the ways in which individuals, their intentionality and action, are shaped by their social context, by supra-personal and impersonal factors. Indeed, recognition of the power of social and historical pathologies provides the opportunity for a reinterpretation of the core of the doctrine of original sin: the dialectic between the 'external' (supra-personal and impersonal) factors and the 'internal'. The traditional formulation of the doctrine speaks of sin's trans-personal reality in metaphysical terms and of its communication in naturalistic ones (biological transmission). In modern reinterpretations that naturalism (judged to be mythological) is translated into social terms.[36] The supra-personal and impersonal reality of sin

---

35. Emil Brunner and Karl Barth both took up the notion of 'life-act' in order to safeguard the *personal* reality of sin. Both argue on that basis for a view of sin which is principally axiological and anti-metaphysical, which appears to ontologise all the acts of a person's life, giving sin a substantial quality (notwithstanding Barth's insistence that it is nothing) *within* the person. See Brunner, *The Christian Doctrine of Creation and Redemption* (Philadelphia: Westminster, 1952), pp. 93, 110; *Man in Revolt*, pp. 116f., 121, 133, 148ff., 300–4; Barth, *Church Dogmatics*, IV/1 (Edinburgh: T. & T. Clark 1956), pp. 394f., 402ff., 490f., 500ff. (where he recommends a change in German theological idiom, from *Erbsünde* to *Ursünde*). This typically Protestant emphasis has been taken up in a number of existentialist, Roman Catholic reinterpretations – e.g., Schoonenberg, *Man and Sin*, pp. 19f., 111; Urs Baumann, *Erbsünde? Ihr traditionelles Verständnis in der Krise heutiger Theologie* (Freiburg: Herder, 1970), pp. 255–9; Mark O'Keefe, 'Social Sin and Fundamental Option', *Irish Theological Quarterly*, 58/2 (1992), 85ff.

36. Kant's notion of a 'kingdom of evil' (*Religion Within the Limits of Reason Alone*, p. 74) was taken up by Schleiermacher, who considered the social 'kingdom of sin' to be a correct translation and interpretation of the traditional concept of original sin (*The Christian Faith*, §71.2). Ritschl, however, abjured such equivocation in stating his own preference for

and the means of its transmission appear here, not as metaphysical or biological, but as social in form.

At the heart of modern, social reinterpretation of original sin, then, lies a new appreciation of the situatedness of the human person. It is not at all a move back from the characteristic modern attentiveness to personal categories. It represents, rather, a reclaiming and redefinition of those categories from the simplicities of an individualist metaphysic that makes the freedom constitutive of personal life and agency dependent on an inner personal core, supposedly untouched by aspects of one's situation. A metaphysic, to put it the other way about, in which situation is in turn construed as something simply external to the asocial and ahistorical internality which constitutes one as a person. In this strand of reinterpretation, the personal is construed as always socially and historically situated; and situated in a way that renders it impossible to speak non-dialectically about inner/outer, personal/supra-personal or personal/impersonal, as if they were simple oppositions. Rather, a human person

> precisely *as* free subject, and not merely *in addition* to this, is a being in the world, in history, and in a world of persons. But this means that he always and inevitably exercises his personal, inalienable and unique acts of freedom in a situation which he finds prior to himself, which is imposed on him, and which is ultimately the presupposition of his freedom. It means that he actualizes himself as a free subject in a situation which is always determined by history and by other persons.

> This situation is not only an exterior situation which basically does not enter into the decision of freedom as such. It is not the external material in which an intention, an attitude or a decision is merely actualized ... Rather freedom inevitably appropriates the material in which it actualizes itself as an intrinsic and constitutive element which is originally co-determined by freedom itself, and incorporates it into the finality of the existence which possesses itself in freedom.[37]

This understanding of the situatedness of the person and of her free action affords the possibility of demythologising the idea of a naturally inherited guilt into ideas of transmission or contamination through

similarly non-metaphysical, social concepts of sin. These he regarded, not as translating, but as *substituting for* and replacing the earlier, 'naturalistic' doctrine of original sin (*The Christian Doctrine of Justification and Reconciliation*, pp. 335, 342f., 350). He also argued that the power of social influence on the will was paralleled by psychological processes of habituation (pp. 343, 349). See also Michael Sievernich's discussion of this theme in his *Schuld und Sünde in der Theologie der Gegenwart* (Frankfurt am Main: Josef Knecht, 1983), 90ff., 249ff., 256ff., 265ff.

37. Karl Rahner, *Foundations of Christian Faith: An Introduction to the Idea of Christianity* (London: Darton, Longman & Todd, 1978), pp. 106f.

concrete processes, structures and institutions of social interaction (which includes the cultural, political and economic).[38] Here there is a thoroughgoing substitution of social categories for the ontological and metaphysical language through which the doctrine of original sin is traditionally expressed. What we inherit are the *consequences* of a past history of freedom as they distort the conditions of communication and relation (and thereby of meaning-, value- and identity-formation) in which we are situated.[39] We inherit this, furthermore, not merely as the external situation upon which we act, but in the internal pre-conditioning of our free agency. Sin is then propagated through forms of sociality distorted through a history of sinning. The social processes, structures and institutions through which we are called into full personhood, the very processes through which we receive the conditions for autonomous and therefore responsible action, are pathologically distorted. They are alienated and alienating from God.

38. Both liberation theologians and the Roman Catholic episcopate in Latin America have framed talk of situational and structural sin in predominantly political and economic terms ('Latin American Bishops' Conference: Medellín Final Documents', in *The Church in the Present-Day Transformation of Latin America*, II (Washington DC: USCC, 1970), I.1, II.1, 2; 'Puebla Final Document', in John Eagleson and Philip Scharper, eds., *Puebla and Beyond* (Maryknoll, N.Y.: Orbis, 1979), 28, 281, 287, 328, 452, 487; John Paul II, *Sollicitudo Rei Socialis*, 36, 37, 46). Whilst the Roman Catholic magisterium had previously recognised a social dimension of sin (e.g., in *Gaudium et Spes: Pastoral Constitution on the Church in the Modern World*, Part 1, ch.3) and subsequently sometimes has explicitly adopted Puebla's language of structural sin (*Reconciliatio et Penitentia* no.16: *Acta Apostolicae Sedis 77* (1985), 213–17), there is real disinclination to acknowledge social and structural sin as anything more than an analogous use of the term. Structural and social sin represent the crystallisation of the confluence of individuals' sins in a situation which then encourages and legitimises (but does not determine) further individual sins. It is these individual sins which are, in fact, here considered to be real sin. Here is designated the structural mediation of the past sins of individuals to individuals in the present in a way which is not deterministic, but which encourages the continued misuse of freedom. So sin remains here correlated with notions of personal responsibility construed in moralistic terms: as the free (i.e., self-determined, rather than socially or structurally determined) acts of moral agents (see, e.g., *Instrumentum Laboris* from the Synod of Bishops, 1983; *Reconciliatio et Penitentia*, 16). It is yet assumed that the kind of agency involved in sin is moral; whereas social structures do not have moral agency (neither would people subject to those structures in a deterministic way). Hence the reality of sin is again identified as residing in the moral interiority of the person, which remains unaffected by structural pathologies, at least sufficient for her assimilation of and shaping by these structures to be characterised in moral terms: as at some level and to some extent a free act. Indeed, liberation theologians themselves sometimes seem to share this equivocation concerning the real sinfulness of pathological structures (see, e.g., José Comblin, *Being Human: A Christian Anthropology* (Tunbridge Wells: Burns & Oates, 1990), p. 219). However, a much less naive interpretation of the concrete nature and operation of individual freedom is suggested in their characterisation of the ideological function of sinful structures – their power to incorporate people by presenting themselves as rational, just or 'natural' – as realities which we cannot free ourselves from, but on which must be predicated all our thinking, relating and acting (see, e.g., Juan Luis Segundo, *Grace and the Human Condition* (Dublin: Gill & Macmillan, 1980), pp. 38f.). For further insightful discussion of the categories of social and structural sin as deployed by liberation theologians, see Sievernich, *Schuld und Sünde in der Theologie der Gegenwart*, pp. 232–82.

39. Segundo, *Grace and the Human Condition*, pp. 107ff.

We receive the means for acting in a manner capable of moral evaluation (i.e., freely) through the processes of social reproduction. But these processes are themselves distorted by sin, and so we receive the distortions of our situation alongside – or, rather, at the very heart of – our personal being. We do not therefore enter the stage of personal action with a clean slate, morally in neutral as it were, but already infected with the pathologies of our situation, alienating us from God and the good. We stand already, prior to any action on our part, in a pathological relationship to God – in sin. Furthermore, through our subsequent, active participation in corporate sin, we ourselves contribute to the building up of a distorted and distorting common life, which passes these distortions on to others.

This is evidently a much more radical construal of the reality of sin than is possible in an individualistic framework. Here sin has more than an axiological and individual reality. The field of reference of the term 'sin' is no longer restricted to individuals' free acts, but now extends to social structures, institutions and processes. And sin is present within the person, not only prior to, but within the conditionality of, his own moral action.

Yet, social reinterpretation has more in common with individualistic counter-interpretation than appears superficially to be the case. To say that both are modern is to say rather more than that they happen to come from a common era or culture. Beneath the surface, both share some of the assumptions characteristic of modernity concerning the inalienability of freedom, coupled with the assumptions of 'natural' morality concerning the conditions for the attribution of moral responsibility.

This is evidenced in the desire of more than a few social reinterpretations to avoid the implication that, by taking so seriously the historical, social and cultural contingency of the person and her action, they might be implying a form of determinism which would obviate the possibility of moral autonomy. Here there is a temptation to revert to notions of the permanent inviolability of personal freedom, whatever the social distortions one is subject to. And so the threat of determinism is countered by permitting the notion of a transcendental personal core to return by the back door. The inner core of a person's free agency is a social transcendental, not corruptible by external contingencies in the situation, by what is passively received from outside their own sphere of free agency.[40]

40. So, e.g., Schoonenberg, *Man and Sin*, pp. 104f., 112–18, 138ff.; Stanley Hauerwas, *The Peaceable Kingdom* (Notre Dame, I: University of Notre Dame Press, 1983), pp. 38–49 (on whose position, see the perceptive critiques of Gene Outka, 'Character, Vision, and Narrative', *Religious Studies Review*, 6/2 (1980), 110–18 and Tina K. Allik, 'Nature and Spirit: Agency and Concupiscence in Hauerwas and Rahner', *Journal of Religious Ethics*, 15/1 (1987), 14–32). See also the discussion of feminist theologies of sin in this regard in a footnote to p. 135, below.

More significant evidence than this, however, is found in the universal reluctance of modern reinterpretations to speak of the social reality and inheritance of sin as something for which the person stands guilty and accountable. This indicates a subtle, though highly significant, shift in the meaning of the term 'sin' when applied to social structures and processes rather than free acts. Certainly, most social reinterpretations term social distortions, 'sin'. But caution should be exercised in assuming that the term is being used univocally of the personal and supra-personal. For, although there may be a preparedness to name the social and historical situation in which one inevitably participates as sin, a distinction is generally made in so doing between passively received, inherited sin and sinning by personal acts. And it is only personal acts for which one is said to be responsible; only through them that one may incur guilt.[41] The

41. Where there is retention of the term 'guilt' for anything other than personal acts, it tends to be applied with neither univocal meaning nor uniform force. Schleiermacher struggles to affirm that original, inherited sinfulness is guilt-bearing sin, and not just evil, by insisting that original sin cannot properly be considered apart from its ratification by the individual's subsequent actual sins. Hence it is never simply passively received. But the knot between original and actual sin begins to unravel in his consideration of infants whose internality is distorted by inherited original sin, but who are yet incapable of actual sin (i.e., of personal, culpable acts) by which they become guilty. Schleiermacher implies that infants are guilty but, until they achieve the maturity to ratify original sin in actions for which they are *personally* responsible, their guilt is of a lesser extent and quality. Schleiermacher appears to hold here (*The Christian Faith*, §71.1; cf. §67.1) that infants are held guilty in *anticipation* of this future ratification, which inevitably follows (assuming what cannot properly be assumed – that maturation is reached) because, in inheriting original sin, actual sin is inevitable as one's own responsible act. Infants appear therefore to be justly held guilty from the perspective, not so much of their situation strictly as infants, but from the standpoint of their future maturation into sinners: on the basis of future acts which meet the moral criteria for personal culpability. It is hard to avoid the conclusion that guilt proper appends, after all, only in regard to morally culpable acts, which explains his later statement that guilt for original sin applies properly not to the individual, insofar as he passively receives it, but to the race (§71.2). Somewhat similarly, Karl Rahner speaks of the 'guilt' of others as a co-determinant of our situation (*Foundations of Christian Faith*, pp. 111f.) which we take on when we act freely. Yet the passive inheritance of a situation already saturated with guilt he considers sin only analogically, since it is not personal (pp. 111, 113). Hence, the guilt of others which determines our situation is guilt-proper only for them; it is guilt for us, after all, only analogically. Weger also is able to affirm that guilt is inherited in our historical situatedness only by making an analogy between original and personal sin, which awaits personal activation before it is guilt, non-analogically (*Theologie der Erbsünde*, pp. 16–23, 28–31, 107, 141). Schoonenberg (*Man and Sin*, p. 181) speaks of original sin as a 'faint foreshadowing of a personal decision'; whilst Vanneste is unwilling to apply the category of sin to infants at all, because – lacking the freedom concomitant with full personhood – they cannot be guilty (*The Dogma of Original Sin*, pp. 26, 30, 82–90, 102, 104; cf. the brief comment by Brunner in *Man in Revolt*, p. 400). See also Marciano Vidal's discussion of official Roman Catholic documents and his own synthetic view in 'Structural Sin: A New Category in Moral Theology?', in Raphael Gallagher and Brendan McConvery, eds., *History and Conscience: Studies in Honour of Father Sean O'Riordan, CSsR* (Dublin: Gill & Macmillan, 1989), pp. 190ff., 194–7; and the brief comment of Michael Sievernich, '"Social Sin" and its Acknowledgment', *Concilium*, 190 (1987), 56f. Marjorie Hewitt Suchocki (*The Fall to Violence: Original Sin in Relational Theology* (New York: Continuum, 1994), pp. 137–42) speaks of

meaning of the term 'sin' shifts when it is applied to the social sphere. In the end, the distinction between passive and active is made against moral criteria concerning the conditions of personal accountability and responsibility. Moreover, it is made in such a way as to suggest that it is, after all, only sin in the sphere of the personal (which, despite the overall affirmation of the social as a dimension of the personal, is nonetheless construed in individualistic terms when it comes to the issue of accountability, responsibility and guilt) for which I am responsible and which therefore holds real seriousness for my personal being.

The social limitations and pressures operating on individuals are here taken seriously as co-determinants of action; nevertheless, it is our own, free action – and not pathological sociality – for which alone we stand accountable, which alone bears guilt. Hence social reinterpretation of the doctrine of original sin actually excises, rather than interprets, the traditional notion of the non-personal transmission and inheritance of guilt. What is not capable of interpretation through the filter of modern culture (with its double affirmation of the inalienability of freedom of choice and that the conditions for attribution of theological guilt conform to those of 'natural' morality) is filtered out. What is socially inherited and communicated, passively received, cannot be guilt.[42] At most, it is a socially mediated deprivation of the good. We share in sin in the form of guilt only when we activate that social inheritance. Sin remains here, then, primarily

'original guilt' in relation to passive participation in sinful social structures and institutions only where there is a developed *capacity* for transcendence and freedom which could and should have been used to resist them. Which is to say that guilt is not, after all, 'ontological', but personal, incurred only where participation in sinful social structures is not as passive as it might seem, but represents a refusal of the power of resistance. Guilt is incurred where participation is a *free act of the person*. Cf. here also Tillich's discussion in *Systematic Theology*, II, p. 59 and Swinburne who (not advocating a social reinterpretation, of course), speaks of our involvement in one another's sins, meaning only to signify a duty to help them atone and find forgiveness (*Responsibility and Atonement*, pp. 145f.).

42. Schoonenberg, *Man and Sin*, p. 196; Schleiermacher, *The Christian Faith*, §71.1; Baumann, *Erbsünde?*, p. 247. The use of terms other than 'sin' for that which is passively received is often a device for avoiding the connotations of guilt properly associated with the term 'sin'. Ted Peters, for example, makes a distinction between the 'essentially moral' notion of sin and the 'pre-moral' notion of defilement (*Sin: Radical Evil in Soul and Society* (Grand Rapids: Eerdmans, 1994), p. 141) which matches his earlier equivocation in switching to the category of 'evil' when referring to a radical, supra-personal malevolence in which one participates through acts of sin and through sinful dispositions (e.g., pp. 24f., 218 n.2). From a feminist and otherwise thoroughly relational perspective, Mary Potter Engel similarly elects to term that which is passively received through social systems and structures 'evil', and to reserve 'sin' for 'free, discrete acts of responsible individuals' ('Evil, Sin and Violation of the Vulnerable', in S. B. Thistlethwaite and M. P. Engel, eds., *Lift Every Voice: Constructing Christian Theologies from the Underside* (San Francisco: Harper & Row, 1990), p. 155). (Swinburne is able to use the language of defilement, but only to refer to the rationally calculable, subjective evil of an intentional act (*Responsibility and Atonement*, pp. 74f.).)

an axiological and moral category after all. We are accountable for sin, in the end not in or by our (social) *being*, but by our *acting* – in this case, our active self-incorporation into the institutionalised processes of social action.

Sin as a moral language

Modern theologies of sin object to any idea of primordial solidarity with others in sin, construed as accountability, responsibility and guilt. The only form of solidarity admissible is that effected through individuals' free acts. Hence, even those modern reinterpretations which retain a sense of the corporate nature of sin suggest nonetheless that I join myself to the pre-history and social reality of sinning in my own freedom, certainly so far as my own accountability for sin is concerned. I am the subject of my own sin insofar as it is something for which I am accountable. In no sense do I find myself already accountable for the supra- or trans-personal reality of sin prior to my free act. In modern theology, the scope of accountability for sin is narrowed to the field of action and immediate situation of each person. That is to say, accountability for sin is restricted to that over which I have some power or control, and in relation to which I am free. It is restricted, in other words, to that which, in personal power and freedom, I transcend, to which I *can* – though may not (which is to say such failure is culpable) – avoid succumbing. Accountability for sin then applies to persons as the *perpetrators* of free, personal acts. It does not apply to *victims*, since they, by definition, do not have the kind of freedom and power in and personal transcendence of their situation necessary for moral culpability. So, when sin passes through the filter of modernity in modern theology, it bears a much closer resemblance than previously to a moral language of blame. The danger attending modern theologies of sin is a total collapse into moral categories, which – in a secular culture – exclude any active reference to God. What appears to be demythologisation of the doctrine of original sin threatens to slide into a de-theologising of sin. And the closer sin approximates to secular, moral categories, the more the onus should fairly be on those who wish still to deploy the language to show that its naming of the pathological is still a means of referring to God.

We can glimpse here the somewhat paradoxical situation that confronts those who approximate sin too closely to moral categories and invite it to be assessed in them. For sin appears to be objectionable at the points at which it resists moral categorisation. But if those points of resistance are eliminated, there seems little point in operating with this theological category at all. If the language of sin functions in the way any other moral language does, then there is a danger that any non-moral element will be so effectively silenced as to be functionally eliminated. It is no defence against this latter possibility to suppose that the language of sin is still functionally theological if God is taken to be the author and legislator of the moral codes and norms against which sin is assessed (especially as these approach universal affirmation and so appear to be an aspect of the universal human situation rather than of divine decree).

Here there is an analogy with a line frequently taken in relation to the doctrine of creation in the face of the capability of modern science to explain the world without reference to God, which settles for an affirmation of God's original authorship of all that is. That leaves God entirely inactive and absent from the world once it has come into being. It abandons any idea that God might yet be involved in the ongoing workings and internal structure of the world, and therefore necessary for a full understanding and explanation of them. The task of a theology of creation had better be construed as interpreting the reality of the natural order (as partially described and theorised by secular natural sciences) in relation to the Christian understanding of God's presence and action, rather than as a collusion with the assumption that secular, pragmatically atheist science is sufficient as a form of explanation.

In the case of the doctrine of sin, the assumption should be avoided that God only has function as the originator of norms for human life which, once in place, function without further reference to God. Were that the case, then sin would be adequately expressed in terms of secular morality, since the only difference between the language of sin and those of secular morality is the question of whence these norms are derived, what legitimates and authorises them.

If sin is a moral language (that is, reducible to the frame of reference afforded by its understanding of freedom of will), then, in a secular culture, Christians might have to exercise extraordinary care in using it to ensure that it retains functional reference to God. But, beyond that, would the reduction of sin to a moral frame of reference be problematic? Perhaps not, provided the challenges of its undergirding conception of freedom as separation may be met in relation to the construal of the intrinsic relatedness of creation (including human creatures) to God and of the fundamental solidarity of humanity before God in salvation as in creation. I am dubious about that, but let me concede the possibility here for argument's sake. In that case, there would be no cause for concern, humanly or theologically, provided such moral frames of reference held sufficient explanatory and descriptive power to bring to comprehensive expression the depth dynamics of concrete pathologies. It is that proviso which, no less than the theological language of sin, deserves to be tested in relation to concrete pathologies. If the result of such testing shows the explanatory power of moral discourse to be limited, then there is an at least prima facie case for reconsidering those elements of sin-talk occluded in its reduction to moral categories. Furthermore, if that limitation relates to the conceptualisation of freedom (identified in this chapter as the founding axiom, both of our culture and of moral frameworks of interpretation) that so chafed against core aspects of the traditional interpretation of original sin, there might be a more substantive case for their reconsideration. In that case, the eclipse of the non-moral might seem humanly as well as theologically problematic.

After a brief, methodological interlude, I shall embark on this task of testing ways of construing the pathological in theological terms (neither limited nor irreducible to the moral) to illuminate the dynamics and nature of concrete pathologies. In the following chapter, I discuss the strategy I adopt in this book for testing doctrine in this way, alongside the broader questions and issues in theological method this raises. I then move, in chapters 4 and 5, to a description of the concrete pathologies in relation to which the explanatory power of the language of sin is to be tested. The methodological discussion in chapter 3 is not essential for the substantive discussion that follows on from there.

3

Testing, testing: theology in concrete conversation

The business of theology is to talk about God. An underlying theme of previous chapters was the temptation facing modern theology of collapsing the transcendent into secular frames of reference – into ways of speaking about the world which pragmatically exclude God. This, in fact, mirrors the other main temptation of modern theology: to sustain reference to the transcendent in a secular culture by withdrawing theology from the empirical and material. So theology withdraws from those domains wherein secular discourses are presumed to have competence into the spheres of personal morality and spirituality. The existential situation of modern theology is to be suspended between these two extremes, which easily appear to be the only alternatives to a fundamentalist refusal to let go of a pre-scientific, metaphysical cosmology. Hence, modern theology is constantly poised between the danger, at one extreme, of collapsing talk of God into secular frames of reference without remainder (appending God as little more than rhetorical flourish) and, at the other, of withdrawing God to the margins of secular competence (a God of the gaps and a God only related to the non-material). In the end, both strategies permit talk of at least some features of mundane, empirical reality to go on without any functioning reference to God. Theology thereby ceases to be discernment of God's presence and activity in and relation to the world. Both therefore let go of the one possibility by which modern theology may live: to draw the secular into dialogue, to live in a critical and dialectical relationship with secular disciplines.[1] That possibility is undermined wherever the

---

1. Cf. here Pannenberg's resistance to theologies which try to identify a 'point of contact' (the phrase is Bultmann's – see his 'Points of Contact and Conflict', in *Essays Philosophical and Theological* (London: SCM, 1955), 133–50) with secular discourses which then enter theology uncritically. Here theology gives up on the possibility of critically transforming the secular through contact and conversation with theology (Wolfhart Pannenberg, *Anthropology in Theological Perspective* (Edinburgh: T. & T. Clark, 1985), p. 19).

basic assumption of our secular culture is allowed to stand: that explaining the world in the world's own terms excludes any reference to transcendence, to God. The twin suppositions that the world in itself is adequately comprehensible without God and that the transcendence of God implies separation from the world are essentially non-Christian and have permitted secularity to become a form of pragmatic atheism. Modern theology colludes with that assumption wherever it refuses to operate a specifically Christian, trinitarian understanding of God's relation to the world which is dynamic, and in which God's transcendence and immanence are always found together.

In the light of this assertion, the statement with which I began must be modified. The task of theology is, indeed, to speak of God. But, since the God of Christian faith is intimately and dynamically related to the world, that talk may not permissibly be carried on in abstraction from the world, nor, therefore, from worldly forms of self-understanding. It is not the business of Christian theology to talk of God only in the abstract or in ways that affirm God's supposed abstraction from the world. Rather, it is to understand both God and reality from the perspective of God's concrete presence and activity in the world, and in relation to our concretely lived experiences of being in the world. Nowhere is that more true than in relation to the doctrine of sin. Sin is a way of speaking of the pathological aspects of the world encountered by human beings as they live in it. It either brings to expression the depth dynamics of the pathologies we empirically encounter, and which secular discourses speak of in worldly terms, or it is meaningless abstraction. If the doctrine of sin has no relation to empirical reality, cannot be tested by it in any way, then it is meaningless.[2] Hence, any appropriate means of testing sin-talk must have an empirical reference. It must be a means of testing its explanatory and descriptive power in relation to concrete pathologies and the secular disciplines by means of which they are analysed, interpreted and resisted.

It is not immediately obvious, however, whether and how doctrines of sin may be considered statements about empirical reality, and therefore subjected to empirical testing.

---

2. There is an obvious similarity here with the principles of verification and of falsification, which assert that any proposition which is not, in principle, capable of verification/falsification is meaningless. My criterion is less severe, however, and admits of a range of possible connections with empirical data through which a theoretical proposition might be tested – a less stringent requirement than direct verification or falsification.

One immediate difficulty relates precisely to the integrity of the world in all its proper distinctiveness from God. The clearer the 'vertical' reference (speaking of pathologies in our relationship to God) in a doctrinal formulation, the more opaque does sin-talk become in its 'horizontal' reference (speaking of pathologies in our relationships one to another), and vice versa. If the fundamental characterisation of sin is rebellion against God, idolatry or the refusal to be a creature, say, it is clear how one might look for empirical instantiation in terms of people overtly rejecting God, worshipping the devil, making graven images and the like. But it is not at all clear whether and how such images of sin pertain to human behaviour beyond the confines of the specifically and obviously religious; not immediately obvious how all pathology is at heart some form of, say, rebellion against God or idolatry. Neither is it immediately or obviously clear how offences against others (murder, rape, adultery) or pathological human situations (poverty, abusive family, racist society) are at the same time, much less in their essence, against God (rebellion, idolatry, refusal of creatureliness). In short, it is not obvious how the very theological character of sin-talk permits a relation to our empirical experience of the profane. Empirical testing asks whether speaking of concrete pathologies as sin (i.e., as pathologies *in relation to God*) holds explanatory or descriptive power and whether doing so also helps illuminate and give more definition to the *theological* substance of sin-talk. In part, what it tests is the extensiveness of the range of reference of sin-talk in relation to pathologies between human beings.

Beyond these difficulties arising from the integrity of creation which tempt us to abstract God from the world, abstraction in another sense represents a difficulty in empirical testing of doctrines of sin. Doctrines of sin (e.g., original sin) are intended as statements concerning the universal condition of human beings before God (contingent, universal, communicable and radical distortion and accountability). Their universal reference is required, is shaped by and mirrors that most basic Christian conviction, the universality of God's salvific action in Christ. Christians are driven towards an account of sin as a means for understanding the pathology they know to be healed in Christ (thus it follows that sin may only be known and should only be spoken of in relation to salvation). Since that healing of salvation applies universally, so must the need for it: sin must be universal too. Doctrines of sin therefore speak of it at this universal level, and so are necessarily highly generalised and abstract formulations. Their task is to represent sin's fundamental character in a way that will be applicable to an infinitely varied range of particular settings. And so sin is presented as a theological pathology permeating every human person, relation, situation, action, event, intention and endeavour at all times and in all places. Doctrines of sin have to give a degree of definition as to sin's fundamental character (they have to indicate what sin fundamentally is), but do so without at the same time losing anything of its universal range of reference. It is therefore necessary for them to work at the highest level of generality and to achieve definition without overspecification.

Thus, doctrinal formulations of sin speak about the empirical (that is, they make claims about the pathological distortions to be found in every particular, empirical setting), but do so at a necessarily general and abstract level. Consequently, they look more like metaphysical claims or grand theory than straightforward strict, empirical descriptions. And so it is difficult to know how the conceptualisation of sin at this level relates to particular, empirical situations, how it might illuminate their concrete, depth pathologies and how it might be subjected to empirical testing. Doctrinal formulations of sin are not without empirical reference, but they tend to be too idealised, abstract and non-specific a representation of reality to admit of direct empirical verification or falsification. That is to say, abstract formulations are empirically irrefutable, cannot receive inductive support, and are not specific enough to function predictively at the level of concrete situations. They register claims about a fact so basic, fundamental and extensive (one might say, metaphysical) that they cannot be directly tested. In addition, they refer to the whole of reality at once, and therefore without any degree of specificity, and their basic symbolism has no clear empirical content. Like the general theories of science (e.g., general field theory, information theory, game theory, systems theory, the theory of evolution), they offer an abstract characterisation of a system's 'gross structure', in their formulation entirely independent of the properties of matter or other aspects of concrete reality.[3] They form a 'generic epistemological framework' aiding the interpretation of a highly varied set of specific situations, at various levels of reality and complexity.

Like general scientific theories, doctrines of sin cannot be subject to *direct* empirical testing, but may yet be capable of *indirect*, empirical confir-

3. I am greatly indebted here to Mario Bunge's discussion of the relationship between grand theory in science and empirical description: 'Testability Today', in *Method, Model and Matter* (Dordrecht and Boston: Reidel, 1973), and to Daniel W. Hardy for putting this text in my hands.

mation or disconfirmation once they are interpreted in the direction of hypotheses, theories or models with more specific reference, which may themselves be empirically tested.[4] That might be a case of deductively unpacking the implications of the general theory already in place, or showing its 'fit' with one or more, more specific hypotheses, models or theories that can be empirically tested directly. At the same time, theory at all levels may be enriched through empirical testing, not only through association with a more specific theory or model (which may amend interpretation of the more abstract one), but through induction from empirical data gathered by these and other means.[5]

Doctrines of sin in their most abstract and general form approximate to the general theories of science. We should not, therefore, expect to be able to subject them to direct, empirical testing. In relation to the doctrine of original sin, for example, its account of sin as distortion and accountability in relation to God that is contingent, universal, communicable and radical is not directly amenable to testing against concrete, empirical phenomena. It is capable of only indirect testing through the mediation of theories or models with more specific and localised reference, such as a theory of intentionality deduced from the claim that sin distorts, but is not a phenomenon of, our freedom (e.g., bondage of the will); or a hypothetical model of sin (e.g., pride, as the interpreted nature of the first, and so all subsequent, sin).

The two situations in relation to which I have chosen to test the doctrine of sin are the sexual abuse of children and the holocaust. Two situations, in order better to ascertain those dynamics which might be generalisable beyond the specific features of a particular pathological situation, not more than two because of the difficulty of doing them full justice within present constraints. Why *these* two situations? Their complexity affords a rich environment for testing the doctrine and means that each has generated an extensive literature attempting to grapple with such complex dynamics. They are almost (although, significantly, not quite) universally recognised as having reality and as being pathological.

---

4. According to Bunge, that may require a number of such interpretive moves. A general theory may be associated with a 'generic, semi-interpreted theory' (e.g., classical or quantum mechanics, general relativity theory, the synthetic theory of evolution) which may itself be still too general and abstract to admit of direct, empirical testing, which requires further interpretation in the direction of a 'specific theory' or 'theoretical model'. See ibid., p. 38.

5. Bunge states that it is by 'showing that they do in fact fit a whole family of specific theories (concerning specific systems) or that they take part in the design of viable systems'. Ibid., p. 37.

The recognition of their pathological character does not depend on a specifically Christian or theological mode of discernment. That fact allows the question of the contribution of a theological language to emerge the more starkly. If these situations may be recognised and described as pathological without the Christian God, then what is the theological task in relation to them? Is there anything more or different that can be said about them when they are brought into explicit relation to the Christian God? Is the secular description of their pathology not adequate? Furthermore, it seemed wise to select situations which invite differences of emphasis and interpretation, thus witnessing to the complexity of the pathology.

Engaging with these concrete phenomena requires an engagement with the secular disciplines in which they are analysed, interpreted and resisted. The conversation with secular thought remains very close to the concrete realities of these two situations. It is more usual for constructive theology to choose as conversation-partners secular disciplines and discussions which are themselves already at a high level of sophisticated abstraction, removed from the concrete situations in which the themes they take up emerge (such as theoretical accounts of the general structure of human existence). That sort of conversation, however, represents a still theoretical testing of the doctrine of sin. It would still remain to be seen whether the resultant correlation of secular and theological theory actually illuminated concrete situations.

What am I doing by constructing a conversation between the Christian doctrine of sin and secular ways of understanding child sexual abuse and the holocaust? What status does such conversation have? What is to be expected of it? What is the status of the concrete situations? Let me be absolutely clear before going any further that *child sexual abuse and the holocaust are not used as examples; they are rather fields of testing encounter*. I am not trying to exemplify an understanding of sin which has been (or could be) worked out independently of the consideration of these concrete situations. Rather, I am trying to understand and to test the doctrine of sin in and through a consideration of these two situations, which draws theology into conversation with secular forms of discernment and description.

To say that the concrete situations are not examples is to say that neither Christian doctrinal tradition nor secular discussion are going to be permitted to enter the conversation with conclusions which are unassailable and unreformable in the light of their interaction with the concrete situations and with one another. All that is to say that this is a dialogue concerning the nature of concrete, pathological dynamics, in which the theological and the non-theological test each other's understanding and are tested by the empirical realities of the situations.

It should also be noted that I am not claiming any form of epistemological privilege for these two situations in relation to sin. Sin is a universally extensive reality and, whilst it is not equally distributed in its quality or intensity, there are no situations of which it may be claimed that they afford privileged insight into sin's reality over against other situations. There is a certain benefit from engaging with two situations in which sin achieves a particular intensity. But there are also dangers. The very intensity of the pathological dynamic in the holocaust and the sexual abuse of children might suggest that the reality of sin is clear, obvious, and requires very little by way of thick description. The opposite is, in fact, the case: the density of sin's dynamic requires corresponding density in interpretation and description, whilst simultaneously provoking systematically embedded ways of hiding its nature and reality. Sin's dynamic complexity makes it incapable of complete understanding or explanation, whilst its intensity makes it appear unbelievable. Sin's complex intensity blinds and masks its own reality in effecting what I shall call later a traumatic confusion in the realm of knowledge and understanding, as much as in practice.

Perhaps the greater danger, though, is that the choice of situations of intense pathology might mislead by suggesting that sin is most real or dangerous where it has this kind of intensity. It is not only just as real, it is in some ways more dangerous, where it has a lower intensity; where it presents itself as a trivial, unexceptional and unavoidable aspect of the mundane and everyday. In the particular situations I have chosen, however, the severe intensity of sin is, in part, evidenced in its colonisation of the mundane, the way in which it insinuates itself, incognito, into the fabric of the everyday, and so appears unexceptional, normal, the way things are and have to be. Thinking through the doctrine of sin responsibly in relation to these particular situations cannot then concentrate exclusively on the horrific details of genocide and of acts of sexual abuse of children. The true horror of both is in a way marked in the low-intensity of an all-encompassing background against which particularly horrific acts take place. And the more we pay attention to this background intensity of sin, the narrower appears to be the difference between these 'extreme' situations and those which we normally take to be mundane or trivial. I hope that the engagement will therefore resist our propensity to regard sin as an interruption of the everyday, as an exceptional event, as something happening elsewhere than here, in the midst of the mundane normality of our own lives. The engagement with situations in which the power of sin achieves a high degree of concentration is intended to facilitate the recognition of sin's reality in situations in which it might achieve (or seem to achieve) a lower intensity.

This process of 'testing' is an engagement with secular discourses in concrete encounter, through which Christian understanding may be shown to be inadequate to the concrete realities of pathology and needing to be reconfigured. Is such preparedness to allow Christian self-understanding to be changed through dialogue a departure from tradition? Only if tradition is misconstrued as the passive receipt of an already co-ordinated doctrinal deposit. Being traditional, being shaped by tradition and handing it on (*tradere*), is an active, historical responsibility that is always, and can only be, worked out in the contingencies of concrete situations and through ad hoc correlations and conversations.[6] Much modern theology operates on the assumption that tradition is a kind of fundament, which already contains all that is necessary for future development pregnant within it. That is as true of more liberal approaches which recover marginalised voices as it is of strategies which take the more conservative view, that the stabilisation achieved in the inherited co-ordination of the doctrinal corpus is fixed and binding.

The point here is not simply that Christian tradition is not the univocal monolith which some conservative theological strategies seem to suppose. The point is rather that tradition is something we take responsibility for in the making. Doctrinal continuity is not something we receive from the past, but something which we find and recognise in the present – not merely in, but for, to meet the demands of, the practical and theoretical exigencies of particular situations.

The present stabilisation of doctrine is not a trans-historical fundament containing all within it necessary for its own future development, and much less should it be regarded as itself the final and complete co-ordination of Christian truth, which requires no subsequent development. Rather, the truth and fixity represented by the stabilisation of doctrine in the tradition (which has never been univocal) occurred in the process of handing on, and discerning the nature of, the faith in a broad

---

6. Cf. here Hans W. Frei, *Types of Christian Theology* (New Haven: Yale University Press, 1992), pp. 3f., 81–91; William Werpehowski, 'Ad Hoc Apologetics', *Journal of Religion*, 76 (1986), 282–301.

range of cultural contexts. It arose, in other words, not out of a process of spelling out a fixed meaning which was a given and necessary property of the gospel, but out of the historical dynamics of mission whereby the gospel moved into a broader range of contexts than it had hitherto known. In that process, it was necessary to agree on a trans-historical, trans-contextual co-ordination of the truth of the gospel. But the fixity so achieved was always a two-term affair, entwining both the content and context of meaning, since it arose out of (and for the purpose of regulating) the dialectical interactions between the gospel and the situations in which it found itself.

The achievement of doctrinal stability arose out of the flux of hearing the Word in a range of concrete situations. Its purpose is not to carry permanently fixed, static meaning. It is to facilitate hearing and responding to God's Word in a range of disparate and highly varied situations. And that purpose is frustrated wherever the stability of doctrine is raised out of its historical dynamic and turned into a static and fixed fundament. Then the theological task is essentially repetition. But if being traditioned actually entails entering an historical dynamic which is still in play, then the theological task becomes at once more deeply oriented both on its context and on the gospel mediated through the tradition. Here we may begin to see that the stability of Christian tradition is not static and fixed, but an act of historical recognition. We see doctrinal continuity and stability after the event, by recognising family resemblances from the perspective of our own situation. Theology, I suggest, is more like the practice of discerning family resemblance by general, shared characteristics than it is a scientific technique for tracking biological relation by taking blood samples and comparing the DNA. Theology is then a reconstructive discipline which tests and reconstrues the continuity and stability of the doctrinal tradition in its concrete task of discerning the reality of God in its specific situation.[7] And such discernment has always been conducted through conversation with non-theological and non-Christian frameworks and disciplines of interpretation and understanding. The truth of God can only be found through conversation with non-theological (and, in our culture, that means pragmatically atheist) contemporary forms of

7. Here I am very close to the position arrived at by Charles Davis in his *Religion and the Making of Society: Essays in Social Theology* (Cambridge: Cambridge University Press, 1994), pp. 96–111. Cf. here the closing pages of Alister McGrath's *The Genesis of Doctrine: A Study in the Foundations of Doctrinal Criticism* (Oxford: Blackwell, 1990), pp. 198–200 and my own 'Truth as Mission: the Christian Claim to Universal Truth in a Pluralist Public World', *Scottish Journal of Theology*, 46/4 (1993), 437–56.

understanding and practice. My claim here is that faith, *in order to be intelligible and true to itself,* has to engage in dialogue with non-theological forms of public explanation, understanding and truth which both confront and permeate the situation of living faith.

To term such conversation dialogue indicates the requirement that the specific identities of the partners be taken seriously, so protecting either one from being subsumed into the discourse of the other. It suggests, further, a double-hermeneutic whereby the conversation may be mutually illuminating. That implies a positive assessment of secular discourses, which allows that they may illuminate Christian theology and prompt the tradition towards new development. But theology is at the same time expected to illuminate secular discourses, drawing them into relation to a theological framework: to the attestation of the triune God's relation to, presence and action in the world. It is assumed, in other words, that theological discourses do refer and apply to reality in a way that makes a significant difference to interpreting and living in it. Here there is an implication of the inadequacies of secular discourses, at least insofar as they have become Godless, pragmatically atheist, in our culture. Drawing the secular into conversation with theology in the way I am attempting affirms secularity, but invites us to think God along with and in the secular. This is the side of Bonhoeffer's search for 'religionless Christianity' which is too frequently forgotten: worldly Christianity, a holiness which is a dimension of this-worldliness; or, as one might say, the Christian God as the truth of secular this-worldliness.[8] Such a conversation is a dialogue which maintains a dialectical tension between the secular and the theological, which resists the imperialistic tendencies of both a religious and a secular self-confidence in their autonomous and enclosed self-sufficiency. Here the integrity and the autonomy of the world (and hence of secular disciplines) is maintained as a correlate (rather than a contradiction) of faith in the triune and incarnate Christian God. At the same time, if the dialectic is to be maintained, the Christian God cannot be collapsed into the world, cannot become simply an aspect of nature accessible through secular means of discernment. Faith is not worldliness without qualification, and neither therefore may theology legitimately be turned, non-dialectically and without qualification, into

---

8. On this theme, see Haddon Willmer's interesting study of the factors preventing English writers from developing and maintaining a notion of 'holy worldliness', or at least one sufficiently dialectical, in the late nineteenth and early twentieth centuries: '"Holy Worldliness" in Nineteenth-Century England', ed. D. Baker, *Studies in Church History*, 10 (1973), 193–211.

psychology, sociology, history, philosophy, literary analysis, phenomenology, or natural science – although it cannot and may not be without
them either.

In testing sin-talk in relation to concrete pathologies, I am asking
whether there is a religious, spiritual or theological dimension to them
which secular frameworks of analysis, interpretation and therapeutic
action are incapable of bringing to adequate expression. If that is the case,
then secular language cannot be adequate to express and interpret the *full*
pathological reality of the pathology. If, however, it is not the case, then
theological language and frameworks of interpretation can have no
descriptive or explanatory power – at least in their specifically theological
aspects and reference. If it could be shown that theological language was
incapable of bringing the core pathological dynamic to expression, of
naming and identifying it, then that would be sufficient for it to fail the
test. Clearly, then, asking whether the tradition is capable of identifying
and naming the key features and aspects of concrete pathology which
emerge in their phenomenological description is one of the first tests to
apply. But, whilst a negative result would be enough for God-talk to fail
the test, a positive one would prove insufficient to pass it. For more is
required of theology than showing that its lexicon includes (or may be
reinterpreted as including) the meanings required by analysis in non-
theological terms. That is a necessary but not a sufficient condition
for passing the test. For, if left at the level of matching terms, concepts
and meanings, theological language is stripped of its theological reference: theological terms substitute for secular ones and are defined and
confined by their referential limits. There is then little point in substituting theological for secular terms, beyond their familiarity in particular
communities, since they would then have no additional explanatory
power as *theological* terms. Whilst the language of sin is here explicitly
retained, its meaning is non-theologically derived and controlled.

The business of the third part of the book is therefore not limited to
establishing whether Christian conceptuality already includes (or may be
extended by reinterpretation to include) the main components of secular
analysis. It must also ask whether specific and explicit theological description is able to recognise and bring to expression aspects of pathology that
secular analysis is ill-equipped to recognise, but which makes deeper and
greater sense of secular analysis and description. Does theology reach the
parts other frameworks of interpretation and description are unable to
reach? Do the concrete pathologies identified in non-theological terms

relate to God in a way that invites and requires theological description in order to comprehend the depths of their full reality?

Let me now be more specific about the kind of claim I am making in mounting this conversation: the concrete pathologies operating in child sexual abuse and the holocaust cannot *adequately* be understood except with reference to the denial of and opposition to God which characterises sin. And so frameworks of analysis, interpretation and forms of therapeutic or political action that (at least implicitly) exclude God will, I contend, have a significant depth-dimension missing. Secular descriptions cannot be accepted as the entirely adequate, pre-theological basis for subsequent theological elaboration, interpretation or commentary. But they must be accepted as the provisionally adequate descriptions which theology is obliged to work with, in and through.[9]

To put my basic contention here simply in a way which returns to the concerns of the previous chapter, and without any of the humility which really should characterise such a venture of faith, the theological task is to discern and then show to secular discourse its own inner truth. If truth is one in God and God is related to the whole of reality, then nothing that is true about the world can be unrelated to God. At the same time, however, the failure of secular discourses in our culture to relate their truth to God, to incorporate into themselves reference to the dynamic being and activity of the triune God, must be judged from this perspective as a failure. And this is a failure, not according to some externally imposed theological standard, but *in relation to secular disciplines' own truth*. If God is the truth of the world and is actively present in and in relation to it, then a secular understanding of the world in its own terms cannot properly exclude God. That is the basis on which the following concrete conversation is conducted. I leave it to the reader to judge, in the end, whether it has proved possible to be faithful at the same time to Christian faith in the triune God, to the concrete situations themselves and to the secular disciplines which attempt to understand and describe them.

---

9. Cf. again Pannenberg, *Anthropology in Theological Perspective*, pp. 19f. Of particular relevance to the theme of this book is his discussion of the theological understanding of the sin of pride in relation to secular psychological description (pp. 91f.).

Part II
―――――――
Concrete Pathologies

4

Bound by silence: sexual abuse of children

In this and the following chapter, I present accounts of the two concrete pathologies against which the theological language of sin will be tested in Part III. These accounts are the fruit of sustained engagement with the relevant secular disciplines and are presented in terms that are not explicitly theological. My purpose is to work up phenomenological descriptions of pathologies in their own terms, without bringing them into immediate, explicit relation to theology. To do otherwise would undermine the possibilities of testing the descriptive and explanatory power of the theological language of pathology in relation to both its concrete manifestations and its non-theological expression. In order to ask whether theology might enrich (and, in turn, be enriched by exposure to) such non-theological description, it is necessary to delay the point at which it is drawn into an explicit theological framework. However, whilst these phenomenologies have been shaped through engagement with secular disciplines, they do not simply replicate their terminology or frame of analysis. The engagement is both constructive and synthetic, seeking to understand the concrete situations described and analysed in secular discourses rather than attempting a straightforward representation of those descriptions.

The pathological effects of childhood sexual abuse can be, and often are, severe, deep-seated and long-lasting. They are also highly particular. What the reality of abuse actually is for any individual child or adult survivor – how it is experienced, the nature and extent of its effects – relates to a complex interaction of factors which will be unique in every case.[1]

---

1. Such as: relationship to the abuser; length of time over which abuse took place; whether the abuser was male or female; whether abuser and child are of the same sex; the nature of

Because the experience of being abused and of surviving is idiosyncratic, it is not possible to give any unitary account that will hold true for all survivors. In what follows, I am not so much offering a description of 'the' experience of childhood sexual abuse, as constructing an account of the core, pathological dynamic in which sexually abused children are trapped. Rather than squashing particularity, I hope that this general phenomenology will help to account for the highly particular and diverse consequences of childhood sexual abuse in the uniqueness of individual lives. More than anything, I hope that survivors (and especially those who have shared their stories with me) will be able to recognise themselves in this account.[2]

Footnote 1 (*cont.*)

the abusive acts; the child's psychology; the age at which abuse began; the number of abusers; the existence of close and stable relationships with other adults; prevailing cultural codes and norms of behaviour; the use of violence or other, more subtle, coercive techniques; the rationalisations offered by the abuser. It is the *interaction* of such factors which is constitutive of the reality, experience and effects of abuse for a particular child or adult survivor. There can therefore be no simple correlation between any single, specific factor and a particular effect. Childhood sexual abuse may affect people, not only in diverse, but in opposite, ways (for instance, one survivor may exhibit obsessional sexual behaviour; another, extreme sexual inhibition). Statistics as to the prevalence of childhood sexual abuse are difficult to gather accurately. However, data from the most reliable research, using classifications similar to the definition offered in this discussion, suggests that a minimum of 10%, and a possible maximum of around 30%, of all children are sexually abused. In little less than half of these instances, the abuser is a member of the child's family, and in approximately 40% of the remainder the abuser is known to the child, though unrelated. The prevalence of sexual abuse among boys has been estimated at something between 3% and 9%; that amongst girls, between 15% and 30%. Girls are more likely to be abused alone; boys to be abused with others, usually their sisters, by a parent. The perpetrators in at least 90% of incidents are men. Women abuse around 20% of female and 5% of male victims. (But on the possible underestimation of both male victims and female abusers, see Matthew Parynik Mendel, *The Male Survivor: The Impact of Sexual Abuse* (Thousand Oaks, CA: Sage, 1995); and on female abusers see: K. Faller, 'Women who Sexually Abuse Children', *Violence and Victims*, 2 (1987), 263–76; L. McCarty, 'Mother–Child Incest: Characteristics of the Offender', *Child Welfare*, 65 (1986), 447–58; Jane Kinder Matthews, Ruth Matthews and Kathleen Speltz, 'Female Sexual Offenders: A Typology', in Michael Quinn Patton, ed., *Family Sexual Abuse: Frontline Research and Evaluation* (Newbury Park, CA: Sage, 1991), pp. 199–219.) Sexually abused boys tend to suffer separately inflicted physical abuse as well, a phenomenon which is more marked when the abuse is intrafamilial. See David Finkelhor, *Child Sexual Abuse: New Theory and Research* (NY: The Free Press, 1984), pp. 72f., 80f., 163–6, 177; Diana Russell, 'The Incidence and Prevalence of Intrafamilial and Extrafamilial Sexual Abuse of Female Children', *Child Abuse and Neglect: The International Journal*, 7 (1983), 133–46; Carol R. Hartman and Ann W. Burgess, 'Sexual Abuse of Children', in Dante Cicchetti and Vicki Carlson, eds., *Child Maltreatment: Theory and Research on the Causes and Consequences of Child Abuse and Neglect* (Cambridge: Cambridge University Press, 1989), pp. 98f., 155f.; A. Baker and S. Duncan, 'Child Sexual Abuse: A Study of Prevalence in Great Britain', *Child Abuse and Neglect*, 9, (1985), 457–67.

2. This account of abuse could usefully be read alongside the testimonies and stories which feature in much of the literature, such as: Carolyn Ainscough and Kay Toon, *Breaking Free: Help for Survivors of Child Sexual Abuse* (London: SPCK, 1993); Mendel, *The Male Survivor*; Yvette M. Pennachia, *Healing the Whole: Diary of an Incest Survivor* (London: Cassell, 1994); Tracy Hansen, *Seven for a Secret: Healing the Wounds of Sexual Abuse in Childhood* (London: Triangle/SPCK, 1991).

What counts as sexual abuse of children?

In popular and media discussion, one finds a good deal of uncertainty, disagreement and 'fuzziness around the edges' about what constitutes sexual abuse of children. Is it limited to the sort of activity that would constitute sexual assault, were it committed on a non-consenting adult (requiring tactile contact)? Does the abuser have to be an adult? Is the term only to be used in relation to pre-pubescent children? Such uncertainty and disagreement may even be found in the professional literature, and is reflected in the variety of definitions offered. Since the definition of childhood sexual abuse is not transparent, I offer the following statement as a clear indication of the definition which operates in and underlies my discussion of the abusive dynamic: *children are sexually abused when they are involved in sexual activity, are exposed to sexual stimuli or are used as sexual stimuli by anybody significantly older than they are.*[3]

Notice that the abuser does not have to be an adult, just significantly older than the child; and that *significant* age-difference is presented as both a necessary and a sufficient condition for sexual involvement to constitute abuse. What is it that makes age-difference crucial to the recognition of a sexual interaction as abusive? It is that age-difference is related to other differentials, such as knowledge, understanding and physical strength as well as differences in social power and status which exist

3. Sexual activity may be defined as anything that would count as such if transacted between adults. For activity to count as sexual does not require the abuser to intend or to achieve sexual stimulation, although such is usually a reliable clue as to the inappropriate and abusive nature of a superficially legitimate act, such as tickling or bathing. It is crucial that a definition should not prematurely exclude any possible instances of abuse, including that of the abuser gaining no sexual stimulation, or such being far from the dominant motivating factor. The abuser's sexual arousal is a sufficient, but not a necessary, condition in identifying a situation as abusive, and so should not form part of any definition used for purposes of clinical classification. Furthermore, making the classification of abuse conditional on something as elusive as the identification of abuser motivation invites a turning of sustained attention away from what has happened to the child to the abuser. A number of studies do, however, make sexual motivation or arousal a necessary condition for classification. See: Baker and Duncan, 'Child Sexual Abuse', 458; Hartman and Burgess, 'Sexual Abuse of Children', p. 97; Jean La Fontaine, *Child Sexual Abuse* (Oxford: Polity Press, 1990), p. 191; Tilman Furniss, *The Multi-Professional Handbook of Child Sexual Abuse: Integrated Management, Therapy and Legal Intervention* (London: Routledge, 1991), pp. 4, 30, 32; Christopher J. Hobbs, Helga G. I. Hanks and Jane M. Wynne, *Child Abuse and Neglect: A Clinician's Handbook* (Edinburgh: Churchill Livingstone, 1993), p. 120; Jean Renvoize, *Innocence Destroyed: A Study of Child Sexual Abuse* (London: Routledge, 1993), p. 36; Emily Driver, 'Introduction' to Emily Driver and Audrey Droisen, eds., *Child Sexual Abuse: Feminist Perspectives* (Basingstoke: Macmillan, 1989), pp. 3–6, whose view is further problematised by the narrowness of its rights perspective.

between different age-groups in society.[4] And where these differentials are significant, it is impossible for sexual involvement *not* to be based on and exploitative of them. So, even where the child is manoeuvred into articulating consent, the consent cannot be unforced or genuinely informed, since the relationship is permeated by these differentials.

Notice also the range of behaviour included. Vaginal and anal intercourse or penetration by objects; oral sex and masturbation, certainly. But also: exposure to pornography; exposure of others' sexual organs;[5] viewing others engaged in sexual activity; receiving an obscene telephone call; being photographed for the sexual use of others. Clearly, sexual involvement, exposure to or use as sexual stimuli can take a variety of forms, not necessarily involving physical contact.[6]

A *definition* of childhood sexual abuse has a clear task to perform: to render criteria by which behaviour may be classified and recognised as sexually abusive of children. It is a heuristic device. Inevitably, it draws attention towards *acts* and gives grounds for identifying them as abusive. The task of a *description*, however, which aims at understanding its full traumatic reality, its pathological dynamic, is somewhat different. And here an emphasis on the *acts* of abuse does not serve the cause of understanding nearly so well as it does that of classification. Here we will be much better served if we think more in terms of *relation* than of *act*. What the abuser does to the child is rather more than subject her to this or that *act*. What he[7] does

4. On the significance of the disparities in knowledge and power in relation to the issue of consent, see, e.g., Finkelhor, *Child Sexual Abuse*, pp. 17–22; Karin C. Meiselman, *Resolving the Trauma of Incest: Reintegration Therapy with Survivors* (San Francisco: Jossey-Bass, 1990), pp. 27, 37; Gay Search, *The Last Taboo: Sexual Abuse of Children* (Harmondsworth: Penguin, 1988), pp. 8, 152f.; Emily Driver, 'Introduction', pp. 4ff.; Cathy Waldby, Atosha Clancy, Jan Emetchi and Caroline Summerfield, 'Theoretical Perspectives on Father–Daughter Incest', also in Driver and Droisen, eds., *Child Sexual Abuse*, pp. 101–5.

5. The sight of significantly older people's genitals need not be sexually abusive. Parents who are not inhibited about nudity, e.g., being seen dressing or bathing, perhaps permitting their children to help in these acts, might be helping their children towards healthy, not artificially repressed, attitudes towards bodiliness in general and nakedness in particular. For exposure to count as sexual abuse some other factor is necessary which sexualises the context and the display. That might be, despite my comments in n.3, abuser motivation or arousal or the way in which it is experienced by the child as having sexual meaning, or as unwelcome, frightening, arousing.

6. The trauma associated with non-tactile forms can be as intense and damaging as that associated with abuse involving physical contact.

7. Since the vast majority of abusers are male, it would not serve the interests of truth to hide that fact by using inclusive language. So, although it is true that the relatively small number of female abusers are incorporated in this male semantic reference and rendered invisible, which may admittedly have certain problematic aspects, the use of male pronouns is more than simply generic. The use of gender-inclusive language would not simply render female abusers visible; it would over-expose them, thus creating the impression, with every equivocation between 'he' and 'she', that they are represented in roughly equal number to the men. In referring to children who are abused, however, I do

by abusing her sexually is to set up a deeply distorting, distorted and damaging relationship.[8]

Sexual abuse of a child effects a distorted form of relationship, the consequences of which may not stop when the abuse does or when any *physical* trauma associated with the acts have healed. They tend not to stop because of the way in which the reality of abuse for the child is raised to significance by what the abuser does (or what may otherwise happen) to close off the abuse and the abusive relationship from other relationships. Where she is prohibited or inhibited from disclosing, or where attempted disclosure is unsuccessful, abusive dynamics press to be internalised and sedimented in the form of a distorted identity and patterns of relationship. It is not merely that the core dynamic of abuse is that of a distorted and distorting relationality, then; it also encloses and traps the child in its distortions. The borders of the relationship are closed, binding the child, and often the adult survivor, in and to the relationship's abusive reality. It is this dynamic of isolation and enclosure which is at the heart of the pathology of childhood sexual abuse. For it is the enforced isolation and secrecy which severely intensify the damage sustained in the inappropriate sexualisation of a relationship with a child and frequently also damage the processes of socialisation and identity-formation.

In order to abuse, and subsequently to avoid detection of the abuse, an abuser must close the context of abuse, must isolate the abusive relationship from other social networks of relationship, of meaning and of action. Because of the differentials in power, status and knowledge, it is relatively easy for an abuser to overcome the child's potential or actual resistance (by offering rationalisations, justifications and false interpretations of the meaning of what is happening; by using or explicitly or implicitly threatening force and violence). That this is rarely sufficient on its own to enable abuse strongly suggests that abuse is seldom, if ever, a transaction between abuser and victim alone. Rather, when a child is sexually abused – especially over time – the failure or distortion of a

alternate between male and female pronouns, even though the best statistics show a preponderance of female victims. To use the female pronoun exclusively for victims and survivors, however, might create the dangerous and misleading impression that abuse of boys is atypical, both quantitatively and qualitatively. Male victims and survivors might then be prevented by such semantic means from recognising themselves in accounts of the abusive dynamic. That, in turn, may reinforce any impression they have that they are insignificant, aberrant, abnormal, and that such abnormality was not just a consequence but a cause of the abuse: that they are to blame or deserved it in some way.

8. Cf. the remarks made by Beatrix Campbell, making a slightly different point, in her *Unofficial Secrets: Child Sexual Abuse – The Cleveland Case* (London: Virago, 1988), p. 147.

wider network of relationships is almost always implicated in some way. The child has to be isolated in some way from functioning networks of relationship that would protect him from abuse. Strategies of isolation take a number of different forms and have the effect of enclosing the child in the reality of abuse before it is actually initiated.

Isolation

The most effective constraints operating in a situation of potential abuse are the psychological and physical presence of others, especially other adults.[9] Unless the constraints arising out of a child's relationships to other adults in her situation can be surmounted, someone who has overcome whatever internal inhibitions he had to abuse will be frustrated in his intentions.[10] No amount of coercion, manipulation or violence directed towards the child will succeed unless the child is already isolated from the effective care, concern and interference of other adults and from the codes, values and interpretive frameworks belonging to normal social relationships.[11] An abuser has either to find a child already in a situation of physical, psychological and social isolation, cut off from effective networks of committed and concerned relationship (at least for the duration of the abuse), or else pursue strategies towards that. Abusers have, in other words, to prepare the ground for abuse by undermining the knowledge, understanding and capacity for effective resistance of other adults. Abuse first happens to particular children, not because of anything about their identity, behaviour or character, but because they have the terrible and tragic misfortune either simply to be in the wrong place at the wrong time, or else to be the victims of a great deal of adult cunning, foresight and ingenuity in planning, manipulating and manoeuvring the adult relationships in their general situation. They find themselves in a wider relational situation that makes them

9. Psychological presence denotes active interest in a child's everyday affairs. As such, it is often mediated by, but does not require, constant or frequent physical presence. On this and the significance of the related factors of supervision, the mother's psychological presence and family non-isolation see Finkelhor, *Child Sexual Abuse*, pp. 57ff.

10. Finkelhor (*Child Sexual Abuse*, ch. 5) establishes a now-standard model of the analytically separable components of a sequence which an abuser has to go through before abuse may begin. An abuser must: have a motivation to abuse children sexually; overcome internal inhibitions; overcome external impediments; undermine or overcome the child's resistance. Cf. J. Kaufman and E. Zigler, 'The Intergenerational Transmission of Child Abuse', in Cicchetti and Carlson, eds., *Child Maltreatment*, pp. 138–41.

11. Where a child is too young effectively to have internalised these for himself, he is reliant on their mediation by adults.

vulnerable to abuse or which is already permeated by the abuser's distortions.

Physical seclusion

The simplest way in which abusers prevent the interference of third parties is by seclusion: the physical isolation of the place and time of abuse from the sight or hearing of others.

Such physical isolation at the time of abuse, however, is neither necessary nor sufficient on its own to facilitate abuse (except in those relatively rare instances where a stranger in a one-off incident abuses a child). Physical isolation of the location of abuse is insufficient alone, since it would not in itself inhibit subsequent disclosure to adults willing and able to intervene to protect this child or other children from future abuse. Where the abuser is known to the child and where a child is abused over a long period of time, the abuser will not abuse unless he is satisfied that the risk of discovery is minimised. So, something further must happen. The power and willingness of other adults to take effective action must be either incapacitated[12] or circumvented, by removing the knowledge-base for action – which generally means inhibiting the child from disclosing (discussed below). When either of those conditions are met, the child is effectively isolated psychologically and socially from other adults, from their care, concern and protection – at least so far as the abuse is concerned.

The capacity and willingness of some abusers to abuse in public space shows that physical isolation is not a necessary condition for abuse. Where the social and psychological isolation of the child is already achieved, her isolation from frameworks of social meaning and action leave unchallenged whatever the abuser presents to her about his actions.

12. Where, for example, an abuser (usually the father or father surrogate) exercises excessive, arbitrary and despotic power over all other members of the family, so intimidating them with actual or threatened (implicitly, if not explicitly) violence from intervening themselves or contacting outside agencies. See Meiselman, *Resolving the Trauma of Incest*; Judith L. Herman and Lisa Hirschman, 'Father–Daughter Incest: A Clinical Study', *Signs: Journal of Women in Culture and Society*, 2 (1977), 735–56; J. Herman, *Father–Daughter Incest* (Cambridge, MA: Harvard University Press, 1981); Janis Tyler Johnson, *Mothers of Incest Survivors: Another Side of the Story* (Bloomington: Indiana University Press, 1992); Search, *The Last Taboo*, pp. 73f; Bruno Cormier, Miriam Kennedy and Jadwiga Sangowitz, 'Psychodynamics of Father–Daughter Incest', *Canadian Psychiatric Association Journal*, 7 (1962), 203–17; Wini Breines and Linda Gordon, 'The New Scholarship on Family Violence', *Signs*, 8 (1983), 490–531; Donna L. Truesdell, John S. McNeil and Jeanne P. Deschner, 'Incidence of Wife Abuse in Incestuous Families', *Social Work*, 31 (1986), 138–40. Here the proper privacy of apparently functional families can operate as a cloak of concealment which seals and isolates the family from a wider social hermeneutic.

Thus, disclosure to other adults present may be inhibited, not only by threatened recrimination, but also by induced beliefs concerning other consequences of disclosure (disbelief, blame, anger) or the normality and acceptability of the abusive acts. This kind of isolation is what makes surreptitious abuse of children without physical isolation possible.[13] Here the abuser trades on the imperceptibility of dissonance between the abusive relationship and the normal social codes operating in the context as a whole. That abuse takes place in a normal sphere of interaction encourages others to interpret what they see as normal, even the child's discomfort and unhappiness (as, say, churlishness, surliness, silliness, lack of respect for elders, in rejecting the friendliness of an older person).

False normality

More common than the presentation of abuse in the guise of normality to other adults, however, is its presentation as such to the child. The differentials in knowledge and understanding permit the abuser to construct for the child a false, but powerfully persuasive, perception of normality, building up the illusion that abuse is acceptable according to social codes governing everyday contexts. In other words, abuse is presented as normal; not isolated in its idiosyncrasies, but indistinguishable from non-abusive behaviour and relationships. The difference between the abusive and other contexts is elided.

Abuse might, for example, be incorporated into the everyday routines of washing, changing and toileting, so that it becomes for the child indistinguishable from normal hygienic procedures.[14] Here the abuser plays on the ignorance of the child concerning the proper limits and nature of hygienic attention, together with her willingness to trust older people to define reality for her. The cloak of normality might also be effective in shielding the abusive reality from inspection by other adults too, since it is not unusual to perform such tasks in privacy. The abuser utilises a form of activity which, by its very nature, is regulated through highly localised rules of interaction, in order to hide abuse from others (what is impermissible elsewhere, such as touching of genitalia, may be necessary in the

---

13. An abuser might sit a child on his lap, in contact with his erection, or might find a way of touching breasts, buttocks and genitals, even inserting digits into anus or vagina, in a way which is either hidden from the direct view of others or appears to others to be a social, even a loving, embrace.

14. David Finkelhor, 'Dynamics of Abuse', in David Finkelhor and Linda Meyer-Williams, with Nanci Burns, *Nursery Crimes: Sexual Abuse in Day Care* (Newbury Park, CA: Sage, 1988), pp. 93f.

bathroom). This has the added effect of presenting it as acceptable and normal to the child, as socially acceptable according to wider social norms, codes and conventions regulating relationships and action. This effect is considerably enhanced when other adults in the situation are tacitly, if not explicitly, giving permission for the 'hygienic' task to be performed. Now the abuse may parasitically draw on the authority structures in the wider situation for its own legitimation.

Much the same processes are at work when abusive acts are incorporated into a well-known game or when given an innocuous name (teasing or tickling, for instance). The abuse appears to the child (and, on disclosure, may so appear to other adults) to be incorporated into the fabric of 'normal' life. In ignorance of what is really going on, other adults may find themselves unwittingly giving it their permission ('get up to the bathroom this instant and stop crying, daddy is waiting for you'; 'you should enjoy ring-o'-roses, I used to when I was your age'; 'you are silly, being so upset when grandpa teases you; it's just his way of showing he loves you'). Thus the abuse may not only be legitimated, but the distress or confusion of the child may be misinterpreted, disallowed or misattributed, deepening the reality of her isolation from other people and from normal codes of social interaction and meaning.

That the child experiences an unbroken connection between the abusive context and the legislative authorities, powers, rules and meaning-frames of all other social contexts actually works to deepen the isolation of the one from the others. The child who is sexually abused in these ways is isolated in his experience and understanding of the world, which others around him will not share. He cannot speak on the basis of a shared understanding of what these hygienic routines, games and innocuously named activities mean to any third party, no matter how close they are to him. For the abuser has undercut the possibilities of their hearing what he has to say by falsely naming the world and his experience of it.

Illusions of consent

Where the abuser is able to convince the child that she has consented in some way to the abuse, she is likely not only to have internalised feelings of guilt, blame and responsibility, but also to feel herself inextricably bound into the realities of the abusive relationship. The illusion of consent traps her, not only at the point of abuse, but subsequently. For she is inhibited from disclosing to others something for which she feels she is to blame. So the relationship to abuse and abuser is raised to central significance. The bonds to this relationship are strengthened, relative to those to other people and realities, from which she is increasingly isolated. Again, this effect is actually heightened by any intimation that the abuse is not acceptable to those outside the abusive context.

Wanting a good relationship

Some abusers find themselves already in a situation in which the bonds of their relationship to the child are stronger than in her other relationships (most obviously, when the abuser is a parent). Others will expend a great deal of time and energy in pursuit of that achievement by targeting children who are emotionally vulnerable, undermining what alternative emotional resources and supports they do have, and isolating them from alternative sources for the meeting of emotional and other needs. Where the relationship to the abuser has become the sole or main functioning source for emotional or material nourishment, the cost of resisting or disclosing the abuse may seem unbearable, even if the child is clear that the abuse is wrong, unwanted or even painful. Here the abuser has socially, emotionally and psychologically bound the child to a relationship in which abuse seems at least an acceptable pay-off against other benefits. She may even see the abuse as an isolated element in the relationship, rather than its defining and determining characteristic: that this is a 'real' and 'good' relationship, in which these activities take place, but in which they have no essential place.[15]

The appearance of consent to the relationship within which abuse takes place is further enhanced when abuse is initiated 'by degrees', so that the boundary between acceptable and abusive behaviour is blurred. Here there is a gradual increment in behaviour that slowly and carefully reels the child into the dynamic of abuse, since there is no significant, discernible difference between the previous act and the next. Since she did not object to the last one, the child feels in a situation of implied consent and acceptance in relation to the next. No great boundary-lines are crossed between one act and the next. Contiguous acts in the sequence hold no significantly different quality. It is only when the next act is placed alongside the first that it is clear that there has been a significant shift in their quality through the sequence as a whole. Once again, any intimation she has that what comes next is 'wrong' does not attach her effectively to norms and resources outside of the abusive context. Rather, that intimation only isolates her all the more completely. For she has

---

15. See Search, *The Last Taboo*, pp. 63–7.

already 'permitted' other 'wrong' acts, from which this is indistinguishable. Intimations of the wrongness of what is happening only help her to see herself as tarnished already by the abuse, as isolated from (and judged by) whatever 'good' norms of conduct and relation she may be aware of as pertaining outside this context.

Rewards

What I have indicated in respect of emotional entrapment applies equally to the receipt of any other kind of benefit, either from the abuse itself or from the abuser. The child's abilities to separate himself (his decisions and acts as a subject – rather than as an object – of abuse, and so his core identity also) from the circle of abuse are severely constrained, and he is consequently inhibited also from attaching himself to others. Inducements (money, sweets or other presents) may be offered to the child immediately before abuse, implying that a contract is being made between the child and the abuser: this is the fee for performing this act. He is trapped into abuse by his desire for the reward (which may even induce the child to 'initiate' abuse on subsequent occasions), fostering the illusion that he is consenting to the abuse rather than to receipt of the reward.[16] By offering inducements, the abuser effects a confused conflation between wanting the abuse and desiring the reward, creating the appearance of mutuality and consent.[17] Any such effect is reinforced if the abuse is accompanied by the physiological effects of sexual arousal. These work to inhibit him from seeing the abuse as something external to him – something which he was subjected to, in which he had no active, effective responsibility and which he did not seek and which has been harmful to him.

Bound in silence

I have been adumbrating the ways in which the sexual abuse of children requires and establishes a dynamic of isolation and entrapment, if not even before the abuse itself is initiated, then in its succeeding course. In

16. The child's desire, of course, is to receive the reward. He has made a correct contextual association between the reward and the activity. So he does not communicate his desire for sweets by asking for them straightforwardly, but by, for instance, touching (or asking to touch) the abuser's penis. The abuser has successfully produced confusion in the child between his desire for sweets and his desire to touch his penis.

17. The effects are not significantly different when 'payment' is made after the event, even if the 'reward' is not accepted by the child but is left by the abuser in the location of abuse. That can be enough to convince her that she has been 'paid', and so must have entered into a contract and consented.

illustrating some of the isolating processes set in train by the abuser, I have already drawn attention to a number of internal inhibitors against the child's subsequent disclosure of abuse and to the abuser's need to prevent it. Where the abuser is not a total stranger and cannot be certain of undermining the capacities for action of other adults in the immediate situation, he has to ensure continuing secrecy (i.e., isolation of the abusive context from wider social networks of relation, frameworks of meaning and action). Disclosure must be prevented, either by fostering in the child inappropriate self-attribution of responsibility or by the use of threats. In either case, inhibiting the child from disclosure intensifies the dynamic of enclosure and isolation already set in train and thereby also intensifies the pathological effects of abuse.

Threats

The temporal mode of any threat is futural. Threats concerning the consequences of disclosure establish a claim on the child in times and places distanced from the context of the abuse. Threats of violence transmit the abuser's power and the reality of abuse into every context the child now inhabits or will inhabit as an adult survivor. They communicate to the child that the abuser is more powerful than she, not only in the immediate context of abuse or when in physical proximity, but in any other context and, since he can overcome the capacity of others to protect her, more powerful than anyone she might tell.[18] She is unlikely to feel safe from the abuser and the threatened consequences of disclosure in any place, in any relationship or with anybody else. Fear of disclosure may invade any and all other relationships. Her fear of the abuser loosens her bonds of trust in and of others, whilst more strongly binding her to the abuse.

All that is necessary to inhibit disclosure is the child's fear of its consequences. That the threatened consequences need not relate to violence from the abuser indicates both the powerful way in which the child can internalise blame, guilt and shame and the way in which she feels enclosed and isolated by the abuse. It is this enclosure and isolation which seem to her to verify the abuser's claims that disclosure would either be disbelieved (representing the claim that the bonds the abuser has to competent adults, their respect for him, his believability, etc. are stronger

---

18. Sometimes such threats may be accompanied by claims of magical powers to know what she is doing at all times and in all places, to prevent disclosure being believed and to exact retribution in any context, regardless of the abuser's physical presence.

than those of the child[19]) or, if believed, would result in her stigmatisation (the claim that abuse now defines and has defiled her identity, cutting her off from the care and love which 'unsullied' children deserve) or her being blamed for its subsequent consequences (such as imprisonment of the abuser and consequent disruption of family life).

Secrecy

In any case, when children are sexually abused, they are almost invariably enjoined to secrecy (implicitly through the intimations they have of the abuser's power, if not explicitly through threats or violence). That injunction to secrecy closes off the immediate context of abuse from other contexts, intensifies the dynamic of isolation which encloses and traps the child in the relation to the abuser and separates her from all other relationships. Enjoining her to secrecy, the abuser weakens her bonds of relation to other people and contexts of meaning and communication; simultaneously, he strengthens the bonds between her, the abuse and himself. And this applies, even if she never sees him again.

A secret is something withheld from public communication, a reality not to be shared with others. Those party to a secret are drawn into a closed circle of meaning which others are prevented from entering by the boundaries of hidden information. A secret is information (or a whole context of communication and relation) isolated from other contexts of communication. Secrecy is designed to prevent others becoming aware of the information, combining it with other information within a framework of meaning which may yield them new understanding and provide new bases for action. Secrecy encloses.

But the social isolation effected by the injunction to secrecy does rather more than silence the child and prevent her from bringing information to public expression. It inhibits not just her *communication*, but her *processes of understanding, judging, evaluating* the information represented by the abuse.

Sexual abuse of a child typically exploits the fact that the child is unsure or confused about the meaning of the sexual acts taking place. That confusion is not brought to an end, but heightened, by the injunction to secrecy. A situation of secrecy usually involves collusion to restrict

19. Janis Tyler Johnson's study of mothers in situations of father–daughter incest (*Mothers of Incest Survivors*) strongly suggests that the strength and form of the bonds of loyalty between mother and father are decisive for resolving how the mother responds to disclosure (she makes an interesting comparison with reactions to bereavement, in order to explain how cognitive acceptance may be accompanied by emotional denial).

shared knowledge and understanding from wider public access. But in this context, the disparities between abuser and child in knowledge and understanding mean that the world of meaning enclosed by secrecy may well be substantially different for each. How they are able to interpret and understand the abuse may significantly differ. The child may simply be unable to understand what has happened to her, what this means, unable even to comprehend it as abuse. It is not necessary for her to have a full understanding of what it is that she is to keep secret, just that she is to keep it secret; is not to refer to it in other contexts. But that is to say that she may find herself holding information which has not for her been encoded in public meaning, combined with other information so that it might be interpreted appropriately. And it is this combination with other information held in public meaning-frames and interpretive frameworks that is rendered impossible by the injunction to secrecy. Secrecy interdicts her access to other frameworks of meaning (which, depending on her stage of maturation, she may not have access to independently already) by preventing her from sharing the information with others who might provide appropriate interpretation as well as action. Consequently, she is prevented from processing the information, since the resources for so doing are unlikely to be in her command already. Secrecy isolates by blocking transcendence.

The secret does not merely isolate the child from the companionship, solace and assistance of others, then, but from the processes of public meaning, communication and exchange through which the meaning and significance of the abuse may be processed. He is isolated from the social means for comprehending and interpreting reality, including the reality of an abusive sexual relationship, just at the point where he has traumatic new information to make sense of and integrate into his sense of himself and his world. The stark realities of abuse, together with what the abuser says to explain, justify and comment on it ('it is all right, it means I love you'; 'I am teaching you what you will need to know about sex'; 'this is your punishment for being such a bad girl'; 'this is happening because you are dirty and wicked') easily become the sole frameworks of meaning by which the child may interpret and evaluate both the abuse and his own identity in its light.

Childhood sexual abuse is almost always confusing, often traumatically so.[20] If the abuse is physically painful or if it breaches public norms

20. Sexual abuse of children cuts across so many of our normal social assumptions concerning power, trust and responsibility that disclosures or suspicions of abuse render

and values already internalised (especially in the case of an older child), then the child is faced with a conflict of claims about what is right and wrong. Even if the child is psychologically developed and settled in identity sufficiently for it to be clear to her that abuse is wrong, she is still left with the confusion engendered by being abused by someone who, on account of significant age-difference (and possibly familial relation or caring role), should be trustworthy.

Secrecy can prevent abused children (especially pre-pubescent children) from interpreting the abuse against wider public codes, norms and values. Yet secrecy also establishes an intimation of dissonance between the codes, norms and values operating in the abusive context and those operating outside. For if there is nothing wrong with this, why can it not be shared with other people? Secrecy itself makes abuse confusing. Even for a child who accepts abuser rationalisations at face value, the injunction to secrecy itself implies that this is not, after all, something good, normal and acceptable. It is something bad and shameful, or else it could withstand public exposure.

Internalising abuse

But with that intimation usually comes another visitor: this is something which the child easily believes that *he* has done, since *he* fears exposure. Therefore he may feel guilt, even if the reason he fears exposure and must keep the secret is that the abuser has threatened him with violence or told him that he will bear sole responsibility for the consequences of disclosure (family break-up; imprisonment of the sole bread-winner; others' emotional reactions, etc.). Here the child is given the illusion of power: all now seems to be in his hands.[21] And it is very hard for him to resist reading that power back into the abusive situation: 'If I am in control of the secret and fear its exposure, then I must be responsible for the abuse.' The injunction to secrecy includes intimations concerning his accountability for the consequences of disclosure (if not directly for the abuse itself), as well as responsibility for policing the borders of the abusive context, and this easily confuses him about the nature and extent of his

adult society prone to traumatic confusion also. For a vivid example, see Campbell, *Unofficial Secrets*, pp. 4ff., 13, 61–5, 69, 93.

21. Thus, in relation to the consequences of disclosure, the child is forced to adopt a 'pseudo-adult role' – so Hobbs, Hanks and Wynne, *Child Abuse and Neglect*, p. 127. See also Furniss' comments concerning psychological participation which might be confused with legal (or moral) responsibility, *The Multi-Professional Handbook of Child Sexual Abuse*, pp. 8ff.

responsibility, accountability and power, as about the nature of causality in relationships.

First, the task of keeping the secret may suggest to him that he has the power to prevent further incidents of abuse (by disclosing previous ones), and so these at least must be based on his freely given consent. Such intimation of freedom may then seem to imply that the 'agreement' to keep the secret was itself an act of free will, since he subsequently wills to keep the abuse secret from others. Further, because he would be the catalyst, the final, precipitating agent, of whatever consequences would follow disclosure, he may easily believe that he is the sole potent agency and therefore culpable for whatever further ills befall others.

Since the child's conflicts and confusions attending abuse cannot be resolved through recourse to frameworks of public meaning, they can only be survived by turning them inward in a series of rationalisations in the form of deep-seated, distorted beliefs concerning her identity and value ('I am dirty'; 'it is my fault'; 'I let this happen'; 'I am evil' and so on). The enclosure of the child in the reality of abuse inhibits the operation of and attachment to norms, values and rules of interaction (as well as personal bonds of loyalty, care and concern) transcending and opposed to the rationality of abuse. This effects substitution of the rationality of abuse for her own rational structures and resources, along with those available in her general situation. By that means her behaviour is eventually (if not from the outset) controlled internally as her rational structures are sequestered by abusive rationality (as I have already intimated in relation to the confusions concerning causation and responsibility effected by the injunction to secrecy).

This is powerfully enhanced by the way in which all the child's resources for survival not only permit the abuse to carry on, but have the effect of confirming and more deeply embedding its reality. All strategies for psychological survival are also in effect accommodations to the abuse.[22] They have to take abuse as the unalterable base-line against which identity must be worked out.

Anything that the child does to survive (even strategies employed during abuse, such as dissociation[23]), all her own energies which are

22. Cf. Meiselman, *Resolving the Trauma of Incest*, p. 90; Furniss, *The Multi-Professional Handbook of Child Sexual Abuse*, pp. 28ff.; Campbell, *Unofficial Secrets*, pp. 79f.
23. Dissociation, the creation of experiential distance from the abuse by effecting an altered state of consciousness or determinedly adjusting the focus of consciousness, is an extremely common strategy for dealing with the trauma of abuse whilst it is happening. An abused child may try to escape psychologically by, say, conjuring up a powerful mental

brought into play in order to create and sustain a meaningful identity in face of the abuse, further concentrate and intensify its damaging power. Yet, as she cannot prevent the abuse and is inhibited from disclosing it to others, that has to be an organisation of identity around the reality of abuse. Abuse thence becomes the prime informant of identity, entering its very core – yet it does so in a hidden and distorting way because it cannot be properly processed. Abuse easily insinuates itself into a child's total way of being, relating to, interpreting and communicating in every context of interaction. It can distort the deepest structures of personhood and identity, and therefore her whole ecology and economy of relating, because, in keeping the trauma secret, she effectively centres her whole life and identity around it.

It is possible to identify four dynamics operating in childhood sexual abuse which are analytically separable but in practice are interwoven: traumatic sexualisation; betrayal; powerlessness; stigmatisation.[24] These four dynamics are intensified when combined with that which I have identified as the core dynamic of childhood sexual abuse: isolation and enclosure.

Traumatic sexualisation

First, childhood sexual abuse introduces children to sexual activity prematurely and in inappropriate ways. It is not only socially inappropriate, but developmentally premature, psychologically, emotionally, spiritually and physiologically. Subsequently, it may become a central feature shaping the development of sexuality (feelings, attitudes, drives, emotional and other associations, sexual identity) 'in a developmentally inappropriate and interpersonally dysfunctional fashion'.[25] For when children are sexually abused the normal processes of social development are inappropriately and prematurely sexualised. Survivors of childhood sexual abuse may be confused about their sexual identities, about the rules, codes and norms applying to sexual behaviour in wider society and about the relationships

counter-image of being somewhere else and doing something pleasant; by imagining that she is 'out of her body', observing what is happening as if to someone else; or she might focus all aspects of her consciousness on some trivial aspect of her surroundings: the wardrobe door, the pattern on the wallpaper, sounds from the street. See Meiselman, *Resolving the Trauma of Incest*, pp. 29, 45f.; Hartman and Burgess, 'Sexual Abuse of Children', pp. 96f., 116–22; Furniss, *The Multi-Professional Handbook of Child Sexual Abuse*, pp. 25–8; Judith Herman, *Trauma and Recovery* (New York; Basic Books, 1992); Lenore Terr, *Unchained Memories* (New York: HarperCollins, 1994).

24. In what follows, I follow closely David Finkelhor and Angela Browne, 'The Traumatic Impact of Child Sexual Abuse: A Conceptualisation', *American Journal of Orthopsychiatry*, 55 (1985), 530–41.   25. Ibid., p. 531.

between intimacy, emotional attachment, pleasure and sexual behaviour. Sex may then become an obsessional preoccupation or something to be feared; it might have heightened and unrealistic emotional significance or else be disembedded from the emotions and so dehumanised and depersonalised (as, say, in prostitution or the use of a prostitute).

Betrayal

All childhood sexual abuse includes an element of betrayal, exploitation and abuse of the trust which children invest in and expect from those significantly older than they. In most instances, however, it includes a more severe betrayal than this, since most victims know their abuser, who either already has or creates bonds of emotional and other forms of dependency and attachment with them. Abused children and adult survivors experience that betrayal if and when it becomes clear to them that this trusted person was to blame for the abuse and that it has harmed and damaged them in some way. On top of the betrayal by their abuser, many children also experience the betrayal of other adults when they attempt to disclose but encounter disbelief or blame. Trust and fear of betrayal are clearly crucial issues for survivors of abuse which may invade all their relationships, creating either a heightened, inappropriate and unrealistic sense of dependency on others (which makes one vulnerable to future disappointment, if not abuse) or an inability to trust.

Powerlessness

Abuse is also an experience of extreme powerlessness, often including actual or threatened use of force and violence. The abuser exploits the differentials in power so that the child's experience is almost invariably of being enjoined in activity which he does not want, but which he is psychologically, socially and physically powerless to prevent. His will and needs, his experience of reality, his power over his own body as well as his emotional, social and physical space are contravened and discounted.[26]

---

26. The clearest example of which is the tendency of abusers explicitly to contradict the child's understanding, experience and perceptions ('this does not hurt'; 'you are enjoying this'; etc.). This represents a systematic disqualification of the child's modes of apprehending, perceiving, understanding and interacting with reality – of his structures of rationality (which may be repeated by other adults' eagerness to discount the child's understanding on disclosure). The child learns that his own modes of apprehending reality are not trustworthy, but also learns that reality itself is (and people specifically are) not to be trusted. Consequently, he is likely to live with some confusion and uncertainty about all aspects of reality, unable to trust his own interpretations, but also wary of placing any trust in others or their interpretations of reality, since he has learned that trust can be abused.

When children learn that they are generally powerless, they may experience abnormal levels of fear and anxiety, together with a lowered sense of self, of being a powerless and passive victim, an object rather than a subject, in all relationships and dimensions of life. Alternatively, the child may identify with the abuser, modelling his own behaviour on the abuser's clues and cues as to what makes one powerful in relationships, what protects one emotionally and in other ways from others, how one resolves one's own emotional issues.[27]

Stigmatisation

What the abuser says to rationalise abuse or to inhibit disclosure frequently communicates negative estimations of the child's worth, internalised as shame and an expectation of public stigmatisation. Moreover, keeping the secret builds up an experience of being different from others and fearful of their finding out which readily plays into the dynamic of stigmatisation. In any case, the attribution of responsibility, whether implied or overtly stated, is frequently internalised in the form of deep-seated feelings of

27. This tends to fall out in gender-related patterns, with revictimisation more common among women survivors; the propensity to become an abuser (not necessarily sexually, and not exclusively of children) more common among men. See: J. Miller, D. Mueller, A. Kaufman, P. DiVasto, D. Pathak and J. Christy, 'Recidivism Among Sex Assault Victims', *American Journal of Psychiatry*, 135 (1978), 1103f.; D. Finkelhor and K. Yllo, *Licenced to Rape: Sexual Violence Against Wives* (New York: Holt, Rinehart, 1985); D. Russell, *Rape in Marriage* (New York: Macmillan, 1982); D. Russell, *Rape, Incest and Sexual Exploitation* (Los Angeles: Sage, 1984). Finkelhor's study in *Child Sexual Abuse* failed to find a statistically significant connection between the genders of abuser and victim, but offers possible explanations for that – see pp. 193f. He also provides evidence of sexual abuse in the history of male abusers (pp. 181ff.). See also statistical data in: M. De Young, *The Sexual Victimization of Children* (Jefferson, NC: McFarland, 1982); P. Gerhard, J. Gagnon, W. Pomeroy and C. Christenson, *Sex Offenders: An Analysis of Types* (New York: Harper & Row, 1965); D. T. Ballard, G. D. Blair, S. Devereaux, L. K. Valentine, A. L. Horton and B. L. Johnson, 'A Contemporary Profile of the Incest Perpetrator: Background Characteristics, Abuse History, and Use of Social Skills', in A. L. Horton, B. L. Johnson, L. M. Roundy and D. Williams, eds., *The Incest Perpetrator: A Family Member No-One Wants to Treat* (Newbury Park, CA: Sage, 1990), pp. 43–64; G. E. Davis and H. Leitenberg, 'Adolescent Sex-Offenders', *Psychological Bulletin*, 101, 417–27; A. N. Groth, W. Hobson and T. Gary, 'The Child Molester: Clinical Observations', in J. Conte and D. Shore, eds., *Social Work and Child Sexual Abuse* (New York: Haworth, 1982); N. A. Groth and A. W. Burgess, 'Sexual Trauma in the Life-Histories of Rapists and Child Molesters', *Victimology*, 4 (1979), 10–16; R. Langevin, L. Handy, H. Hook, D. Day and A. Russon, 'Are Incestuous Fathers Pedophilic and Aggressive?', in R. Langevin, ed., *Erotic Preference, Gender Identity and Aggression* (New York: Erlbaum Associates, 1983); T. Seghorn and R. Boucher, 'Sexual Abuse in Childhood as a Factor in Sexually Dangerous Criminal Offences', in J. M. Samson, ed., *Childhood and Sexuality* (Montreal: Editions Vivantes, 1980). Matthew Mendel persuasively accounts for the differences in the attempted resolutions of male and female survivors as they integrate their experience of powerless victimisation with the gender-differentiated roles assigned to masculinity and femininity in wider culture, particularly those related to power and protectiveness. The tasks of integrating the experience of abuse with an identity shaped by the socially constructed reality of masculinity and one shaped by femininity differ. See *The Male Survivor*, pp. 204–12.

guilt and shame, low levels of self-esteem and a heightened sense of not fitting with and being psychologically isolated from, out of tune with, others.

In easily distorting identity in these ways, childhood sexual abuse creates the means whereby the effects of abuse may be transmitted into all relationships, and thence to other people. Abuse has the capacity to invade and distort the entire ecology of relating. It presses the survivor to reconfirm the distorted, but fragile, identity structured in order to survive the abuse (incorporating deeply internalised beliefs about worth, blame, guilt and what can be expected from others) in every relationship, even those which are potentially therapeutic. This happens most obviously in adopting patterns of revictimisation or abuse, but also in patterns of heightened empathy and attunement to others' needs to the point of sacrifice of self;[28] less obviously, in the whole gamut of imbalances in personal identity and relation, from domination to 'loss of self'.

The dynamic of isolation and enclosure which runs through the other four dynamics I have delineated makes this distorted personal identity very robust against disconfirmation from others. The experience of keeping abuse secret often encourages the formation of the view that it is not just the abuse which is hidden from others, but 'the real me'. So the child is able immediately to discount any apparent contradiction of her negative view of herself as responding to her presentation of a 'fictional', good self which protects both herself and her secret. Yet, the extent to which abuse systematically created distance and dissonance between herself and her body, the abused and the real self, might also generate a sense of alienation from and confusion about who she really is. As I have tried to show, she may therefore encounter difficulty,

---

28. Which arises, not out of an unambiguously positive sense of relation to another, but as a strategy to protect oneself in a situation of felt alienation from others. N. D. Feshbach's discussion of physical abuse is instructive here: 'The Construct of Empathy and the Phenomenon of Physical Maltreatment of Children', in Cicchetti and Carlson, eds., *Child Maltreatment*, pp. 349–73. Meiselman, *Resolving the Trauma of Incest*, p. 35, and Emily Driver, 'Through the Looking Glass: Children and the Professionals who Treat Them', in Driver and Droisen, eds., *Child Sexual Abuse*, pp. 112, 116–19 both suggest a gender differentiation in the construction of empathy amongst survivors of sexual abuse. Both empathy and its opposite (abuse) are regarded as ways of escaping from the sense of isolation, alienation, hopelessness and powerlessness inflicted through abuse, either through a mirroring form of attachment to others' needs, involving a distancing from oneself, or an enacted dissociation or isolation from others' needs through power over others. Cf. here also John McDargh, 'Desire, Domination, and the Life and death of the Soul', in Richard K. Fenn and Donald Capps, eds., *On Losing the Soul: Essays in the Social Psychology of Religion* (Albany, NY: State University of New York Press, 1995), pp. 218f.

not only in integrating herself with a wider network of social relationships and meanings, but in the internal integration of the experience of abuse.

Abuse, then, easily distorts the child's sense of reality in all its aspects – social, moral, personal, physical.[29] What is good and bad, normal and impermissible, right and wrong, injurious and healthy; criteria for evaluating oneself and others; the senses of responsibility, power, guilt and shame; awareness of body-states and identification with the body; sexuality; the boundary between oneself and others; the patterning of loyalty and trust, of anger, gratitude, resentment, of inhibition and disinhibition; the handling of intimacy and of affection; self-esteem; perception of risk, especially in personal relationships; autonomy in relationships; how one relates to time[30] – all may be distorted and changed by the pathological dynamics of abuse. Hence, all possibilities and processes of cognition, communication and action are liable to distortion, the basic life-orientation of the person prone to profound disorientation. In addition to finding that he may no longer be able to be sufficiently in control of himself to exercise will effectively (because of the disabling and possibly unpredictable intrusion of traumatic memories and a heightened and sometimes inappropriate startle response), he might also potentially find that abuse modifies his motivational complex.

> It is the transformation of the self as autonomous agent that is perhaps the most apparent in survivors of trauma. First, the autonomy-undermining symptoms of [Post Traumatic Stress Disorder] reconfigure the survivor's will, rendering involuntary many responses that once were under voluntary control ... The loss of control ... alters who one is, not only limiting what one can do (and can refrain from doing) but also changing what one *wants* to do.
>
> A trauma survivor suffers a loss of control not only over herself but also over her environment – a loss that, in turn, can lead to a constriction of the boundaries of her will. If a rape victim is unable to walk outside without fear of being assaulted again, she quickly loses the desire to go for a walk ... what she is able to will post-trauma is ... drastically altered. Some reactions that once were under the will's

29. Susan J. Brison speaks in terms of 'epistemological reversals' in relation to being raped as an adult ('Surviving Sexual Violence: A Philosophical Perspective', *Journal of Social Philosophy*, 24 (1), 5–22).
30. The significance of the intrusions of traumatic memories and the manifold other ways in which the past remains present in strategies for survival (heightened awareness of the risk and a pervading sense of not being safe in every situation, etc.) are frequently underestimated in their effects on identity, as is the sense of being so fundamentally altered and defined by the abuse that one loses one's past.

command become involuntary, and some desires that once were motivating can no longer be felt, let alone acted upon.[31]

Summary

This journey through the complexities of what happens when children are sexually abused has taken us through the dynamics of isolation, through the false construction of normality (the sense of what is good, right, true) to the internalisation of abusive dynamics in reconfiguring identity and life-intentionality, disorienting desire and will. In Part III, I shall begin the task of testing whether it is possible to bring these dynamics to expression through a theological frame of reference (by speaking of them as sin), and whether, in doing so, a dimension of depth is revealed that was hitherto hidden. Given the amount of detail presented in the course of this analysis, it may help to provide a summary of its most significant points before passing through a similarly lengthy consideration of another concrete situation en route to Part III. That will help sharpen our focus on the main features of the terrain just passed over before continuing and also provide a ready means of reference to it as we proceed.

The key findings of this chapter may be summarised thus:

· The sexual abuse of children is fundamentally an abuse of trust and of power which exploits the age-related differentials between child and abuser, as well as enlisting, abusing, distorting and disorienting the child's needs for intimacy, affirmation, security, trust and guidance.

· Abuse is not adequately construed in terms of acts which might then have certain consequences; it is better thought of in terms of an expansive dynamic of distorted relationality which may affect all of the child's relationships (including that to herself) and invade the relational ecology of other sets of relationships. (It is thus impossible clearly and cleanly to separate act from consequence.)

· Its core dynamic is that of entrapment and isolation, through which social and psychological transcendence may be blocked.

· That dynamic effects a form of traumatic confusion concerning the nature of reality in all its dimensions (social, moral, personal, material).

· A particular source of confusion is the incorporation of the child's

31. Brison, 'Surviving Sexual Violence', pp. 27f.

active agency in psychologically 'accommodating' to the abuse and in keeping it secret.

· As a consequence, abuse easily leads to a radical distortion of the very core of self-identity,[32]

· which becomes the means of transmission of the consequences of abuse into an entire ecology of relating and is capable of passing on the effects of abuse trans-generationally.

32. I use this phrase to indicate that it is one's own sense of who one is which is liable to such distortion, and not only one's presentation or others' perception of one's self which is at stake. For further technical clarification of this term see my *The Call to Personhood: A Christian Theory of the Individual in Social Relationships* (Cambridge: Cambridge University Press, 1990), pp. 98, 105, 135, 136, 181, 318.

5

What was the problem? 'The Final Solution' and the binding of reason

Rational racism

Ideas first?

Between the 'euthanasia' programme directed against the mentally handicapped in 1939 and the ending of the war in 1945, the Nazi state had organised the systematic murder of approximately eleven million people, among them six million Jews. How could such a monstrous act be contemplated, much less implemented? There seems to be no single, comprehensively satisfactory answer to that question. But the most convincing approach begins by bringing the two halves of the question – contemplation and implementation – together and resisting the notion that ideas are primary, always preceding action. For there appears to have been a much more complex interplay between ideas and action than that. The *idea* of genocide against the Jews and other 'degenerate' races, groups and individuals was not a fully formulated action-guiding principle, a programmatic intention of Hitler's, from the start.[1] The idea itself took shape in the context of concrete, social, political and material processes of action and interaction; in other words, it appears that, in the development of a policy of genocide, practice drove the incremental development of ideas as much as the other way about.

1. Contra the 'intentionalist' school, who attribute Nazi genocide to the clarity of Hitler's ideological purpose and the power and efficacy of his leadership to implement his intentions. The root cause of the holocaust then lies in ideas and intentions which *subsequently* are married to the right kind of institutional, political and social power to put them into practice. Ideas are here primary; the social and political processes of human action and interaction, secondary. See, e.g., Klaus Hildebrand, *The Third Reich* (London: Routledge, 1984); Hermann Graml, 'The Genesis of the Final Solution', in Walter H. Pehle, ed., *November 1938: From 'Kristallnacht' to Genocide* (New York: Oxford University Press, 1991), pp. 168–86; Eberhard Jäckel, *Hitler's Weltanschauung: A Blueprint for Power* (Middletown, CT: Wesleyan University Press, 1972).

Genocide as a policy was arrived at only gradually, as previous policies proved to be inadequate to 'the Jewish problem'. The pre-war encouragement of Jews to emigrate to Palestine, to other European nations or to the USA were unlikely ever to represent a total solution, given the reluctance of other nations to receive them or to permit their movement in appropriate numbers. The plan to expel all Jews to Madagascar, on the other hand, was seriously entertained as an adequate solution until relatively late,[2] eventually proving impracticable with the failure to defeat Britain (since the necessary diversion of resources could not then be contemplated, nor the necessary military and merchant shipping be exposed to the risk of attack by the Royal Navy).

Running alongside these plans were those (implemented between 1939 and 1941) for a massive resettlement of various populations. Ethnic Germans were to be reunited in a Greater Germany, and were to settle in areas to the east of then-current borders. To permit this, the present population (Poles) of areas designated for Aryan *Lebensraum* had to be moved further eastwards and Slavs, in their turn, would have to be moved to accommodate them. Jews were eventually to be resettled in the Eastern extremities of the conquered territories.

By the invasion of Russia, however, the plan for Jewish resettlement had encountered many frustrations. Without yet having the priority it was later to achieve among Nazi objectives, the resolution of 'the Jewish question' had to compete for resources with the military and with other resettlement plans. Furthermore, the number of Jews 'in transit' in various camps and ghettos, whom it was not possible to move further onwards because of the resourcing problem, created a vast 'bottleneck'. Moreover, the scope of military successes in the East, especially after the invasion of Russia, increased the size of 'the problem' (since it brought many more Jews under German control). It also inspired more grandiose plans for *Volksdeutsche* resettlement (*Generalplan Ost* suggested settlement as far east as Lithuania, Leningrad and the Crimea), requiring rethinking of the location and very idea of Jewish resettlement. At the same time, the programme of pacification through the elimination of cultural and ideological elites (carriers of cultural, ideological and national identities which might focus resistance), which had been carried out already by the *Einsatzgruppen* against the Polish intelligentsia, was to be applied in Russia to

2. Hitler approved a memorandum from Himmler to this effect on 25 May 1940. See Christopher Browning, *The Path to Genocide: Essays on Launching the Final Solution* (Cambridge: Cambridge University Press, 1992), pp. 16–20.

leading Jews as well. For, in Nazi demonology, Russian commissars and Jews were one: 'the political and biological manifestations of the same "Jewish-Bolshevik conspiracy."'[3] It was in this context, and with victory in the East looking secure, that the search for a Final Solution to 'the Jewish question', necessitated by the frustrations of earlier ones, turned towards extermination.[4] From the end of 1941, when the decision about the instrumentation of destruction had been made and bureaucratic procedures set in place, the movement of Jews from West to East was no longer part of a resettlement programme, but one of mass extermination.

So the *idea* of genocide took shape only in the context of the failure of previous attempts to resolve the 'Jewish problem' that the Nazis believed they had, and in the face of almost certain victory in continental Europe. The progressive radicalisation in ideas was intimately intertwined with the radicalisation in measures which seemed a matter of *practical* necessity in order to resolve a practical 'problem'. The *idea* of mass extermination was not arrived at through a process of abstract speculation; rather, it was the fruit of *pragmatic, instrumental,* and not theoretical deliberation. And the idea's palatability cannot be accounted for apart from the previous experience of attempting to solve 'the problem' by increasingly radical methods – in the context of a society at war and with a consciousness of its supposed historic mission and destiny (itself related, both to racist ideas and to concrete, historical experience, especially of the ending and aftermath of World War I).

Fantasies of perfection

This account of events suggests that genocide was not a clearly formulated policy goal of Nazi ideology from the outset. However, that is not to say that the decision and implementation of genocide bore no connection at all with Nazi ideology.[5] The racial ideology of the Nazis forms the

---

3. Ibid., p. 25. See also pp. 101f.

4. Finally agreed to by Hitler in summer, 1941. So ibid., pp. 27, 88ff., 111, 113; Christopher Browning, *Fateful Months: Essays on the Emergence of the Final Solution* (New York: Holmes & Meier, 1985), pp. 8–38.

5. This is contrary to the views of those who regard the emergence of the programme of destruction as a purely instrumental-bureaucratic process, independent of the ideological framework within which policy goals had been set ('functionalists'). See, e.g., Arno Mayer, *Why Did the Heavens Not Darken? The 'Final Solution' in History* (New York: Pantheon, 1989); Martin Broszat, 'Hitler und die "Endlösung" Aus Anlass der Thesen von David Irving', *Vierteljahrshefte für Zeitgeschichte*, 25/4 (1977), 739–75; Hans Mommsen, 'Die Realisierung des Utopischen: Die "Endlösung der Judenfrage" im "Dritten Reich"', *Geschichte und Gesellschaft*, 9/3 (1983), 381–420; Ian Kershaw, *The Nazi Dictatorship: Problems and Perspectives of Interpretation* (London: Edward Arnold, 1985).

context within which the perpetrators of the genocide in particular, and the German population in general, believed that there was a 'Jewish question' to be solved by the action of the state. To speak of social problems requiring resolution through programmatic social planning and action already suggests that the holocaust differs significantly from the more ancient forms and currents of violent, emotion-driven anti-Semitism in Europe, which were not widespread in Germany in the period immediately prior to the rise of Nazism.[6] The holocaust was not a pogrom on a massive scale, depending on the incitement of popular emotion in the form of violent blood-lust; not, in fact, the slippage of a modern, civilised nation back into the barbaric, violent irrationality of a less civilised time.[7] The holocaust was the product of a society in the grip, not of irrational violence and uncontrollable passion, but of a highly rational project for the betterment of society. Hence it stands in deep continuity with that highly optimistic assessment of the possibilities of reason in human affairs characteristic of modernity. Outrageous though it may appear, the holocaust was a triumph of rationality in planning and action, which was threatened wherever irrationality – even that of over-zealousness – intruded into and interrupted efficient organisation.[8]

Throughout the nineteenth and well into the twentieth century, Western culture developed a tremendous faith in the capacity of the 'pure, objective' rationality of the natural sciences, not only to increase pure knowledge, but, through the practical implementation of the lessons of science in technology and technique, progressively to free humanity from its bondage and vulnerability to the irrational (nature, superstition, arbitrary authority). The advance of 'objective reason' raised

6. For generations before the Nazis, Germany had become something of a *relatively* safe haven for Jews in Europe, who were formally and fully emancipated under Weimar. Violent anti-Semitism was largely absent and structural anti-Semitism appears to have been less of an impediment in Germany than most other countries, with its thriving Jewish intelligentsia and professional class. Precisely this fact would be used by the Nazis as evidence of Jewish conspiratorial control of national and international society. See, e.g., Michael R. Marrus, *The Holocaust in History* (London: Penguin, 1987), pp. 9f.

7. Contra Lucy Dawidowicz, *The War Against the Jews, 1933–1945* (New York: Bantam, 1975), p. 30.

8. Unlike a pogrom, genocide requires the efficient detachment of administrative functionaries; feelings and emotions being too inefficient and unreliable to be the basis for sustained and systematic action. 'Contemporary mass murder is distinguished by a virtual absence of all spontaneity on the one hand, and the prominence of rational, carefully calculated design on the other. It is marked by an almost complete elimination of contingency or chance, and independence from group emotions or personal motives.' Zygmunt Bauman, *Modernity and the Holocaust* (Cambridge: Polity Press, 1989), p. 90, cf. pp. 17, 20, 74. Cf. John R. Sabini and Maury Silver, 'Destroying the Innocent with a Clear Conscience: A Sociopsychology of the Holocaust', in Joel E. Dinsdale, ed., *Survivors, Victims and Perpetrators: Essays on the Nazi Holocaust* (Washington: Hemisphere, 1980), pp. 328ff.

hopes for controlling, managing and planning the world on a rational basis which seemed to be, in principle, unlimited. Any problem was solvable, since all problems were amenable to rational understanding and thence to rational resolution, provided that science and technology were sufficiently advanced. And society itself began to look like a series of problems amenable to technical-instrumental solution, given sufficient centralisation of power and resources in modern nation-states. Increasingly, it becomes the business of government to intervene in order to pursue the goal of a rational social order, as opposed to one based on the givenness of nature and tradition as we receive them.

Amidst the evident successes of applied rationality in reshaping so much of the modern world – from agricultural through surgical to centralised administrative techniques – the dream of a society secured on a purely rational and objective basis, purged of unreliable irrationality and emotional subjectivity in the conduct of human affairs, became immensely powerful. How is the world seen in the perspective of a dream for a perfectly rational order of life? Zygmunt Bauman suggests gardening or modern medicine as analogues. Modern bureaucratic culture 'prompts us to see society as an object of administration, as a collection of so many "problems" to be solved, as a "nature" to be "controlled", "mastered", "improved" or "remade" as a legitimate target of social engineering, and in general a garden to be designed and kept in the planned shape' by the active cultivation of plants deemed desirable and the elimination of those deemed weeds.[9] Weeds occupy the same status in the world of the gardener as does the cancerous cell in that of the surgeon: a pathogen which cannot be cultivated or turned into a benign organism.[10] They are more than elements which do not fit; they pose a threat to the proper rational order of the garden or organism. If not uprooted, expelled or eliminated, collapse into the chaos of disorder is threatened. Jews were to be removed from the social body as one 'would remove a gangrenous appendix from a diseased', physical one. For 'the Jew is the gangrenous appendix in the body of mankind'.[11]

> All visions of society-as-garden define parts of the social habitat as human weeds. Like all other weeds, they must be segregated,

9. *Modernity and the Holocaust*, p. 92.
10. Just as Jews were depicted as cancer eating away at the Aryan body, so cancer cells appeared in health promotion campaigns depicted as Jews. See Robert N. Proctor, *The Nazi War on Cancer* (Princeton: Princeton University Press, 1999).
11. The words of Fritz Klein, quoted in Robert J. Lifton, *The Nazi Doctors: Medical Killing and the Psychology of Genocide* (New York: Basic Books, 1986), p. 16.

contained, prevented from spreading, removed and kept outside the society boundaries; if all these means prove insufficient, they must be killed.[12]

Nazi policy towards Jews, Gypsies and the mentally handicapped was designed to eliminate pathogens which threatened the realisation of the dream of a perfectly rational social order based on the purity of race. The mentally handicapped, the first of the victims of a policy of murder, were targeted because they weakened the racial state in two ways. They imposed a burden on the state and on families, drawing off energies and resources which should be being employed for the benefit of the nation; and they represented a dilution of the pure, Aryan racial character, which (if permitted to breed) would pass on into subsequent generations. But why were Jews and, alongside them, the Gypsies, seen as posing a greater threat to the Reich's racial order than the other races deemed inferior in Nazi ideology?

'The Jewish question'

Hitler's view of history, which effectively shaped Nazi ideology, appears to have been based on an interpretation of social Darwinism along racial lines, nourished by various nineteenth-century, scientific conceptions of race and its ontological status: a struggle for survival between races, some of which were judged superior (Aryan races); others, inferior (Jews, Slavs, Poles).[13] The Nazis proposed the reunification and revivification of the nation by gathering the scattered *Volksdeutschen* and recovering and celebrating their essential spirit and characteristics. Such a revivifying and refocusing of racial spirit required the removal from the extended homeland of all impediments to the purity of racial order: enemies of true Aryanism (communists, liberal democrats), as well as inferior races (Slavs and Poles) and racial enemies (Gypsies and Jews). The Nazis articulated and then planned the re-creation of the 'Garden of Eden',[14] an artificial social order which recovered the proper, 'natural' order of a human community based on racial identity. The implicit naturalism of the Nazis' project of social engineering (and, indeed, its scientific basis) was immensely significant. Although presented as an *historical* (indeed, historic) project, requiring committed will and agency, it belonged also to

---

12. Bauman, *Modernity and the Holocaust*, p. 92; see also pp. 18, 70f., 73.
13. See, e.g., Eberhard Jäckel, *Hitler in History* (Boston: University Press of New England, 1964); Browning, *The Path to Genocide*, pp. 79, 84f. (discussing the views of Arno Mayer).
14. The phrase was used by Hitler in his 'victory speech' of 16 July 1941. See Alan Clark, *Barbarossa: The Russian–German Conflict 1941–45* (New York: Signet, 1966), p. 155.

the realm of *nature*, of cosmology, ontology and – above all – of biology, as well as history.[15] Hence, Nazi rhetoric could abound with the sense of the unavoidable and irresistible nature of its project – to bring things into accord with the way they really are, with the underlying, unalterable reality of the world's proper order and being from which we have fallen away.

Jews (particularly, but also Gypsies) represented a greater threat than other races to this dream of a perfect society ordered along racial lines. For, in Diaspora, Jews had become a nation without a state.[16] Jews, like Gypsies, did not belong anywhere. Without a nation-state, they lacked the basis for participating in the Darwinian struggle between the races through the normal means of diplomacy and war. Therefore, Nazi ideology maintained, they must utilise covert means.[17] Jews, it was maintained, conspired against other races, not as one nation-state in open confrontation with another, but through *international* conspiratorial action to undermine or take over the nations of the world. Thus Nazi rhetoric abounded with images of Jews as agents of internationalism (i.e., acting against a world-order based on nationality), whether, paradoxically, in its Capitalist (the free movement of capital across national boundaries) or its Communist (the global revolutionary ambitions of Bolshevism) guise.

The Jews were not only dispersed. In Western Europe, they were becoming increasingly integrated and secularised. Unlike their co-religionists to the East, German Jews were abandoning the markers of identity associated with personal appearance and the practices of communal separation in increasing numbers. Even religious practice could no longer reliably be used as an identifier in a situation where, for increasing numbers of Jews, Jewishness had no connection to the Synagogue and sometimes little meaning for them at all. In Nazi ideology, integration fuelled rather than diminished the demonology of Jew as pathogen. That it was hard to tell Jewish apart from 'true' Germans merely evidenced their deviousness in acting to undermine the nation; the danger of diluting the Aryan blood-line through inter-marriage. By straddling the racial boundaries constitutive of racial order, they were both resistant to and undermining of it.[18]

---

15. See Darrel J. Fasching's portrayal of the Nazis' 'mythic narrative' in *Narrative Theology After Auschwitz: From Alienation to Ethics* (Minneapolis: Fortress Press, 1992), pp. 146f.

16. Hannah Arendt, *The Origins of Totalitarianism* (London: George Allen & Unwin, 1962), p. 22.

17. Bauman, *Modernity and the Holocaust*, p. 35, who cites *Hitler's Secret Book* (London: Grove, 1964); cf. Marrus, *The Holocaust in History*, pp. 13f.

18. Patrick Girard, 'Historical Foundations of Anti-Semitism', in Dinsdale, ed., *Survivors, Victims and Perpetrators*, pp. 70f.

In relation to the rationality of the Nazi project of social perfection, the Jew was a surd, a counter-rational element. Jews were construed, then, not merely as a misplaced race, but as undermining the very idea of race and of social order organised along pure, racial lines. The Jews could not be ordered into this society. Their very presence contradicted and resisted the rationality in the redesign of Germany, as a weed does that of a garden; a cancerous cell, that of the body. And yet Jewishness, unlike membership of other religious groups which Hitler considered pathological in their sapping of the Aryan spirit, was a biologically derived identity and not a matter of volitional affiliation. It was not something which would prove amenable to treatment by means of social processes and programmes of therapy or development, such as education. Since Jewishness was an onto-biological condition, it was amenable to social engineering only by exclusion. Jewishness could not be cultivated out of the Jews.[19]

Nazi racial ideology and policy could certainly draw on a long history of anti-Semitism in pre-modern, Christian Europe, but did not stand in a straightforward line of descent from it. They were of mixed parentage, descended also from the Enlightenment's hopes for a perfect, rational order of society, in which the givenness of social and natural order is not to be received uncritically and unquestioningly. Nature and society become projects, to be re-created and re-ordered in line with either a superior, artificial rationality or the original and true, natural order which has been lost or distorted, to be recovered by rational artifice. The vitality of this dream of perfection, characteristic of modern faith in rationality, is directly related to the development of technological *means* by which reality might be brought under rational control – transport, engineering, chemistry, all the technologies associated with modern warfare and, most importantly, centralised bureaucratic, administrative and managerial procedures, instruments and devices which made categorisation and then orderly and

---

19. Bauman, *Modernity and the Holocaust*, pp. 59f., 65. Cf. Arendt, *Origins of Totalitarianism*, p. 87. In practice, however, since Jewish blood looked no different from Aryan, the Nazis had to rely on ties to religious institutions – that is, social and not biological characteristics – as the prime indicator. However, since it was the religious affiliation, not of the present generation, but of its grandparents which was the decisive factor, this did contain an element of heredity. And for that reason, 'the Jews' as a clearly delineated group who could be a single object of Nazi policy was a social construction of the Nazis themselves, containing those who would not have considered themselves to be Jewish, together with those for whom it was the core of identity. On this, see Kenneth Jacobsen, *Embattled Selves: An Investigation into the Nature of Identity Through Oral Histories of Holocaust Survivors* (New York: The Atlantic Monthly Press, 1984), pp. 8, 161–232; Victor Klemperer, *I Shall Bear Witness: The Diaries of Victor Klemperer, 1933–41* (London: Weidenfeld & Nicolson, 1998), p. 128.

systematic action against a large, specifiable segment of various populations possible.[20]

Acting against all Jews required a systematically co-ordinated and
total policy. Nazi Jewish policy did not and could not rely on whipping up
the emotions of the rest of the population to murder Jews, turning the
majority of Germans from the self-consciously civilised to a bloodthirsty
mob, capable of face-to-face murder. Instead, it presented itself as a
matter of rational planning and action towards the betterment of society.
Consequently, on the whole, it turned Aryan Germans into participants
in or bystanders to a bureaucratic, administrative process which dealt
with the commonly perceived 'Jewish question' in a rational, and therefore apparently civilised – above all, legal – manner.

Totalitarian reason

Rational problem solving: means, not ends

Modern means of technical-instrumental action, and the utopian
visions associated with them, then, were necessary, constitutive elements of the holocaust. They were more, however, than pre-condition
and instrumental means. Beyond that, the rational character of Nazi
attempts to solve 'the Jewish question' was the core, constitutive
element of the pathological dynamic in which Aryan Germans and Jews
were caught up in genocide. In the Nazi's Final Solution, we not only
encounter the politics of a totalitarian ideology; we also find the totalitarian tendencies of technical-instrumental reason, of rational expertise
in establishing and implementing means towards the end set by the
political agenda.

The situation in the Third Reich was very little different in respect of
policy formulation and implementation than it is in any other modern,
centralised government. Once broad policy goals were formulated, the

---

20. Bauman, *Modernity and the Holocaust*, pp. 76f.: the Nazi world-view required 'a total and
uncompromising isolation of the pathogenic and infectious race – the source of disease
and contamination – through its complete spacial separation or destruction. By its nature,
this is a daunting task, unthinkable unless in conjunction with the availability of huge
resources, means of their mobilization and planned distribution, skills of splitting the
overall task into a great number of partial and specialized functions and skills to co-
ordinate their performance. In short, the task is inconceivable without modern
bureaucracy . . . *The murderous compound was made of a typically modern ambition of social design
and engineering, mixed with the typically modern concentration of power, resources and managerial
skills.*' Italics in original.

matter was handed over to technical and administrative advisers to devise the most expedient and efficient means for implementation.

The task of rational administration and planning is identifying the appropriate concrete programmes that fulfil general political objectives and the means of their most efficient implementation. This is not a matter of first-order politics, where one might find a discussion of appropriate societal goals according to ideological or moral criteria. For administration is a matter of 'objectivity', of rational instrumentalisation of policy, not of subjective opinion or values. Hence, the concrete programmes which social planners come up with are presented as the rational resolution of commonly agreed problems. If they are to be argued with, that must be against 'objective' criteria concerning the *means* of implementation, not the ends being implemented. The various programmes and procedures set in place to enable resolution of 'the Jewish problem', up to and including the Final Solution, were developed in accordance with the normal rules for technical-instrumental deliberation. Whether one liked or approved what was being done was a question that merely intruded non-rational, personal and subjective elements into the picture.

The matter of Jewish policy was not handed over to bureaucrats only once the programme of genocide had been decided; they, and therefore the techniques of instrumental reason, were a part of the decision-making process itself. Hitler tended to articulate highly general policy wishes, in the expectation that others would charge their corner of the bureaucratic machinery with thinking the matter through practically and come up with concrete proposals.[21]

> Physical extermination was chosen as the most feasible and effective means to the original, and newly expanded, end. The rest was the matter of co-operation between various departments of state bureaucracy; of careful planning, designing proper technology and technical equipment, budgeting, calculating and mobilizing necessary resources: indeed, the matter of dull bureaucratic routine.
>
> ... *the choice of physical extermination as the right means to the task of* Entfernung *was a product of routine bureaucratic procedures*: means-ends calculus, budget balancing, universal rule application. To make the point sharper still – the choice was the effect of the earnest effort to

21. Raul Hilberg, *The Destruction of the European Jews* (New York: Holmes & Meier, 1985), III, p. 996; Browning, *The Path to Genocide*, pp. 7 (n.120), 120f., 142ff.

find rational solutions to successive 'problems', as they arose in the changing circumstances.[22]

Wherever instrumental reason is employed, there is a shift of attention from the ends of action to the means, accompanied by a shift in the criteria for evaluating action, from the moral and political to the instrumental. In short, technical-instrumental expertise and bureaucracy has an ideological function. It may act as a cloak and rationalisation for the real action-guiding values. But its ideological function takes an additional, more insidious, form still. Once a matter becomes merely a matter of the application of rational, technical expertise, of how-to rather than what-to, technical-instrumental rationality may easily colonise the area, expelling competing rationalities. Once set a task, bureaucracy is programmed to find the optimal solution with recourse only to its own innate criteria for evaluating efficiency and efficacy. When freed from the challenges and constraints of the sort of moral and political scrutiny which naturally results where there is political pluralism (and so discussion of basic values and appropriate ends), access to non-instrumental rationalities (which intrude criteria and considerations not germane to the efficient expedition of goals) is blocked. Unless challenged by moral or political discussion of appropriate ends and means, bureaucracy substitutes its own rules for the game. And the game may well be redefined in the process of deliberation concerning means. Non-bureaucratic criteria of judgment and evaluation of action and policy are eliminated. Once engaged, technical-instrumental rationality is only entitled and equipped to ask 'objective' questions concerning efficiency. And without any sustained debate or disagreement in public discourse (where non-instrumental criteria might be brought to bear on policy, on ends), an instrumental discourse quickly becomes totalitarian, redefining ends without the intrusion of competing

---

22. Bauman, *Modernity and the Holocaust*, pp. 16f. (emphasis in original; *Entfernung*, even in the context of Hitler's earliest usage in relation to the Jews, is usually translated as 'elimination'. The noun is ambiguous in German and may also be translated 'expulsion' or 'removal' – in any case, eliminating Jews from the Reich initially carried this latter meaning, but there was no need for a substitute term when it later came to bear the meaning of extermination); Bauman tends towards the position of Karl A. Scheunes (*A Twisted Road to Auschwitz* (Urbana: University of Illinois Press, 1970)), Raul Hilberg (*The Destruction of the European Jews*) and others that the decision was made only by bureaucratic means and did not require decision and permission from Hitler. Against such an interpretation, see Browning's more persuasive account in *The Path to Genocide*, ch. 5. In any case, it is clear that German administrators in each Ministry (including many who were not even notional Nazis) enthusiastically greeted the proposed Final Solution as the rational way forwards at the Wannsee conference (20 January 1942). See e.g., Hannah Arendt, *Eichmann in Jerusalem: Report on the Banality of Evil* (Harmondsworth: Penguin, 1976), ch. VII; Richard Rubenstein, *The Cunning of History*, new edn (New York: Harper & Row, 1978), pp. 4f.

rationalities. In the discussion about means, which has the effect of rede-fining ends for practical purposes, technical-instrumental reason does not present itself as an ideology of values, but as an objective (value-free) consideration of means. So, the moral, political or theological never come into direct and open conflict with matters which seem the domain of those with relevant expertise.

Indeed, morality is redefined for those working within the adminis-tration of the solutions to 'the Jewish question'. Instead of subjecting the implementation of means to scrutiny by external standards, the requirements of efficient functioning in the bureaucracy are themselves moralised, functioning with all the force of moral axioms. The technical-instrumental becomes the criteriological base for a morality and expe-diency and efficiency become moral criteria. Here there is an eclipse of transcendent or external criteria of judgment or frames of reference, as truth and goodness are equated with intra-systemic values. There is no more foundational, primary environment to turn to, which could supply criteria of evaluation.[23]

Standing by a reasonable policy

In the Third Reich all matters relating to the Jews, including those of oth-erwise normal, daily intercourse, were regulated and governed by a single agency of bureaucratic action. The State's Jewish policy and its single, overarching instrument constituted a total environment for everything pertaining to the Jews. The possibilities for effective appeal to or interven-tion by other institutions were thereby undercut, as Jews' interface with organised society had a single point of mediation. The norms of interac-tion appropriate to bureaucratic rationality, as a supposed realm of pure objectivity, displaced those related to subjectivity and intersubjectivity (emotions, preferences, moral values, psychological dispositions, passion, interpersonal commitments). That was, of course, assisted by the earliest anti-Jewish legislative measures that separated German Jews from the biological, psychological, social and then geographical bonds of a common, or even neighbouring, community. The physical disappearance of the Jews from the processes of common life in Germany was paralleled

---

23. Clearly what I, following Bauman, am suggesting approximates to what Peter Haas calls an ethic. Yet his understanding of the *nature* of that ethic and its *origin* in the Just War moral tradition (*Morality After Auschwitz: The Radical Challenge of the Nazi Ethic* (Philadelphia: Fortress Press, 1988), pp. 14f.) are unpersuasive, since that tradition precisely accepts values transcending war aims and nation-states, to which war and treatment of the enemy must be subject.

by their disappearance as *persons* in what increasingly became their only context of interaction with Germans.[24] Efficient bureaucracy deals with people, not as human persons, as *subjects*, but as *objects* (i.e., the recipients) of its action. The key to efficient administration of people in massive numbers is their reduction, for the purposes of this action at least, to objects. The targets of instrumental action are not dealt with on the basis of their individuality, but by conglomeration with others whose case for these purposes is similar. So, people appear before bureaucracies in forms amenable to handling via technical-instrumental criteria – in the form, say, of statistics, of figures on a balance sheet, of tonnes per kilometre on the railway.

> Reduced, like all other objects of bureaucratic management, to pure, quality-free, measurements, human objects lose their distinctiveness. They are already dehumanized – in the sense that the language in which things that happen to them (or are done to them) are narrated, safeguards its referents from ethical evaluation. In fact, this language is unfit for normative-moral statements. It is only humans that may be the objects of ethical propositions.[25]

Since Jews under Nazi rule were dealt with through the co-ordinating action of a single bureaucratic body dedicated to addressing 'the Jewish question' by technical-instrumental means and criteria, the avenue of appeal to other agencies and spheres of action and to alternative criteria for evaluating action was blocked. So Jews gradually disappeared as human subjects, whose needs and interests as such might transcend and place a brake on the possibilities of bureaucratic action.

Moreover, the existence of an 'objective', and therefore rational and 'just', way of dealing with Jews (itself based on 'objective' scientific views concerning race) encouraged other Germans, albeit often reluctantly, to lay aside their 'irrational' moral scruples in favour of the 'rationality' of state action.[26] Alternatively, an appeal might be mounted to exempt particular Jews from programmes of action as exceptional cases (for example, that they had been incorrectly classified; were veterans; were economically or culturally valuable and productive). However, arguing for exemption on exceptional grounds in a *particular* case tacitly affirmed the

---

24. Bauman, *Modernity and the Holocaust*, pp. 188f.   25. Ibid., p. 103.
26. The case was somewhat different in a number of occupied territories, where political, ideological and clandestine military resistance to the occupation could also be combined with a strong retention of civic and humanitarian values which still extended by bonds of community to their Jewish neighbours. This was especially marked in Denmark and in Italy (once the Germans had pushed the Jewish question on to their Fascist allies, even before their occupation of the country) and achieved institutional expression in Romania.

general rule – that Jews as Jews are properly to be subjected to these measures. Appeal could then only effectively be made by using (and so accepting) the criteria afforded by the legal framework enacting the measures (by, say, producing a genealogy showing Aryan descent). Appeals could only be registered by raising procedural questions concerning proper application of the rules, not by questioning the propriety of the rules according to some external criterion of value.[27] Moral motivation, to be effective, had to be translated into technical-instrumental action, in relation to which different rules and criteria for action apply.

Rationally compelled to dirty work

There is, nevertheless, very strong evidence to suggest that the ideological and bureaucratic dehumanisation of Jews, together with their removal from the proximities of moral community prior to the Final Solution, was insufficient to prevent glimmers of human (or, perhaps, only animal) solidarity troubling those charged with face-to-face killing.[28] The psychological effect of pity on those charged with the task of face-to-face murder was a matter of very great concern to Himmler. His concern was at once both pastoral and managerial, a genuine concern for both their humanity and for the efficient furtherance of the programme, to be driven by rational, systematic action and unfettered by 'animal' fellow-feeling.[29] Protection of those working at the 'coal-face' of the Final Solution was the primary reason for the adoption of impersonal, technological means of extermination by gas.[30] It had the added benefit of re-inforcing the claim that those involved were engaged in euthanasia (since this was the means employed in the programme of 1939)[31] or pest control by the most humane means, designed to minimise the suffering of the victims (as well as the psychological turmoil of the directly proximate perpetrators).

How did those whose work required them to kill face-to-face overcome their moral inhibitions and sense of disgust? The prior removal of

---

27. Arendt, *Eichmann in Jerusalem*, pp. 132f.; Bauman, *Modernity and the Holocaust*, pp. 187f.
28. Such glimmers appear to have been much more pronounced, and so much more troubling, when the victims were culturally assimilated German Jews (considered superior to the non-assimilated or those assimilated to inferior cultures), women or children. See, e.g., Arendt, *Eichmann in Jerusalem*, p. 96; Bauman, *Modernity and the Holocaust*, pp. 184f.; Dinsdale, ed., *Survivors, Victims and Perpetrators*, pp. 301f.; Hilberg, *Destruction of the European Jews*, III, pp. 215–19.
29. Arendt uses the term 'animal pity' to characterise Himmler's concern: *Eichmann in Jerusalem*, p. 106.   30. Browning, *Fateful Months*, p. 69.
31. See Lifton, *The Nazi Doctors*.

Jews from moral and social community, together with their ideological and bureaucratic dehumanisation, is one strong clue. The conviction that theirs was a necessary hygienic and sanitary task, carried out amidst the national emergency of total war, also contributed to the alleviation of moral scruples. Desperate problems required emergency measures which would solve them once and for all: 'These are battles which future generations will not have to fight again', Himmler told those working to solve 'the Jewish problem'.[32]

The fact that the task was distasteful to its perpetrators could actually work as a sign, not of a moral judgment immanent to conscience, but of its transcendence of moral criteria. Concern is shifted away from the victims to the burden of pity borne by the perpetrators.[33] The distastefulness of the task seems to have been construed, not as a sign of its impermissibility, but of its necessity in pursuit of the greater good: 'we would not be asked to do such terrible things, were it not strictly necessary'. Hence, experienced distastefulness (the sharpness of which was eroded with every participation, as well as blunted by heavy use of alcohol) worked, not in the direction of self-accusation, but of exoneration: 'this cannot be a matter of my personal will, inclination or uncontrolled passion; it is rather a burden laid on me through a chain of command and through historical destiny'. Significantly, acting against subjective feelings required the suppression of animal instincts (blood-lust and pity) by disciplined self-control and increased the sense that one was acting in accord with objective principle. Individual wills and tastes were matters to be overcome in fulfilment of the great task, the sacrificial cost of which members of the killing units saw as being borne by themselves. This was not so much a matter of personal will, then, but destiny, responsibility for which rested elsewhere.

Some, especially among the SS and SS-derived units, would have had an ideological component to their willingness to discharge unpalatable duties for *Führer* and *Volk*. More common and more decisive than that, however, was loyalty to one's peers. Members of killing units had to consider the effects of their refusal to carry out their tasks, not only on future generations to whom an acute 'Jewish problem' would be bequeathed, but on other members of the unit who would have to carry an increased

---

32. As remembered by Eichmann (Arendt, *Eichmann in Jerusalem*, p. 105).
33. So Arendt, ibid., p. 106. She later notices the capacity of perpetrators of the holocaust to experience themselves as its victims, citing Eichmann's sense of the way in which the Nazi leadership had abused his 'virtue' of obedience (p. 247f.).

share of the burden. The dynamics of group loyalty were of much more significance than ideology or military discipline (there is hardly any evidence that reluctance to participate would have resulted in execution; whereas there is evidence of opportunities for self-exemption), abetted by the sense of taking part in an historically necessary task, playing a part in destiny. The fact that one had to perform troubling tasks together would work to embed further group pride and loyalty: we bear these burdens together (which others may not understand or even be permitted to be aware of); we rose above our feelings about the work and achieved great successes, intensified by all the processes which knit people into an in-group whose experiences, not being shared, could not be understood by those outside. In addition, participation in mass killings appears to have rapidly desensitised those responsible (i.e., introduced a psychological distance between them and their actions and the humanity of the objects of this action), becoming quickly a matter of routine. Again, such distancing was the more easily enabled where there was a division of labour – say, between those rounding up, escorting and shooting Jews.[34]

Separating means and ends again: participating at a distance

The 'Final Solution' was the act of a society, not just its representatives or members of a few organisations. For genocide required the participation of vast numbers of ordinary Germans in ordinary civilian and state occupations and ordinary military formations.[35] The holocaust would have been impossible without the railway employees working out train timetables, driving trains, maintaining track; accountants; mechanics; engineers; and the multitude of clerks in the civil service and elsewhere dealing with bits of paper and passing them on to the next desk. For the most part, people performing routine, humdrum operations perpetrated the holocaust. Their tasks looked exactly the same as did their counterparts' in other countries and, more significantly, as their own had done prior to their incorporation into genocide. Amidst the mundane normality, the entirely routine nature, of their tasks, the majority of the participants in the Final

34. On all of this paragraph, see Christopher Browning, *Ordinary Men: Reserve Police Battalion 101 and the Final Solution in Poland* (New York: HarperCollins, 1992).
35. According to Arendt (*Eichmann in Jerusalem*, p. 159), Nuremberg (and the subsequent trial of Eichmann) failed to comprehend the reality of the Third Reich by identifying as criminal those organisations with peculiar responsibility for the holocaust; whereas, 'there existed not a single organization or public institution in Germany, at least during the war years, that did not become involved in criminal actions and transactions'.

Solution evidently found it difficult to appreciate the abnormal ends towards which their work was being co-ordinated. And even had they been able to appreciate them, it would have been hard for them to take responsibility for those ends because of the nature of bureaucratic processes. This breaks tasks down into differentiated functions that may then be performed by a functionally differentiated and specialised labour force. Any action is the co-ordinated outcome of a process which includes any number of highly varied, contributory tasks carried out by a workforce whose functionally separated tasks may require them never to meet or to understand what others are doing.

The efficiency gained by functional specialisation and division of labour would be threatened should the functionally specialised cogs concern themselves with more than their own immediate sphere of action and interaction, or apply criteria for evaluating their contribution other than the intra-systemic ones of technical-instrumental action. Functional division and specialisation alienates the workforce, not just from other aspects of the process, but from the end product of their own work. It intrudes a distance between the separable tasks and between them and the end result of their total co-ordination. In a sense, it would be true to say that the *meaning* of one's activity is hidden. For meaning is derived from relating one's action to its ultimate consequences, which bureaucratic process draws attention away from. The horizon of concern and attention narrows to the single task, the functioning of the separable cogs, which, being applicable to a range of possible associations and outcomes, holds no *intrinsic* meaning.[36] Meaning being expropriated, moral evaluation and responsibility are also somehow externalised.

> In a functional division of labour, everything one does is in principle
> *multifunctional*; that is, it can be combined and integrated into more
> than one meaning-determining totality. By itself, the function is
> devoid of meaning, and the meaning which will eventually be
> bestowed on it is in no way pre-empted by the actions of its
> perpetrators. It will be 'the others' (in most cases anonymous and out
> of reach) who will sometime, somewhere, decide the meaning.[37]

One performs functions, decided and determined by a superior (whose function in turn is determined by others), not actions for which one is personally responsible. But since there is an infinite regress of responsibilities here (both up and down the hierarchy), personal responsibility is

---

36. George L. Mosse, *Toward the Final Solution: A History of European Racism* (London: Dent, 1978), p. 226.   37. Bauman, *Modernity and the Holocaust*, p. 100.

simply not locatable at all. It is obliterated in the machinery that produces many acts that no-one may consciously appropriate.

Even in the case of those with direct responsibility for killing, the meaning of whose actions cannot be hidden from them by bureaucratically produced distance, an experience of *personal* distance from acts and consequences was still possible because of the chain of command. Hence, rather than experiencing their killing of Jews as acts of their *person* (of their own will), they appear to have experienced their actions in non-personal categories: as the *impersonal* means of instrumentation of others' intentions.[38] As such, they experienced them, not as subject to moral, but technical-instrumental criteria of evaluation and accountability, absolved of all moral responsibility once satisfied that they were in receipt of legal and procedurally correct orders from properly constituted authority. Thus, in being distanced either by bureaucratic and/or by hierarchical organisation, administrative and military functionaries could experience themselves as removed from the compass of moral criteria of evaluation, which were displaced by those dictated by technical-instrumental rationality.

> Technical rationality differs from moral rationality in that it forgets that the action is a means to something other than itself. As outer connections of action are effectively removed from the field of vision, the bureaucrat's own act becomes an end in itself. It can be judged only by its intrinsic criteria of propriety and success. Hand-in-hand with the vaunted relative autonomy of the official conditioned by his functional specialisation, comes his remoteness from the overall effects of divided, yet coordinated labour of the organisation as a whole. Once isolated from their distant consequences, most functional specialized acts either pass moral tests easily, or are morally indifferent. When unencumbered by moral worries, the act can be judged by unambiguously rational grounds.[39]

With the exclusion of morality proper, there is an effective colonisation of moral space by technical-rational criteria, which now perform a surrogate moral function. So being 'good' comes to be equated with efficiency in functional performance, coupled with a proper diligence to procedural technicalities (e.g., that orders and actions received and communicated are

---

38. Ibid., pp. 25 (drawing on John Lachs, *Responsibility of the Individual in Modern Society* (Brighton: Harvester, 1981), pp. 12f., 58), 162f.

39. Ibid., p. 101. Richard L. Rubenstein now accepts that the holocaust had this rational character – see the second edition of *After Auschwitz: History, Theology, and Contemporary Judaism* (Baltimore: Johns Hopkins University Press, 1992), p. 136. See also Arthur A. Cohen, *The Tremendum* (New York: Crossroad, 1981), p. 41.

legal and legitimate). Moral concern no longer relates to the consequences of activity. It is concerned with the technical proficiencies necessary for carrying out one's function. The principal 'moral' virtues are the functional ones of loyalty, discipline and obedience, particularly in the face of conflict with one's own wishes or views.[40] For efficient functioning requires a rational co-ordination of persons as functions rather than of *persons as persons*; bureaucracy is an objective, rational process which requires the submersion of subjectivity to the objective rationality and legitimacy of the process. This functional specialisation with its concomitant exclusion of the moral enables the full motivational engagement of people's skills, professionalism and expertise, unencumbered by their moral or political stances, which are disengaged within the ambit of their work. The person is metamorphosed from a moral agent functioning within a moral community into a functional object within a technical-instrumental process. Morality is not altogether obliterated here, but sequestered by technical-instrumental criteria. Bureaucratic cogs do not lose their motivational interest in right and wrong. Rather, morality is given a new criteriological basis. Right and wrong are redefined: am I doing my job well and efficiently; am I pleasing my superiors?

> [A] bureaucratic system of authority does not militate against moral norms as such, and does not cast them aside as essentially irrational, affective pressures which contradict the cool rationality of a truly efficient action. Instead, it . . . re-deploys them. *Bureaucracy's double feat is the moralization of technology, coupled with the denial of the moral significance of non-technical issues.* It is the technology of action, not its substance, which is subject to assessment as good or bad, proper or improper, right or wrong. The conscience of the actor prompts him to perform well and prompts him to measure his own righteousness by the precision with which he obeys the organizational rules and his dedication to the task as defined by the superiors.[41]

Incorporating the rationality of victims

What is the significance for the victims that they faced, not an old-style pogrom, but the rational implementation of a state policy? Unlike a situation in which irrational hatred and violence of a mob is faced, the creation of a rationally regulated world invites the belief that one may attempt to influence the outcome by the utilisation of one's own rational

40. Bauman, *Modernity and the Holocaust*, pp. 21f.
41. Ibid., p. 160, applying the findings of the Milgram experiment to the bureaucratic process of the holocaust (italics in original).

resources; that, in short, one may play the game, even if one may not alter it, with some hope of gaining an influence on its outcome, even if it is impossible to win it outright.

In the very initial stages, the Nazis' utilisation of legislative measures to identify Jews, and even their plans to solve 'the Jewish problem' through deportation, were considered by some Jews to be potentially beneficial, even though there can have been few who regarded the Nazis as pro-Jewish, since they bore some approximation to Zionist hopes and aspirations.[42] Some German Jews considered the early policies to be fortuitous, if not entirely benign in their intention and justification, and actively co-operated with their implementation for that reason.

The incorporation of their victims' reasoning and willing in the cause of their own destruction was a deliberate aspect of Nazi policy, which supported, enhanced and sometimes created the authority of Jewish leadership to manage Jewish affairs in the ghettos. Securing Jewish compliance in administering the ghettos was a much more efficient and effective means of implementing anti-Jewish measures than deploying (non-Jewish) Germans to do all the necessary work of administration, selection and implementation by open force.[43] Jews in many ghettos co-operated in ensuring the orderly continuation of normal life under abnormal conditions of segregation from surrounding populations and a population massively swelling by German resettlement policy. But they also administered and policed the processes of deprivation of property and of selection for 'transport', even where the meaning of that euphemism was clear to all.[44]

For the most part, Jewish leaders co-operated out of a sense of responsibility for their community, in the hope that Jewish administration could ameliorate the effects of the measures they were instructed to implement or, at the very least, make their implementation more humane.[45] In any case, it was clear that such measures would be taken, with or without Jewish co-operation. Each ghetto was eventually sealed and isolated from interchange and interaction with every aspect of its

42. An assessment echoed by Eichmann, who appears sincere in his belief that he was, not only pro-Jewish, but a Zionist (see Arendt, *Eichmann in Jerusalem*, pp. 40–7, 61f.). See also Victor Klemperer, *I Shall Bear Witness*.

43. Which is to say neither that open and brutal force was never used nor that there was no Jewish resistance (in the form of violent rebellion and of passive, non-compliance and covert undermining of Nazi objectives).

44. Bauman, *Modernity and the Holocaust*, p. 115; cf. pp. 117f., 125.

45. On the Jewish Councils generally, see Isaiah Trunk, *Judenrat: The Jewish Councils in Eastern Europe under German Occupation* (London: Macmillan, 1972).

wider social environment, including the jurisdiction of civilian and military authorities – with the one crucial exception of the ghetto's Nazi administration. Within the ghettos, the Jewish Councils' authority in regulation and administration was total – but only within the parameters set by the State. It was left entirely to the Councils to decide how to administer each new decree. Thus the Nazis co-opted and colonised the authority, power and administrative competence of Jewish leadership. The fact that their power and responsibilities within these parameters were *formally* total almost certainly made it all the harder for members of the Councils to sense their *material* powerlessness, their inability to influence the substance, extent or duration of Nazi measures.

Given the closure of the ghettos, the instructions and regulations of the local Nazi administration (which held complete jurisdiction) formed the constricted parameters of possible action, the base-line and single reference-point of reason.[46] Access to transcendent power, authority and criteria of evaluation had been blocked. Hence, the rational calculation of the best options was thoroughly circumscribed. And yet the fact that such deliberation as to the best means to implement directives was required of the Jewish Councils helped foster the sense that there was some real and significant freedom to manoeuvre in and influence the situation to make the conditions of ordinary life in an overcrowded, under-resourced and under-nourished ghetto bearable. They did this by first arranging accommodation for increasing numbers; finally, by ensuring orderly compliance with and discharge of selection orders (enforced by the ghetto's Jewish police force) in the belief that selections could be made according to criteria which might injure the Jewish community least, that those selected would be treated more humanely by Jews than Nazis and that, by co-operating, they were increasing the chances of survival of those not selected.[47] Co-operation was rational, so long as Jewish involvement in the process of implementing policy against themselves seemed to have a chance of making a difference to the chances of survival of the remainder. Significantly, where Nazi intentions eventually to liquidate the entire population were known, where the illusion that Jews could influence and mitigate their fate collapsed, there was resistance even in the face of

---

46. Bauman, *Modernity and the Holocaust*, pp. 123f.
47. Helen Fein notices how 'the threat of collective death was not anticipated because the social organization of political economy of the ghetto created differential death chances every day. The chance of each to survive depended on his or her place in the pecking order' (*Accounting for Genocide* (New York: Free Press, 1979), p. 319). See also Bauman, *Modernity and the Holocaust*, pp. 140ff.; Arendt, *Eichmann in Jerusalem*, p. 42; Eric H. Boehm, *We Survived* (New Haven: Yale University Press, 1949); Aharon Weiss, 'Jewish Leadership in Occupied Poland: Postures and Attitudes', *Yad Veshem Studies*, 12 (1977), 335–65.

certain lethal and total retribution (of which the rising of the Warsaw ghetto is perhaps the best known, but by no means the only, example).

Hence, the Nazis were uncommonly careful always to place Jews in a situation of apparent choice. In such totalitarian circumstances as this, the rationality of the victims utilised in choosing could only be incorporated into the service, not of self-interest, but of self-destruction; any option taken would have served Nazi purposes.[48] For any exercise of rationality would be sequestered by the rationality of the Nazi policy against the Jews. The real ends of this policy, and their primacy in relation to other aims of the regime, were usually hidden from the Jews. That is to say, the appropriate calculus for the reckoning of rational strategies for the pursuit of the self-interest of the Jewish community were hidden from them. Without knowing what were the ultimate intentions of the Nazis towards them, and the place these had in relation to other of their major objectives, it proved impossible to calculate the 'rationality' of various options. So, for instance, the attempts by various ghetto Councils to make their labour indispensable to the German war effort appeared to be absolutely rational and should, on that basis, have succeeded.[49] But its rationality was only apparent, not real, since it relied on the primacy in the Germans' objectives of ensuring a successful prosecution of the war and the survival of the German state. For rationality in that situation is restricted to its technical-instrumental form, a means–ends calculation. Since it is clear that one cannot influence the ends, rationality in the service of Jewish self-interest necessarily restricted itself to demonstrating that survival served these ends. With the emergence of the Final Solution as the real end of Jewish policy and its primacy over all other objectives, including military ones, all attempts by Jews to operate a rational calculus were doomed to failure. There is here, then, only the rationality already in the service of Nazi ends.[50] The appearance of choice, of plural options which could be exercised, was ultimately illusory.

48. Bauman, *Modernity and the Holocaust*, p. 135; Hilberg, *Destruction of the European Jews*, III, pp. 1036–42; Raul Hilberg, 'The Judenrat: Conscious or Unconscious "Tool"', in Yisrael Gutman and Cynthia J. Haft, eds., *Patterns of Jewish Leadership in Nazi Europe, 1933–1945: Proceedings of the Third Yad Veshem International Historical Conference, Jerusalem, April 4–7, 1977* (Jerusalem: Yad Veshem, 1979), pp. 33, 36.
49. See the discussion in Bauman, *Modernity and the Holocaust*, pp. 137ff.; Trunk, *Judenrat*, pp. 401–19, on whom Bauman draws; Browning, *The Path to Genocide*, pp. 75f.; Yisrael Gutman, 'The Concept of Labo', in Gutman and Haft, eds., *Patterns of Jewish Leadership*, p. 162.
50. Or, as Bauman puts it, 'the *rationality of the ruled is always the weapon of the rulers*' (*Modernity and the Holocaust*, p. 142, italics in original). In this regard, he notes 'a distinction between the rationality of the actor (a psychological phenomenon) and the rationality of the action (measured by its objective consequences for the actor). Reason is a good guide for individual behaviour only on such occasions as the two rationalities resonate and overlap' (p. 149).

In the death camps themselves, the dehumanising process of corrupting the victims was both more individualised and more stark – and, for that reason, more intense in its capacity to evoke heightened senses of complicity and of moral bankruptcy, guilt, shame and self-accusation. Individual co-operation (as *Sonderkommando* or *kapo*, or in merely discharging routine obligations without demur) was based on a similar calculation of self-interest, where one could sometimes make one's own survival more likely, but could do nothing to aid the survival of others or to inhibit the orderly operation of the camp. Often, choosing to optimise one's own chances of survival meant acting in ways that decreased others'. In the camps, rationality in the service of personal survival was forced to oppose itself to moral and religious criteria and obligation towards others. That is one reason why, for those who were not gassed straight away, the experience of active or passive collusion, co-operation or acquiescence dehumanised 'by pressing [them] to use the logic of self-preservation as absolution for moral insensitivity and inaction'.[51]

This dehumanisation, whereby instrumental ran counter to moral reason, was matched by that carefully woven into the design and ordering of the conditions of life in the camps. Prisoners were removed from the normal supports of humanity: from friends and relations; from possessions; from clothes; from their hair; even from their name, replaced by a 'cattle-brand' number;[52] from a normal diet; from normal eating utensils;[53] from adequate toilet facilities;[54] from the normal rights and duties attaching to the human person – especially freedom from arbitrary violence.

> Imagine now a man who is deprived of everyone he loves, and at the same time of his house, his habits, his clothes, in short, of everything he possesses: he will be a hollow man, reduced to suffering and needs, forgetful of dignity and restraint, for he who loses all often easily loses himself. He will be a man whose life or death can be lightly decided with no sense of human affinity, in the most fortunate of cases, on the basis of a pure judgement of utility.[55]
>
> ... it is no longer man who, having lost all restraint, shares his bed with a corpse. Whoever waits for his neighbour to die in order to take his piece of bread is, albeit guiltless, further from the model of thinking man than the most primitive pigmy or most vicious sadist.

51. Ibid., p. 205, italicised in original. Cf. p. 206.
52. Primo Levi, *If This is a Man/The Truce* (London: Abacus, 1987), p. 32; *The Drowned and the Saved* (London: Abacus, 1988), p. 95.   53. Levi, *The Drowned and the Saved*, pp. 90f.
54. Ibid., pp. 89f.; Rubenstein, *After Auschwitz*, pp. 54; 186f.
55. Levi, *If This is a Man*, p. 33. Cf. *The Drowned and the Saved*, pp. 33, 90.

> Part of our existence lies in the feelings of those near to us. That is why the experience of someone who has lived for days during which man was merely a thing in the eyes of man is non-human.[56]

Before inmates were selected for gassing or died from a combination of malnutrition, cold and overwork, a concerted attempt had been made to obliterate and to crush their humanity. They were reduced to 'suffering and needs', the alleviation and meeting of which drew them into open competition – unrestrained by any considerations other than one's own survival – with other inmates, thus weakening further the social foundation of their humanity in ties of human solidarity. In a world where only the fittest and the useful would survive each new selection, a clear invitation was issued to divest oneself of every semblance of common humanity and to experience relief at, if not actively to celebrate and prey upon, the weakness of others.[57] Survival, even until the next selection, was a hardwon prize; survival as a human being, even harder. For that, a prisoner would have to be able still to draw on resources not confined to, transcending, the total situation of the extermination camp.[58]

The deliberate destruction of the human spirit prior to the destruction of their bodies and completed in the industrial use of some Jewish remains was a practical expression of the ideological denial of Jews' humanity which, in the end, Nazis required Jews themselves to experience. This was an attempt to eliminate the distinction between victims and perpetrators by making the Jews complicit in their own destruction. This helps to explain why so many survivors are haunted by feelings of shame and guilt – not only at what they themselves may have done in the camps, but at what they witnessed and lived and at the very fact that they survived whilst others did not.[59] Significantly, the experience of guilt and shame is awakened by survival, by the cessation of the animal-like existence of the camps and the re-integration into contexts of meaning and value which allow and require survivors to measure their dehumanisation according to criteria other than those operating in the camps. As they were re-introduced to human society and its normal standards, so what became of them and was done to them in the camp could appear unbearable. How is it possible to live with faith, trust and hope as a human being beyond the enormity of the evil which survivors were subjected to?

---

56. Levi, *If This is a Man*, pp. 177f.   57. Levi, *The Drowned and the Saved*, pp. 25f.
58. This glimmer of transcendence, of humanity intact and drawing on the reality of a world outside of the camp, is the ministry which Lorenzo performed for Levi. See Levi, *If This is a Man*, pp. 127f.; cf. pp. 177f.
59. Levi, *The Drowned and the Saved*, pp. 54, 56–9; *The Truce*, p. 188.

Summarising concrete pathology

Whereas in the previous chapter I was principally concerned with pathology from victims' perspectives, here I am concerned primarily (though not exclusively) with the perspectives of perpetrators. Notwithstanding that, the following list of the main features of the concrete pathology I have described in this chapter bears a close resemblance to that described in the last.

· The pathological dynamic of the holocaust was historical, social and material, not individual or ideational.

· It utilised and captured desires and intentions, such as the creation of a good, secure and ordered society, the preservation of nation and pride in ethnic identity (on the parts of both victims and perpetrators).

· The whole fabric of German society was incorporated into this pathological dynamic.

· The application of a supposedly neutral, objective and omni-competent technical-instrumental rationality blocked access to transcendent norms and sources of value and evaluation – involving a confusion and conflation of the technical and moral.

· Perpetrators were often incorporated into the pathological dynamic as *functionaries*, rather than as responsible *subjects* of action. The hierarchy of military command and the depersonalisation and compartmentalisation of bureaucratic action together eroded the possibilities of perpetrators experiencing themselves as *subjects* responsible for the process and outcomes of bureaucratic action as a whole.

· Yet the opposite was often true on the part of victims, who were incorporated in ways which were capable of artificially heightening their sense of responsible freedom, of being subjects capable of acting to influence their own destiny,

· but whose every action, intention and desire could in fact only serve the cause of their destruction – that is, was incorporated after all into the pathological dynamic which was aimed at their destruction.

Part III

Testing the Inheritance

6

Willing

Preliminary to engagement

Turning to testing

Does the language of sin hold explanatory and descriptive power in relation to the phenomenologies of abuse and the holocaust delineated over the previous two chapters? This chapter will begin opening up that question. Answering it requires the doctrine of sin to engage with the descriptions of concrete pathology in testing encounter. However, since it is neither immediately obvious what should be brought into the conversation from either side, nor what it should be about, some preliminary deliberations are necessary before we can know how best to proceed.

What is the site on which the encounter is to take place, the theme of the conversation, and how is that to be identified? The previous chapters' discussions of concrete pathologies show them to be multidimensional and complex, resistant to encapsulation without remainder under a single, synthesised, thematic heading. Yet there is too much specific detail and it is too varied for it easily to be engaged with simply as it presents itself. What is needed is a specific dimension of pathological dynamics that may be discussed without falsely systematising the individual pathologies or synthesising the two (if common to both). At the same time, this dimension must be *significant* – close to the heart of the pathology – so that, in discussing it, one is forced into consideration of the whole.

There are similar issues in relation to theology. There is more than one doctrine of sin to choose from, and any particular one is extant in a number of variations. Many have the same kind of complexity and multidimensionality in their account of sin. Furthermore, as I argued in chapter 3 (see above, pp. 46f.), full-blown doctrinal formulations of sin are too abstract and general to admit of direct testing in relation to the concrete particularities of specific situations. They can, however, be indirectly tested through the mediation of models, theories or hypotheses (more specific in content and reference) that may be derived deductively from the more theoretical formulations of full-blown doctrines of sin. But a number of such models, theories and hypotheses are likely to be deducible from any single doctrine. Again, they are likely to be too varied all to be easily testable simultaneously and in relation to the same concrete pathologies. It would be tempting to opt for one common to all doctrines of sin, but there is no obvious candidate for that and such would not necessarily represent an aspect of theologically described pathology operative (and therefore testable) in every concrete situation. There is no model, hypothesis or theory about sin common to all of its doctrinal formulations. In order to find something all doctrines of sin hold in common, we have to move back for a moment to considerations that are more formal, have less substance, and are further removed from the empirical. We have to move back, in fact, to the formal essential of sin-talk, that it is a theological language. That does not help us directly. But it does suggest that, whatever model, hypothesis or theory we choose to test, it must bring God into the conversation. If it fails in that, not only will it fail to test sin as a *theological* language, it will also fail to hold any generalisable significance for all doctrines of sin.

This returns us to the concerns with which this book opened. In Part I, I argued that the sources of the formal and substantive challenges to speaking of the pathological in relation to God in our culture were related to its understanding of freedom. A consideration of the doctrinal formulation found culturally most offensive (original sin) showed it to chafe heavily against the basic axiom of modernity: the primacy and inalienability of freedom, defined as a freedom from determining influence and so founded on an ontology of separation. It is, indeed, freedom conceived of as consisting in separation that makes it so difficult generally to speak of God and world together, without appearing to compromise the integrity of one or the other. In relation to original sin, the difficulties are focused in its articulating an understanding of accountability before God that will not confine itself to the circumference of moral culpability. Sin is presented, not as a phenomenon of our freedom, an object of choice, but as an unavoidable reality conditioning and shaping freedom. And yet, the doctrine insists that we are nevertheless accountable for sin. One of the constituents of this conflict is a difference in understanding what makes our action and our incorporation or participation in situations, events and relationships *personal,* and thereby matters for which we may be held personally accountable. There is only one possible answer to that from the perspective afforded by our culture's ontology of freedom: we are personally joined to action, participation and incorporation through the freedom of the will. It is precisely the will's freedom that the doctrine of original sin contests and, in so doing, proves its resistance to translation into a secular (in our culture, pragmatically atheist), moral language.

Through a rather convoluted route, I have now come to a point where I can identify a strong candidate for the site on which the language of sin may engage and be engaged by the descriptions of concrete pathologies: the phenomenon of human willing. Why does that commend itself?

From the theological side, the general theory of sin that affords the best chance of testing the *theological* referent of sin-talk is that which most forcefully resists translation into secular terms: the doctrine of original sin, in its traditional interpretation. It is not a representative doctrine. Indeed, it is chosen precisely because it is *un*representative of modern theologies of sin that tend to conform themselves to the prevalent understanding of freedom and associated conditions for the attribution of personal responsibility. It is not that it is absolutely impossible for modern theologies of sin (including modern reinterpretations of original sin) to be translated into moral categories and to function theologically. But it is much more difficult within a moral frame of reference to operate an *intrinsic* relation between God and pathology, through which sin-talk may interrupt and make a difference to moral discourse and assumptions. Therefore, with the traditional understanding of original sin, we maximise the opportunity for testing sin-talk at its most distinctive. Insofar as that distinctiveness is derived from its *theological* character, the results are potentially generalisable for all doctrines of sin. Beyond formally validating the theoretical referent of sin-talk, however, a positive result for original sin might prove ambivalent for those doctrines that conform their interpretation to a moral frame of reference. For what we are testing is the explanatory and descriptive power of an understanding of sin irreducible to the moral. Or, to put it the other way round, we are thereby testing also the assumptions of the moral critique of original sin and the descriptive and explanatory power of the moral frames of reference on which most modern theologies of sin depend.

But the traditional doctrine of original sin is too far abstracted from the empirical and particular to be amenable to direct concrete testing. We therefore need to select a specific hypothesis or model of theological pathology, deducible from original sin, with a localised range of reference close enough to the empirical to be amenable to direct empirical testing. We also need to select an hypothesis or model that is deducible from (so in testing may represent) the doctrine's understanding of personal accountability where it chafes so severely against the moral. In addition, that needs to bear relation to key aspects of the descriptions of concrete pathology. From the perspective of the doctrine's conflict with moral frames and standards of reference, what most commends itself is the model of or hypothesis about the way that willing operates in relation to sin: the bondage of the will.[1] That is specifiable enough to admit of concrete testing by asking whether, in the concrete situations, people are *personally* incorporated into pathology only through their free willing, or whether their wills are operative, but not free. This sort of issue certainly emerges through the discussions of concrete pathologies, but whether it merits consideration as an aspect of their core dynamic is less clear at this stage. Whether interpreting what is happening in these situations through a consideration of willing holds explanatory power, whether it illuminates the depth pathologies or proves merely peripheral, is something which itself will be tested through this encounter. If this is to prove to be an appropriate field of testing encounter, then we should expect core pathologies to become more clearly specifiable by approaching them through the portal afforded by a consideration of the role and dynamics of willing.

A similar comment may be made on the theological side. The hypothesis concerning the bondage of the will has a localised field of empirical reference and has been deduced from a more general, theological theory. However, it is in itself neither transparently theological nor highly specific in its content. It is more a general and, in an empirical setting, somewhat vague hypothesis than a model. We know that it refers to the operation of the will and its freedom, but it is vague as to how bondage of the will concretely manifests itself, what non-incapacitating binding of willing involves. Whilst the hypothesis has a specific, empirical referent (the phenomenon of willing), it will require more substantive specification as to what the binding of willing means and how it is to be recognised

1. For good examples of this deduced hypothesis deployed in disputes with those rejecting the general theory of original sin, see, e.g., Martin Luther', *On the Bondage of the Will* (against Erasmus) and Jonathan Edwards, *Freedom of the Will* (New Haven: Yale University Press, 1957 – against New England Arminianism).

in practice. In the very process of testing it as a heuristic device for understanding pathological dynamics, it will have to acquire more clearly specifiable content. In other words, if it is to illuminate and enrich our understanding of concrete pathologies, in the very act of so doing, it must itself be illuminated and conceptually enriched by being given more specific reference in a concrete setting. That is to say, concrete testing is simultaneously deductive and inductive. But if sin-talk is to survive concrete testing, it is necessary that such amplification of the hypothesis points in a theological direction, back towards the superstructure of Christian doctrine.

Moral languages and the circumference of explanatory power

What I have delineated above is a means of testing the explanatory and descriptive power of sin-talk as it escapes the circumscription of moral languages. At the same time, therefore, the descriptive adequacy of moral languages, frames and standards of reference is also being tested. Testing the explanatory power of the hypothesis of bound willing means implicitly asking whether a moral framework (including a moral rendering of the language of sin) principally interested in the tracking of moral culpability is adequate *as a framework for understanding* pathological situations.

The descriptive interests of moral languages are primarily oriented towards the location of blame, and so towards events and situations that are the consequences of behaviour that fulfils the criteria for locating culpability. Crucial among these criteria is the relationship of free willing to acting. Moral interest in willing is limited to agents' (perpetrators') free exercise of will, so that lines of moral causation and of responsibility may be traced. It is tempting to reduce the question demanded by the strictures of concrete testing to whether anyone's willing in the situations enjoys sufficient freedom for them to be held morally culpable. The real question is far broader. It is whether morality's limitation of interest in the phenomenon of willing does not miss some of its key pathological aspects, aspects that require naming if the concrete pathology is to be brought to adequate expression. If the answer to that is in the affirmative, then there is an at least prima facie case that moral languages have limited descriptive and explanatory power in relation to these concrete pathologies, and that a language which is not restricted by the limitations attending moral interests might be needed to perform the task of comprehensive interpretation and description.

In this chapter, then, I am implicitly asking after the *descriptive adequacy* of a framework and language which is interested in willing only insofar as it helps locate moral responsibility, to answer the question 'who is to blame?' To ask whether a moral language and framework of interpretation are adequate to the task of description and understanding is not to ask whether it is *possible* to locate moral responsibility in these situations, but whether doing so is *sufficient* to describe the nature of the pathology at work.

This manner of concrete testing therefore opens up the possibility that there might be other significant descriptive and interpretive tasks for which different modes of discernment and a different language might be necessary. That much is likely to be readily accepted by all and in a sense states the obvious. Complementing moral languages with others dealing with non-moral pathology may readily be admitted without weakening the case for a moral interpretation and delimitation of the language of sin, provided the other discourse does not intrude on the 'subjective' terrain of the moral, but names 'objective' aspects of pathology. But that delimitation does not apply in relation to the language of sin, which presents itself as a language of personal accountability. Precisely what I am testing through the hypothesis of bound willing is whether sin, as a language of personal accountability, might extend to the non-moral aspects of the pathological. That is, in effect, to test one of the major moral criticisms of the doctrine of original sin: that it erodes the difference between the (supposedly) moral language of sin and the non-moral languages of evil or sickness, that for which we are not accountable. To put it the other way around, it is to test the delimitation of the referential scope of the language of sin (which is a limitation of the sphere of our accountability before God) in modern theologies of sin to the moral. A focus on willing is a good device towards this end, since it allows us to examine the performance of the organ of personal accountability in concrete pathology and to ask whether a moral frame of reference is sufficient for recognising all forms of personal participation (and therefore accountability) that arise through willing.

In the following discussion, then, I am not primarily concerned with establishing who is to blame, but with characterising the way in which willing is operative in the concrete situation, in order the better to appreciate the nature and depths of its pathological reality. To risk repetition: my concern is not with the question of whether legal or moral culpability can be established, nor with the conditions for so doing. But that does not mean that I am uninterested in or antagonistic towards the establishment of legal and moral culpability. As a Christian theologian, however, I am bound to object to the supposed universal competence of moral questions and frameworks to deal adequately with these situations: the implicit supposition that, once people have been tried, judged and sentenced in the moral or legal dock, there is no more work to be done. To put the matter simply: being theological about these situations requires us to bring them in their totality, so far as we are able, before God, to relate them to God. And for that purpose, moral frameworks are inadequate – *not redundant, but inadequate*. A fuller and richer description of the pathological dynamics operating in a situation is required than is afforded by a purely moral interest in establishing blame. Moreover, in this theological task, the moral is to be contextualised by the purpose of relating a situation to God (in practice as well as cognitively). That will mean that the practice and the purpose of blaming are not self-standing, self-validating or self-referring. They are legitimate only within the broader compass of attempting to relate a situation to the creating and saving action of the triune God. What it means to locate moral responsibility and to blame, how, when and why we do so, should then be reshaped by this primary theological purpose.

I have taken the time to set all of this out because I feared that otherwise my comments concerning willing (particularly any intimation of my reservations concerning the adequacy of moral frameworks) would be prone to be fed immediately into the dichotomy of blame and understanding, whereby it is supposed that to seek comprehensive understanding necessarily implies a reluctance to locate moral responsibility. I want instead to be free of the moralistic agenda before I begin, so that I may ask *how* will is operating in the concrete situations, without such deliberation being drawn immediately into the agenda of locating moral culpability and being defined by its standards. That means, in particular, that I do not accept that the exercise of will is coterminous with the contours of moral accountability.

Sexual abusers of children

The portrayal of childhood sexual abuse in chapter 4 concentrated on the experience of the child, rather than on that of the abuser. In part, that was because accounts of abusers' points of view are inadequate, partial and not always reliable characterisations of their significant pre-histories and motivations. In part, it was because understanding what brings abusers to will to abuse does not help to clarify the nature of the abusive dynamic as it entraps the child. Indeed, it may draw attention away from the experience of the child to the pre-history of the abuser in a way which disables any appropriate characterisation of what is happening to the child. That is to make more concretely the point that the agenda of tracing culpability for abuse is not identical with that of descriptively explaining its pathology. Hence, the willing of abusers featured only somewhat fleetingly in the description of the pathology of childhood sexual abuse. The paucity of reliable information concerning the general categories of abusers' motivational complexes makes it impossible to make any general statement that would hold true for most or all abusers. The information we do have, however, is sufficient to make some statement as to the nature of pathological willing in the case of *some* abusers. Whilst that cannot stand as representative of all cases, it nonetheless tells us something about the nature and operation of willing which might be of broader applicability than the sexual abuse of children.

The incidence of sexual, physical or emotional abuse in the pre-history of sexual abusers of children is high. As I indicated in chapter 4, childhood sexual abuse often has severe, long-term traumatic consequences; consequences that affect a person's basic pattern and direction of dynamic life-intentionality (their spirit), including their will and its operation. The presence of a history of abuse in the background of a significant proportion of abusers strongly suggests that their own disposition to abuse is not an artefact of their pure internality, having no explanation other than their free and arbitrary decision. Rather, the personal history of these abusers seems to have shaped their basic patterns of intentionality, their character or personal identity, the framework within which will operates.

Furthermore, relatively few abusers appear to be possessed of an innate sexual attraction to children. Abuse is sometimes, though rarely, driven by straightforward (though distorted) sexual desire. More commonly, however, than the alleviation of sexual appetites, abuse seems to be a means for resolving issues of personal identity that reflect distorted identity structures sedimented through histories of distorted interaction.[2] Whilst the means of resolution have become sexualised, neither

2. For those abusers who are themselves survivors of *sexual* abuse, it is likely that they are modelling their own behaviour on that of their abusers. See, e.g., David Finkelhor, *Child Sexual Abuse: New Theory and Research* (New York: The Free Press, 1984), p. 41. The association is particularly strong where abuser and victim are of the same sex; hence, the modelling of abusive behaviour is to be found more often among male than female survivors.

they, nor the issues being so resolved, are intrinsically or specifically sexual. Issues concerning security, trust, worth, vulnerability are resolved through power, domination, humiliation or the semblance of intimacy.

In the cases of those who do experience a prior sexual interest in children, imaginative rehearsal of sexual acts whilst masturbating, whether through fantasies or the use of child pornography, can significantly shape and condition the willingness to realise the acts of imagination, as well as incrementally increasing the kind of activity which is imaginable as being pleasurable and permissible – at least in imagination. Through masturbation, the experience of arousal by children may be reinforced in a way which desensitises potential abusers to feelings of guilt or shame which might act as impediments to active willing,[3] so more deeply embedding the will in this orientation. Masturbation is capable of reinforcing initial sexual interest or arousal by reworking the original situation which caused arousal into a pleasurable and well-rehearsed fixation in which the actual and imagined events become overwhelmingly associated with pleasurable feelings, rather than with those of guilt or shame. Subsequently, abuse itself can provide material for new masturbatory fantasies which serve to reinforce the abusive behaviour further.

Whether abuse is the vehicle for the satisfaction of specifically sexual appetites or a field for resolution of other issues, the physiological effects on abusers of their sexually abusive behaviour are likely in themselves to be reinforcing and habit-forming, even without rehearsal and replay through imagination whilst masturbating. The force of habit is likely to involve an experienced displacement of active willing, not only at the extreme of the spectrum where habit turns into obsessive, fixated and compulsive behaviour. The sexualisation of the means whereby abusers experience release (temporarily) from the stresses and pressures associated with the issues in personal identity ('referred' in the form of physical tension and therefore relievable by physical means) can create psychological dependence. That is likely also further to desensitise the abuser to the child as human person and to increase the sense that the sexual behaviour is unwilled, cannot be helped and may even run counter to his conscious willing. It is likely that the way in which the routinisation and normalisation of abuse affect the victim have their parallel in the

---

3. Ibid., pp. 41ff.; S. C. Wolf, J. R. Conte and M. Engle-Menig, 'Community Treatment of Adults who have Sex with Children', in L. E. A. Walker, ed., *Handbook on Sexual Abuse of Children: Assessment and Treatment Issues* (New York: Springer, 1987). See also the more anecdotal evidence (drawn from a wealth of experience) presented in Gay Search, *The Last Taboo: Sexual Abuse of Children* (Harmondsworth: Penguin, 1988), p. 67.

habituation of the perpetrator's will to abuse and in his experiences of a displaced or impotent will.[4]

Willing the holocaust

Leaders and planners

The account given in chapter 5 of the holocaust makes it clear that Hitler and other Nazi planners and ideologues willed the elimination by mass murder of Jews and other enemies of and dangers to the regime. It could not and would not have happened without or against their explicit willing. But it also makes it clear that the story of the formation of that will is not one of simple causation, of a will formed independently, that stood outside of and originated the process leading to the implementation of extermination, freely choosing it from a neutral standpoint. Rather, the willing of genocide was itself shaped and formed through the process of planning and implementing solutions to 'the Jewish problem', which turned out to be inadequate in the changing circumstances of the war. Willing did not belong here to some neutral sphere, suspended above concrete reality; it was immersed in and inseparable from it.

(And if we ask after the origin of the prior willing to solve 'the Jewish problem', we are again directed to the enmeshing of will with the broader, concrete and ideational interactive dynamics shaping history, societies, psychologies and ideas: the historical relationship between the churches and the Jews; the defeat of Germany in World War I and the conditions of the armistice; the perceived threat of Bolshevism; social Darwinism; the science of eugenics; the rise of rationality and its fantasies of perfection.)

It is not, then, that genocide happens without Hitler's and others' wills, much less against their wills. But the willingness to conceive and implement the Final Solution was born out of a prior commitment of will to address the Jewish problem through less drastic actions, alongside the commitment to technical-instrumental planning. That the logical development of these previous solutions could lead, under the conditions which later prevailed (if not in any case), to genocide was almost certainly inconceivable to all at the beginning, Hitler included. The conceivability and possibility of willing genocide belongs to the creeping incremental-

---

4. Tilman Furniss, *The Multi-Professional Handbook of Child Sexual Abuse: Integrated Management, Therapy, and Legal Intervention* (London: Routledge, 1991), pp. 32ff. speaks of a dynamic of addiction operating for abusers in a way which matches that of secrecy for the child.

isation of anti-Jewish measures (coupled with acclimatisation by the 'euthanasia' programme, experience of mass death in war, commitment to fight a war in Russia unrestrained by normal codes and conventions). Commitment to no previous measure (resettlement, concentration, sealing the ghettos) entailed a commitment to genocide, even though the enforcement of those policies did include the murder of Jews, individually and in large groups. But each successive measure further conditioned the will to accept the next; and with each incremental commitment, it was all the harder to separate the will from the gradually unfolding logic of genocide as the Final Solution. For the will was already enmeshed in options which, when looking back from the perspective of genocide, appeared consistent with it. The incremental incorporation of willing in this dynamic of planning and frustrated implementation clouded the point at which a decision was being taken and at which there was social or personal commitment to a specific course of action. The significance of this observation as regards the will is that incrementation in planning and action helped cloud *what* it was that one was willing and the *point* at which one willed it. The capacity, even of policy-makers, to recognise their willing as responsible for actions which differed from and were distanced by a lapse of time from those they originally willed was probably severely impaired. Later actions might well have appeared to be the result, not of one's pre-history of free willing and its consequences, but of the irresistible, logical drive or unpredictable drift of events.

Any intimation that the Final Solution belonged to the sphere of necessity (whether rational, natural or historical) rather than the arbitrary whim of free will would have the likely effect of relocating the place and redefining the nature of willing in relation to it. Willing is not obliterated when confronted with the irresistibility of logic or nature in the rhetorical guise of historical destiny. For destiny is not fate. Fate merely befalls us in disregard of our will. Destiny, on the other hand, requires our *wilful* submission to its dictates and demands. The presentation of anti-Jewish measures as being in accord with the proper order of nature or as the proper means towards the resolution of a problem (according to technical-instrumental criteria) invited the subjection of subjective willing to the objective truth of 'how things really are'. It invited people, in other words, to subject themselves to 'reality'. Willing was not entirely displaced here, but its function changed. As 'objective' and 'rational', the ends were beyond dispute. Since, however, deliberation concerning means also proceeded by 'objective', technical-instrumental criteria (efficiency towards the given end of re-creating natural racial order), these too appeared to reside outside the sphere of free, choice-making willing, except in the most formal sense. Will could not function as a free choice between competing ends, selecting the ultimate horizon and orientation of action. Instead, it was restricted to a formal freedom in 'choosing' that path which commended itself as the most rational, as the 'best' choice according to criteria related to the efficiency of means (which nonetheless has the capacity for redefining ends). The only room for choice lay in the voluntary (meaning simply an exercise of will, of *voluntas*, as opposed to *liberum arbitrium indifferentiae*), responsible acceptance or irresponsible rejection of 'reality' – which appears as no real choice at all. So willing becomes here the voluntary acceptance of reality; the addition of one's committed action to 'necessity', to 'reality' (its reconstruction along these rational lines and by these rational means).

The rationality of the vision of a Europe purified of Jews and of the means to be eventually employed to that end operated to prevent most participants from experiencing themselves as in a position of free choice concerning their participation. This prevented them also from experiencing their participation in genocide as related to a mode of active willing which would render them *personally* accountable and responsible for their actions. For willing appears here more like a passive acceptance of reality, the order of which is constituted outside of the self, than a decision which rests ultimately on the internally generated freedom of the self in its willing. Yet that description misleads, since willing is not really passive here. It denotes instead the active entrance into 'reality'; the addition of subjective commitment and personal energies to the extra-personal dynamics, structures and orders of 'reality' and the planned recovery of its proper order.

Cogs

The constriction and redefinition of willing and its field of effective operation may also be observed in the situation of those who were 'cogs' in the genocidal process. In the context of bureaucratic functionaries, action was assessed, not according to moral criteria and values concerned with ultimate ends, but according to intra-systemic criteria of technical-instrumental rationality concerned with means. Willing, it seems, ceased to be active in relation to the ends of action, attending only to the efficient execution of means. That is to say, willing was constricted in its sphere of operation with the eclipse of transcendent frameworks of evaluation and the disappearance of the ultimate ends of action from the horizon of the immediate task. So restricted, it ceased to function to direct agents towards some more ultimate framework of meaning (and so ceased to perform a moral or religious function). Yet, it did not cease to function altogether. It was redirected and sequestered in its functioning, not annulled. Willing here functions, not in the making of choices concerning the ends to which action is oriented as well as means, but as the medium through which energies of subjective, personal commitment are added to the discharge of objectified, depersonalised means. *Willing turns function into vocation*; efficiency, expediency and loyalty into virtue. Will is what turns the highly localised and specialised role and work of the cog, robbed of any wider reference (to the ultimate co-ordination of tasks, the end to which this work will be put, as well as to transcendent moral or religious criteria), into *personal* activity to which a moral framework may be applied, in which there is good and bad, right and wrong – but only according to technical-instrumental criteria and applied only within the restricted ambit of the cog's functioning. What we observe here, then, is not the exclusion of either morality or willing, but their sequestration, colonisation and co-option, their total orientation towards fulfilling the allotted task, and doing so well – beyond what is merely demanded. So willing, virtue and the moral are not functioning here as portents and agents of transcendence. They are entirely bent towards and thereby 'redouble' the dynamics into which they are – even unwittingly – incorporated.

Killing units

Somewhat similar processes appear to have been in place amongst the groups of men who carried out face-to-face mass murder. Here also there was the experience of being in a chain of command, of being the mere instruments of the will of those who give orders. Like the chain of bureaucratic process with its separation of tasks and specialisation of labour, hierarchical chains of command function to expropriate decisive willing. The point at which will is appropriately active is far removed from the point at which participants act. In the cases of the perceptions of both bureaucratic cogs and members of killing units, it was not they who had and exercised will in the sense of the ability freely to choose what should be done. That was an attribute and a responsibility borne by those much higher up the hierarchy and far removed from the final point of action. Indeed, the killing could be accompanied by acute counter-sensations of will: that this was not what one would will to do *if* one had a choice. But the existential situation of members of killing units, at least as they themselves experienced it, was of not having choice – or at least not one which they could responsibly exercise. Genocide itself was regarded as belonging to the realm, not of choice, but of necessity and destiny. And so refusing to carry out the task that had been allotted to one's unit was a shirking of the responsibilities of that destiny, as well as those attaching to group loyalty – for if one refused, who was going to shoulder that share of that burden which it had fallen on Germany (and specifically on this unit) to discharge?

To mention the virtues of loyalty and responsibility is to suggest that neither willing nor morality are inoperative here; but neither are they functioning as mediators of transcendence (the ideological and bureaucratic means of eliminating the humanity of victims as bearers of transcendence is also significant here). Their scope is radically circumscribed. Moral claims no longer belong to a sphere transcending the policy and practice of genocide and are certainly no longer mediated by its victims. They are instead self-referring: the greater good in relation to which one subjects one's contrary will and desire is that of a Europe reordered on racial lines, now to be achieved through the genocide of the Jews (mediated also through the sub-morality of loyalty to comrades). So willing functions here too as *voluntas*, as the addition of personal and subjective commitment to that which one experiences as being outside the realm of one's own free choice in the strict sense (*liberum arbitrium indifferentiae*).

The story of the killing units reveals also the speed with which repeated participation in mass murder normalised it, desensitising perpetrators to any intimations of transcendence which might have been borne by pity for the victims – helped along by alcohol and by a culture of *machismo* which regarded the overcoming of scruples (weakness of will) as a sign of strength, inability so to do as weakness and cowardice.

Willing victims?

In the preceding two sections, I have suggested that the willing of sexual abusers of children and perpetrators of the holocaust is more complex than a simplistic moral framework, interested only in will as an independent organ of causal agency, could account for. For perpetrators' willing is ‥rative in ways other than the deliberate exercising of free choice, as the simple cause of certain effects. I draw attention to this as I turn to consider the willing of victims, in order once again to undercut any supposition that this can only mean that victims are going to be blamed. Just as there are aspects of perpetrators' willing which do not fit neatly into the agenda of simple moralism and its search for blame, so there may be ways in which victims exercise will which help us to understand the pathological dynamics of their situation but which do not imply causal responsibility for what happens to them.

Sexually abused children

The definition of childhood sexual abuse I gave in chapter 4 held abuse to be coincident with age-related disparities in power, status and knowledge. Those disparities mean that the child's willing cannot be operative as a cause of abuse. It also means, incidentally, that she is unable effectively to resist the abuse. For her will simply does not have the required potency, given her lack of power, status and knowledge relative to those significantly older than she is, either to initiate or to resist. Since it is impossible for the child to free herself from these disparities, there is no possibility here of genuine consent – of her freely willing to permit the abuse. But the fact that her willing cannot have the kind of efficacy which would be of interest to a moralistic agenda trying to establish clear lines of causation and blame does not mean that it is inactive or that its activity is inconsequential. Indeed, the fact that childhood sexual abuse tends to effect a distortion in survivors' basic patterns and structures of intentionality (including willing) constitutive of identity strongly suggests that the distortion of willing might be traceable back into the situation of abuse itself.

Feminism and sexual abuse of children

Feminist treatment of childhood sexual abuse is instructive here.[5] Unsurprisingly, feminism finds itself in alliance with the mostly female victims against the mostly male perpetrators in its struggle against the oppressiveness of male sexuality. It is hardly surprising that feminist analyses are uncompromising in locating blame with the abuser, identified as the only participant who had sufficient causal agency either to initiate or to prevent the abuse. What is perhaps surprising is the readiness simultaneously to advert to supra-personal, causative factors (the social, material

5. See, e.g., Emily Driver and Audrey Droisen, eds., *Child Sexual Abuse: Feminist Perspectives* (Basingstoke: Macmillan, 1989).

and cultural practices of patriarchy) which shape and condition the willing of abusers. That the overarching social, cultural and political context of 'patriarchy' receives a share of the blame for the sexual abuse of children is not taken to absolve abusers from causal responsibility for abuse. Nonetheless, there is here an at least tacit acceptance of the view that the perpetrator's will is not neutral and self-moving, but has been predisposed and shaped through the processes of male socialisation which, it is argued, tend to encourage men to exercise power oppressively (especially over women and children and in the family setting) and to use sex as a means of expressing such power.

In attempting to do justice to the supra-personal shaping of personal intentionality and action, feminism operates with a more complex understanding of causality and willing (although such is seldom explicated) than that of a straightforward moral framework. In order to do justice to the wider pathological dynamics which operate in sexual abuse of children, feminists working in this field take the risk of suggesting that abusers' willing is not something for which they bear sole responsibility. That is a risk because it could easily be misinterpreted as absolving abusers of blame.

Having rejected a simplistic correlation of pure, uncaused willing and causation in relation to abusers, feminists take a further, similar risk in relation to the situation of abused children. If it is accepted that the only significant forms of agency and of willing are those which are sufficiently potent in a situation to act as cause, then it would follow that abused children, in order to be protected from blame, must be taken to be purely passive and impotent. Feminist commentators tend to realise that restricting the account of willing and agency to that which locates blame squarely with the abuser is not unambiguous for the abused. Certainly, the abused need to be freed of inappropriate feelings of guilt, related to inaccurate senses of their power and agency in the situation (possibly fostered by the abuser). But a description of abuse which suggests that, because they are in no way the cause of abuse (being incapable of consenting), abused children exercised no agency or will renders them as powerless, passive objects, not subjects – of therapeutic processes as of abuse. The feminist strategy of renaming those sexually abused in childhood as survivors is guided by a concern about the future therapeutic consequences of self-narration in the mode of victim. But it is also, in part, a commitment to a more realistic rendering of what happens in abuse: the child is not merely passive; not only done to. She does something. She survives. And so renaming victims as survivors draws attention to the positive, personal achievement of survival. And that achievement can only be judged a *personal* one if it was the achievement of both will and agency; if she shaped it as well as being shaped by it. Otherwise survival too would be just one more thing happening *to* and befalling her through chance, luck or the natural (i.e., not requiring willed participation) operation of forces and processes, the effects of which are passively received. Then she would, in a sense, be a *victim* of survival, which could not then be something which could be reclaimed as her own act and built on therapeutically as a resource for regaining control over her life. Hence it must be implied that surviving required some agency and willing on her part.

The significance of feminist discussions of childhood sexual abuse for the concerns of this chapter does not lie so much in their implicit account and conception of abused children's willing. It lies instead in the risky affirmation that the child's willing may be operative in abuse and that, beyond that, the denial of operant willing does not protect him from blame but confirms, repeats and further embeds abuse by continuing to narrate him as a passive object. Whatever might be the understanding of willing and its freedom with which feminist analyses and responses implicitly work, I wish to take up this risky insight and ask, in relation to the pathological dynamics described in Part II, how victims' willing functions and what the significance of that might be.

Confusion of willing and illusions of consent

The age-related disparities in knowledge and understanding are exploited by some abusers in order to effect a confusion in their victims' willing. That happens most obviously where the child is manoeuvred into a situation where the relationship with the abuser seems to be a benefit outweighing the abuse; where there are rewards, inducements or other benefits; and where initiation of abuse is seductively incremental.

In the first two cases, there is a deliberately induced confusion concerning the objects of willing, about *what* the child wills, *what* constitutes the orientation, horizon and meaning of his willing. His willing for perceived 'benefits' of the relationship (e.g., intimacy with and affection from an older person) or for rewards and inducements may be confused and conflated (if not at the time, then subsequently) with willing abuse. This confusion becomes particularly and traumatically entrenched where the strength of desire for the benefit, inducement or reward encourages him to 'initiate' abuse in order to secure it. For then a virtual equation in the practice of willing has been achieved between abuse and reward as its objects: there is an elimination of the practical difference between means and ends where they are so closely related.

This confusion concerning the objects of willing (combined with any confusion concerning the nature, meaning and consequences of abuse), let me be clear, is not merely an epistemological one. It is a *practical* one. In practice, the child's willing is employed in the cause of abuse. The abuser bends the child's willing for non-abusive objects to abusive purposes by eliding the difference between them, so that the child's willing and intentionality is incorporated into those of the abuser. Childhood sexual abuse abuses the child's active willing and intentionality, and this is why it can have such long-term traumatic consequences.

Where abuse is initiated by gradual increments in abusive behaviour, the child's willing may also become habituated to abuse 'by degrees'. The abuser sets up a long sequence of acts leading from the safe to the abusive, but in which each successive act appears insignificant in its difference from the next. In this way, the child may be confused about the difference between abusive and non-abusive acts, so that she may find herself willingly permitting abusive acts without understanding their nature. The gradient of incrementation is so shallow that it obfuscates, not only the point at which acts become abusive, but the point at which her willing is operative. Even when she becomes aware that she does not want the abusive acts to continue, she may feel pressed to consent because she senses that she has, in a sense, already consented to them by accepting those which now, from this perspective, appear not so different. As she looks back, she is easily convinced that she was willingly accepting abuse from the outset and so she may feel trapped in the trajectory, not of the abuser's coercive manipulation, but of her own willing.

Secrecy and confusion in willing

Confusion in willing does not only attend illusions of consensual willing already in place, however. As I argued in chapter 4, the almost universal injunction to secrecy places the child in a situation where he has to exercise will against discovery. And this can apply even in instances where abuse has clearly been instituted by threatened or actual use of force and violence; where the illusion of consent to abuse is absent. That notwithstanding, willing and acting to keep the secret may subsequently produce just such an illusion. The child may experience difficulty in distinguishing between willing secrecy (in order to avoid threatened or prophesied consequences) and having willed abuse, and may suppose that the exercise of committed willing, in any case, implies freedom in choosing the objects of willing in a way which implies causal responsibility. But, in reality, secrecy encloses abuse as a total context for all the child's willing, and so no willing in relation to abuse can be free from it. The inescapable reality of abuse sets the parameters for and then requires the exercise of willing. That means that the child cannot choose an object of willing which is not itself constrained by and confirming of abuse, yet is obliged to exercise will in another mode.

That the child's own willing is operative, even within the totalitarian framework of abuse, is what makes psychological survival through the reconstruction of identity possible. And yet, because the context of willing is totalitarian, this achievement may only be a form of accommodation to abuse. Identity, including the basic structure of intentionality (and so of future willing related to oneself, others, the world and God), is organised around the reality of abuse, which becomes the prime informant of identity. Hence every act of future willing only further strengthens abuse's power, reconfirms and more deeply embeds it. Removed from the realm of *liberum arbitrium indifferentiae* it becomes, then, a prime constituent of *voluntas*, so that her willing cannot free itself from it.

Through the use of her own internal energies and resources which enable survival, she internalises the damaging and distorting energy of abuse (which can neither be processed nor 'earthed' by being connected to other energy and information sources) within the very basis and structure of future willing – an abused identity. That is to say that there is here a sequestration of the child's internal structures and energies – including that of willing – by abuse. Again, it appears that the will is not disabled, but disoriented in its operation.

Jewish willing

Towards the end of chapter 5, I suggested (following Zygmunt Bauman) that one effect of the holocaust's rational character was its capacity to incorporate its victims' willing. Significantly, that frequently was possible only because the Nazis were duplicitous concerning their actual intentions, the ends to which Jewish action would actually be oriented and contributing. The basis for making rational calculations concerning action was hidden in order to effect an apparent confusion and conflation between Jewish and Nazi interests, so that the real orientation of their active willing could be masked from the Jews. At the same time, every indication was given that rationally based and oriented action and willing could be effective. But, since the hidden, guiding rationality of Nazi actions constituted an all-encompassing and inflexible environment and framework for Jewish action, active Jewish willing was certain to be incorporated into its service. Again, I think it appropriate to characterise this phenomenon as the deceptive *appearance* of the capacity to exercise freedom in willing as material choice between different possible *ultimate* objects of willing – even if this was obviously fettered by the restrictions imposed by declared Nazi policy and practice, there was yet the *apparent* retention of the possibility of actively willing and changing possible outcomes from the situation. In reality, however, such freedom was entirely formal, since there could be but one object and destination of Jewish willing once Nazi policy had become (and been realistically accepted as) the closed orbit of Jewish living and dying. Willing and acting in any way other than resistance and rebellion had the effect of adding internal energies and resources to those of the Nazis and to their eventually genocidal intentions.

In the extermination camps, where the co-option and collusion of Jewish willing in the prosecution of the genocide was made explicit, this became a tool for the destruction of the integrity of Jewish identity and humanity. There it was explicit that, for those not gassed immediately upon arrival, willing one's own survival meant an at least passive willing of others' destruction; that one's active willing had been incorporated into the Nazi destruction of Jewish humanity; that giving up on this willing to survive would also secure a Nazi victory, for nothing was more fatal in the camps than loss of will to survive.

Some interim comments

What has emerged from revisiting the pathologies described in chapters 4 and 5?

First, I think this discussion has decisively shown the descriptive inadequacy of any simplistic notion of willing as the exercise of completely free decision and of the underlying notion of the will as a neutral organ of arbitrary choice (*liberum arbitrium indifferentiae*). Willing in these two situations appears bound up with situation. Description of the pathological dynamics operating here cannot restrict its attention to acts and to their simple, internal causes (such as free decisions of will). The pathological dynamics at work appear both broader and deeper than a focus on free acts of will could possibly allow for. Abuse potentially implicates abusers' significant histories of relation (and by implication the personal identities of key participants – and, in turn, their histories – in this history) as well as potentially distorting survivors' futures of relation; the holocaust implicates the broad history of European anti-Semitism, the conditions of defeat in World War I and the terms of armistice subsequently imposed, the social, economic and political conditions under Weimar, and particular scientific theories and practices; more immediately, it implicates the dream of a perfect, rational society, rational means of administration, a society at war and penultimate attempts to solve 'the Jewish question'.

Situation permeates will in a way and to an extent which makes it descriptively inadequate to name personal pathology (or, indeed, the person as pathogen) without at the same time naming the overarching pathological dynamics in which the person is incorporated and incorporates herself through her own willing. Indeed, it might be said that these concrete situations redefine what it means to say that willing renders action genuinely *personal* – not on account of its internal purity, neutrality and arbitrariness, but as an act of the concretely situated, whole person. Inseparable from the orientation and structure of personal identity, consequently willing is inseparable also from the processes and accidents of person-formation (the wider relational dynamics) current in wider society and in individual life-stories which have shaped particular structures of identity, intentionality and life-orientation. Distortions in willing evidence distortions at the core of personal identity, in the basic trajectory and pattern of intentionality. In turn, these evidence distortions in significant identities, relationships, social structures and social, historical and psychological processes which have shaped a specific identity and its dynamic of life-intentionality – including, of course, its willing.[6]

Willing may become pathologically habituated (often, but not always, incrementally) by incorporation into concrete, social and material processes of action and by the trajectory of past action. Willing is not merely a personal dynamic; we find it arising out of and being incorporated into pathological dynamics which are inter-, trans-, and supra-personal. Such incorporation into pathological dynamics which one's willing has not created (although it may sustain them), which are there already, appears

---

6. On this general theme see my *The Call to Personhood: A Christian Theory of the Individual in Social Relationships* (Cambridge: Cambridge University Press, 1990), chs. 3–5.

to effect a disorientation in willing. Willing may retain a *formal* capacity of free choice between potential objects of willing. But in the totalitarian, pathological dynamics operating in the holocaust and in sexual abuse of children, the personal power to make choices may be subject to a more powerful field of force which sequesters, colonises and captures it. Here willing is not so much disempowered as 'bent' by a superior attractive force, pulled into the vortex of a pathological dynamic and oriented towards its service. The effect which this may have in restricting the number of possible objects of immediate choice is far less significant than its capacity to appropriate the means and criteria by and direction in which choices are made (by defining 'reality', 'normality', 'the good' or 'rationality') as all immediate objects of possible choosing are incorporated into the dynamic of this pathological orientation.

In a moral framework, willing is generally taken to be a purely internal, personal dynamic, the exercise of which carries moral responsibility: wherever there is willing, therefore, there is culpability. But the case in these two concrete situations is nowhere near as simple or neat as that. For both victims and perpetrators exercise will – and not only, and arguably not primarily, in ways which render them morally culpable. The pathology in both situations appears to involve confusion in, of and concerning willing and its disorientation in dynamics that are not merely personal. That, in turn, is related to confusion in the construal of reality at all levels, including the moral: confusion concerning what is good, right, true and the criteria by which that might be judged; a total spiritual disaffection and disorientation which incorporates and distorts willing from the inside, although it may not have originated there. A moral language (and indeed, the modern priority accorded internal freedom of decision) is descriptively inadequate to the complex reality of willing in these pathological situations.

The fact that aspects of willing escape its sphere of reference is significant in indicating that the limitation does not correspond with the expected limitations of moral language: the proper boundary between subjective and objective, personal and impersonal, forms of pathology. For in the phenomenon of willing we are not dealing with a passively received pathogen; we are dealing with the active contribution of the self – albeit not one characterised by the sort of freedom of self in relation to act which might make it a morally culpable act. But that is precisely the force of my point. Here we are faced with personal activity that escapes the criteria of moral evaluation. And if sin is to function as a moral language, then this is an aspect of the pathological dynamic into which both perpetrators and victims may be *personally* incorporated, which will remain unnamed; which will not be brought into relation to God through the act of naming.[7] And if we are unable adequately to name the personal pathological dynamics in which we participate, we cannot be personally accountable for them before God. Once we have freed ourselves from the limitations of moral conceptions, we might construe this accountability in terms other than those of personal culpability. If we fail to comprehend the ways in which our willing (and so we as persons, as subjects) are opposed to God in sin, then we shall be unable comprehensively to comprehend the way in which the dynamics of salvation address our situation; the way in which we are addressed by God in our sin and what we are called to through that address. We shall fail, in other words, to take appropriate forms of accountability for the sin we find ourselves embedded in. And, as I have already begun to hint, that responsibility, whilst it might well be personal, need not be construed in moral terms.

The hypothesis, deducible from the doctrine of original sin, that pathology binds willing looks to have some real explanatory and descriptive power in relation to both concrete pathologies. Moreover, this discussion of the phenomenon of willing in concrete pathologies has indicated the explanatory and descriptive inadequacy of the standards and frame of reference of moral languages. In the course of this examination of concrete pathology through the heuristic of willing, what it means for the will to be bound rather than free, the nature and scope of personal participation thereby effected have achieved some clarification, though further conceptual definition would be helpful. What has not really become any more clear, however, is the *theological* content and context of the hypothesis. Whilst the hypothesis may be deduced from the doctrine of original sin, proof of its explanatory power through concrete testing does not necessarily lead us inductively to retrace our steps back to a theological framework of understanding. A case still remains to be made as to the explanatory power of theological frames and standards of reference, criteria and language in relation to the mode of personal participation in

---

7. This concern runs through Andrew Sung Park's *The Wounded Heart of God: The Asian Concept of Han and the Christian Doctrine of Sin* (Nashville: Abingdon, 1993); see especially pp. 13, 72f., 177. His substitution of the category of *Han* (broadly, shame) for sin in relation to the effect of perpetrators' sin on victims, however, actually embeds further the assumption that sin is a moral category, requiring the sort of potency and freedom in willing which victims tend not to possess. Only sin, not *han*, therefore incurs guilt and only *han* may be passed on through the generations (pp. 12f., 76–80, 82).

pathology that escapes the circumference of moral interests. Do they enrich our understanding of the pathological binding of willing? With this question in mind, I turn now to consideration of the most vibrant, contemporary discussion of sin, which focuses on issues of personal participation, though both its strengths and its theological inadequacies will lead us into more ancient debates and back on to the terrain of original sin.

7

Power and participation: feminist theologies of sin

The criteria and standards of judgment afforded by moral frames of reference suggest that we participate and engage in sin *personally* only where we have sufficient freedom for self-determination in action. Freedom is here closely correlated with power. In the context of the standards of moral judgment, freedom means a freedom *from* the determining influences of internal impulses and external pressures. It denotes the power to retain self-direction and control and to resist being overpowered by: psychological drives; biological instincts; other people; the social, economic, ideological and cultural forces operating in our general situation. Freedom is here taken to be synonymous with autonomy, involving a positive differential in power between myself (construed as an independent centre of power) and all the other forces exerting an influence on me. Put negatively, it indicates my capacity to resist determination by other forces. More positively, it is the power to implement my will (independently derived and self-directed) in action, regardless of resistance. Construed within the limits of the interests of moral judgment, then, freedom as autonomy means the power to instantiate alternative courses of action which are neither coerced nor determined: the power to implement one's self-determined will in action.

Where I enjoy this freedom from determination and coercion, then, it is supposed that I live and act essentially in my own power – that I am self-determining, both in my action and in the basic orientation of my life-intentionality. That means that I have sufficient power to effect my will. But it also means that my will is itself in my own power; that, in my willing, I am in possession of myself, rather than possessed by some alien, controlling power. So neither my willing nor the expression of my will in action are coerced or determined. I am the sufficient cause of both. It

See I. Berlin

follows that, on this view, I may be held accountable (culpable) for my action (or non-action) only where there is a positive differential between my personal power and all other forces operating in and upon me: where I have made autonomous choice resting on the *liberum arbitrium* of my will.

Such a view need not be naive concerning the strength either of internal drives or external forces operating on us. It is perfectly possible for moral frameworks to recognise that an action may be determined rather than free (although in practice they tend to operate with an assumption that action is more often personal than it is determined by impersonal, extra-personal or supra-personal forces; and so the burden of proof tends to lie in the direction of establishing the exceptions to the normal conditions of personal culpability rather than the other way about). But a moral framework so defines will in terms of relationally pure self-determination that any willed act meets the criteria for the attribution of moral accountability. If will operates at all, it does so in unconstrained self-determination, following the law (*nomos*) of its own uncoerced desires and motivations. Hence, voluntary action is synonymous with autonomy. And so the crucial question which moral interpretation asks of an action is: notwithstanding all situational influences and pressures, was this a willed and therefore free act of the person? Here the relationship between the internal dynamics of a person's self-directed life-intentionality (including will) and the dynamics operating in his situation is understood in terms of opposition. So the task of establishing whether someone is morally accountable for their behaviour rests on discerning the relative potency of personal *against* other forces. Was the thief overpowered by the influences of criminal sub-culture, impoverishment, hunger, an unhappy childhood, the threat of his accomplices, such that his action was not really his own? Or did he nonetheless retain sufficient independent, personal power that, whilst the deleterious influence of other forces might be acknowledged, he remains self-determined and directed, rather than subject to the play of other forces? No matter how complex the entanglement of operative factors might be, we are, in the end, faced here with a sharp and simple dichotomy between personal power and other forces. *Either* internal, personal dynamics are potent relative to other forces and dynamics *or* I am overpowered by them. *Either* I have personal power, exercise will and am therefore culpable *or* I am the innocent victim of my situation, irresistible drives or the superior, coercive force of others. Accountability, as I have already suggested, is here a function of the differential between personal power and all other forces operating in and on one: the ability to implement one's will. To put it slightly differently, we might say that it is a function of personal transcendence of one's situatedness and mode of embodiment.

The last three chapters strongly suggest the descriptive and explanatory inadequacy of such a framework of understanding. For, in relation to concrete pathologies, it appears particularly problematic to speak of personal power, will and life-intentionality as independent and transcendent of concrete situatedness and relatedness. There seems to be a much more complex interrelationship between the 'internal' and the 'external' (the interpersonal, political, social, historical) than may be allowed for in the oppositional dichotomy assumed by moral frameworks. As I have described them, these are situations in which what happens is often not the *overpowering* of the will (of both victims and perpetrators) by the superior force of internal drives, other people or social pressures. Action is not coerced *against* the will. Will is not *disembedded* from action (now under the control of impersonal or extra-personal forces) whilst remaining opposed in its innermost orientation which it now finds itself powerless to implement in practice. Moreover, the internal dynamics of willing and of life-intentionality cannot be separated from those operating in relation and situation. Personal and extra-personal dynamics do not so much stand in simple opposition as co-operate. Will, in these situations, is co-opted into a more potent and more highly energised dynamic. Bent, not broken off, will remains embedded in action. Action therefore remains *personal*, since it is the centrally organised direction of energy which expresses the internal life-intentionality of the person. To the extent that personal centredness permits self-direction and orientation, it is not wholly misleading to speak here of autonomy. Yet, this organisational centredness and internal orientation are not generated out of some relationally pure internality. Whilst not heteronomously determined, they are nonetheless determinate: situated and embodied within the concrete and particular situational dynamics within which we live. Hence, if we speak here of autonomy we must be careful not to import the highly individualistic assumptions with which the term is conventionally saturated. For what was encountered in the expositions of concrete pathologies in chapters 4 and 5 was precisely the influencing of the internal dynamics of life-intentionality by the pathological dynamics operating in interpersonal relationships and in wider society. This influence is exerted in such a way that the pathological dynamics of situation and relation do not remain straightforwardly external; they do not operate by overpowering will and internal life-intentionality, but by incorporating and thereby reorienting them.

The traditional doctrine of original sin recognises just this dialectic between the active contribution of the person and what she receives as a consequence of her situatedness. This insight concerning the complex interplay between person and situation receives some contemporary support from what might be considered a surprising source: theological feminism. The support is surprising, since feminist theologies tend to be wary of the traditional doctrine of original sin, chiefly on account of its supposed opposition between nature and grace and consequent slippage into naturalistic rather than moral categories. Indeed, some feminist theologians expressly prefer to speak of 'original blessing' instead of original sin.[1] Nonetheless, an acknowledgment of the tension between autonomy and situatedness has always marked feminist theologies. Deep attentiveness to the significance of situation (social, cultural, material and historical embodiment) is characteristically set in the context of an overarching strategy for the recovery of the conditions for women's subjective agency, and vice versa. This sense of the interrelatedness of person with situation has been particularly evident in feminist discussions of sin. There is good reason to suppose, therefore, that feminist theologies of sin might have developed ways of speaking of the pathological that avoid the limitations of moral frameworks of interpretation. Might the conceptualities operating there have descriptive and explanatory power in relation to the 'co-operation' between personal and extra-personal dynamics that featured so prominently in the phenomenologies of concrete pathology in chapters 4 and 5 and discussed in the last chapter? And will such conceptualities prove to be functionally theological as well as richly illuminating?[2]

Pride: the problem

The most extensive, explicit and best known feminist discussion of sin concerns the self and its pathologies. Issues related to identity, integrity,

1. The phrase originates with Matthew Fox's 'creation spirituality'. See his *Original Blessing: A Primer in Creation Spirituality* (Santa Fe: Bear, 1983).
2. The following exposition of feminist theologies seeks to clarify the undergirding conceptuality of feminist discussions of sin. It therefore presses beyond the understandings which appear explicitly on the surface and is what might be termed a creative act of interpretation. Whilst, on the one hand, I suggest that feminist theologies of sin have potential to illuminate the discussion so far, on the other, the terminology and agenda thrown up by that discussion help illuminate the conceptuality implicit in feminist theological discourse.

power, autonomy and relationality are of central importance to it. The significance of this discussion for theological feminism is clear from its relative extensiveness, but also from its prominence in what is generally regarded as the founding document of feminist theology, Valerie Saiving's programmatic, 1960 statement.[3] The question she first raised concerning the appropriate and adequate naming of sinful structures of selfhood focused attention on the traditional insistence on pride as the paradigmatic sin.[4] Subsequent discussion has continued to centre itself on this traditional image for sin.[5]

Pride in this context indicates idolisation of the self or (where self-identity is equated with group identity) of that which one identifies oneself with (e.g., ethnicity, socio-economic class, human species). Hence pride means putting oneself (or the group identity one represents) in God's place. The proud self (or that with which it identifies itself and mediates) is construed, in practice as well as in cognition, as the ultimate

3. Valerie Saiving, 'The Human Situation: A Feminine View', *Journal of Religion*, 40 (1960), 100–12.

4. The emphasis on pride is a continuing characteristic of orthodox Christian traditions. For example amongst major modern theologians, see, e.g., Karl Barth, *Church Dogmatics*, IV/1 (Edinburgh: T. & T. Clark, 1956), pp. 142, 358, 412–19, 419–23, 431f., 745; Paul Tillich, *Systematic Theology*, II (London: SCM, 1978), pp. 47–50; Reinhold Niebuhr, *The Nature and Destiny of Man*, I (London: Nisbet, 1941), pp. 198–220; Emil Brunner, *Man in Revolt: A Christian Anthropology* (Philadelphia: Westminster, 1939), pp. 129, 136, 262f., 272f.; Wolfhart Pannenberg, *Systematic Theology*, II (Edinburgh: T. & T. Clark, 1994), pp. 243ff., 250f., 260f.; (Pannenberg's construal of pride as any fixation on the self stretches it to cover what looks least like pride – e.g., anxiety occasioned by lack of self-worth and self-loathing – on the grounds that these are all forms of self-willing without God; cf. here Søren Kierkegaard's comments in *Sickness Unto Death* (Princeton: Princeton University Press, 1980), pp. 14, 20, 49), Wolfhart Pannenberg, *Anthropology in Theological Perspective* (Edinburgh: T. & T. Clark, 1985), pp. 88f.

5. Wanda Warren Berry, 'Images of Sin and Salvation in Feminist Theology', *Anglican Theological Review*, 60:1 (1979), 25–54; Judith Plaskow, *Sex, Sin and Grace: Women's Experience and the Theologies of Reinhold Niebuhr and Paul Tillich* (Lanham, MD: University Press of America, 1980); Susan Nelson Dunfee, 'The Sin of Hiding: A Feminist Critique of Reinhold Niebuhr's Account of the Sin of Pride', *Soundings*, 65/3 (1982), 316–27; Mary Daly, *Beyond God the Father: Towards a Philosophy of Women's Liberation* (London: the Women's Press, 1986), ch. 2; Daphne Hampson, 'Reinhold Niebuhr on Sin: A Critique', in Richard Harries, ed., *Reinhold Niebuhr and the Issues of our Time* (London: Mowbray, 1986), pp. 46–60; Daphne Hampson, 'Luther on the Self: A Feminist Critique', in Ann Loades, ed., *Feminist Theology: A Reader* (London: SPCK, 1990), ch. 18; Daphne Hampson, *Theology and Feminism* (Oxford: Blackwell, 1990), pp. 121–6; Mary Grey, *Redeeming the Dream: Feminism, Redemption and Christian Tradition* (London: SPCK, 1989), pp. 15–19, 27, 91; Susan Brooks Thistlethwaite, *Sex, Race and God: Christian Feminism in Black and White* (London: Chapman, 1990), ch. 5; Lucia Scherzberg, *Sünde und Gnade in der Feministischen Theologie* (Mainz: Grünewald, 1991); Marjorie Hewitt Suchocki, *The Fall to Violence: Original Sin in Relational Theology* (New York: Continuum, 1994), pp. 26, 31ff., 39f., 43f., 83f., 96; Barbara Hilkert Andolsen, 'Agape in Feminist Ethics', *Journal of Religious Ethics*, 9 (1981), 69–83; Susan L. Lichtman, 'The Concept of Sin in the Theology of Paul Tillich: A Break from Patriarchy?', *Journal of Women and Religion*, 8 (Winter, 1989), 49–55. Cf. the earlier work of John C. Raines, 'Sin as Pride and Sin as Sloth', *Christianity and Crisis*, 29 (1969), 4–8.

good, as the arbiter and criterion of the worth of everything else and as the good towards which all other goods (already defined in terms of their utility relative to it) are to be dedicated. Because pride involves active referral of all goods to the self, it denotes worship of the self. The mainstream of the theological tradition takes pride to be a rebellion of self-assertiveness: human beings' usurping the place of God, claiming for themselves that sovereignty which properly belongs to creator rather than creature. Pride is simultaneous refusal to be a creature and to acknowledge God as God. It is the attempt to be like God: to live without limits as the source of one's own life, law and goodness – indeed, to live as the ultimate location of all life, law and goodness, the attempt to order everything around the supreme value of the self. Pride is therefore construed in the mainstream of the tradition as overabundant self-assertion: the attempt to live as a completely autonomous self, without reference to God or to any external realities, values or claims.

To view sin as having a paradigmatic form is implicitly to invoke a normative standard of reference for the good, over against which pathological deviations may be discerned. If pride is the paradigm form of the pathological and we know what pride is, then we may infer the normative standard of reference which validates the construal of sin as always, at bottom, some form of pride. To put it another way, we may infer the *logos* which is pathologically disordered in pride; the good, the corruption of which always amounts to pride. If the paradigm form of sin is overblown self-assertion to the point of self-idolisation, then the good which pride disrupts and opposes (the normative standard of reference for pathology) seems to its feminist critics to be its simple opposite: self-abasement to the point of self-abnegation. Where pride is sin because it usurps the place of God, the correlate good would then appear to be the acknowledgment of creatureliness in the self-abnegation of total obeisance to God's sovereignty.

If pride is the paradigmatic form of sin and stands for an overpowering form of self-assertion which oppresses others, then (stereotypically considered) women may be judged innocent; indeed, not only innocent, but virtuous. For, according to standard feminist critique, women are not full of themselves, making the world revolve around *their* needs or making it conform to *their* definitions of what is good, normal and true. Women are those whose sense of self is not overabundant. More typically, their sense of self is submerged in relationships to others, whose identities, desires and needs displace their own to the extent that one may speak of a loss, dissipation or diffusion of self and of identity: a virtual collapse of self into relationships.[6] Whilst men are actively sinners in the perspective of the emphasis on pride, women exercise the 'virtues' of passivity and self-abnegation, of serving others' needs and interests to the detriment of their own.[7] We may now understand why feminist theologians might regard the declaration of women's innocence as rather dubious and wish to critique its basis in the construal of sin and virtue which follows from the traditional emphasis on pride.

First, taking pride to be the paradigm for sin expresses what is the predominant or stereotypical experience of men, not women. It therefore belongs to a 'patriarchal' mode of doing theology – naming the world, including sin, from the perspective of men's point of view and of action. Hence, second, women are absent from theological discourse in a double sense. Women are neither *subjects* of theological discernment, naming the world from the perspective of their own experience, nor its *objects*. If women experience what the feminist literature terms 'loss of self' rather than pride, then they do not exercise the form of self-will and autonomous agency which is generally considered worthy of consideration in relation to a doctrine of sin. So women whose sense of self has been dissipated appear unworthy *objects* of theological consideration in relation to an understanding of sin. They are the victims of sin, not its perpetrators. Third, if pride is the paradigm for sin, then the surrender of self and the lack of self-assertion are surely the normative standard of reference for the human good. The appropriate mode of relation to others and to God may then be construed as requiring us to be passive objects rather than active subjects exercising will and agency. The virtue of subjection to heteronomy appears to be commended in place of the sin of proud autonomy. Just

6. I shall discuss the significance and meaning of the notion of 'self-loss' more fully below. For its occurrence in the literature, see, e.g., Plaskow (who uses the term 'self-abnegation'), *Sex, Sin and Grace*, pp. 3, 87f., 95, 109, 135, 149, 156f.; Dunfee, 'The Sin of Hiding', pp. 320f.; Bernice Martin, 'Whose Soul is it Anyway? Domestic Tyranny and the Suffocated Soul', in Richard K. Fenn and Donald Capps, eds., *On Losing the Soul: Essays in the Social Psychology of Religion* (Albany, NY: State University of New York Press, 1995), p. 71; Linda A. Mercadante, *Victims and Sinners: Spiritual Roots of Addiction and Recovery* (Louisville: Westminster/John Knox, 1996), pp. 38f., 148–55. Cf. Saiving, 'The Human Situation', p. 109 and Annelies van Heijst, *Longing for the Fall* (Kampen: Kok Pharos, 1995), pp. 7f. The idea that the self may be lost stems from Kierkegaard's dynamic construal of the self in terms of activity rather than substance. Where one is not active in one's self-relation in choosing and taking responsibility for one's own life, he speaks of an absence or loss of self (*Either-Or*, II (Princeton: Princeton University Press, 1987)) and of this form of the sin of despair as before God not willing to be oneself (*Sickness Unto Death*, pp. 49, 77), construing the 'not willing' as also implying some defiance, so that the distinction between sins of weakness and of defiance is only relative (p. 49).

7. So, e.g., Rosemary Radford Ruether, *Sexism and God-Talk* (London: SCM, 1983), pp. 185f.

as is the case in relation to divine grace, in the face of oppression one is not to be 'wilful'. Any act of women's resistance to oppression, victimisation or abuse is therefore likely to be construed as the sort of self-assertiveness and self-concern which counts as pride.[8]

Feminist theologians agree that pride accurately names the stereo-typical sin of men, and therefore appropriately names men as sinners. However, they simultaneously recognise that, ironically, naming pride as sin may nonetheless work to preserve male dominance. For, ironically, the possibilities of women's liberation are undercut in the very basis of the recognition of the male sin of pride. Since all self-assertion is deemed sinful pride, the self-assertion necessary for women to protect or to liberate themselves from men would fall under the same condemnation as does male pride. For the corollary of 'male' pride is the 'female' virtue of submissiveness and self-surrender. Oppressive men may be sinners, but women are to preserve their 'innocence' by practising the 'female' virtues of self-denial. The teaching of the tradition appears to be that the sin which belongs to the male role of 'heroic' (Promethean) agency is to be met by the patient virtue of female passivity: don't resist when he beats you, for that would add your pride to his. And so theological feminism finds the declaration of female innocence works to keep women passive in the face of their own oppression.[9] Whilst it is men whose sin is named, it is women who are to continue to bear the burden of that sin. For women are commended for declining autonomy and self-assertion. So women appear to be expected passively to wait on the agency of God or the conversion of men in a way which denies to them any personal intentionality or agency. But if the *appropriateness* of naming pride as sin is undisputed, the adequacy of this naming most certainly is. Theological feminism therefore does not dispute the tradition's characterisation of pride, nor its designation of pride as sin. Instead, it critiques the *emphasis* which pride has received in the tradition.

8. Saiving, 'The Human Situation', pp. 109f.; Plaskow, *Sex, Sin and Grace*, pp. 85–90, 92f., 135, 151f., 156f.; Dunfee, 'The Sin of Hiding', pp. 321f.; Hampson, 'Reinhold Niebuhr on Sin', p. 49; Rita Nakashima Brock, *Journeys by Heart: A Christology of Erotic Power* (New York: Crossroad, 1992), pp. 19f.; Christine E. Gudorf, *Victimization: Examining Christian Complicity* (Philadelphia: Trinity Press International, 1992), p. 91.

9. Hence, I think Angela West slightly overstates her case against theological feminism. Whilst her argument that it frequently constructs an implicit myth of female innocence and 'natural' blessedness is often persuasive and insightful, she seems sometimes to miss the subtlety of a good deal of feminist theology which is alert to the dangers of such a myth and works to deconstruct it (although admittedly there is a strong tendency for it to reappear under another guise). See *Deadly Innocence: Feminism and the Mythology of Sin* (London: Cassell, 1995), pp. 30, 35f., 54, 56, 60, 106, 120.

Sloth

Feminist naming of women's sin

It is hardly an unambiguous blessing, then, for women to be exonerated of sin through the traditional emphasis on pride. For their innocence is based on the assumption that, insofar as they are victims of oppression, women are entirely passive (without committed will and intentionality of their own). The strategy of reclaiming the traditional image of sin as sloth must be understood, in this context, as an attempt to do justice to the ways in which women contribute personal agency and committed intentionality *as victims*. In the feminist recovery of sloth to name the experience of 'self-loss', the term undergoes a shift in meaning as it is inserted into a feminist register. In the seven deadly sins tradition, sloth denotes indolence; not so much doing the wrong thing as failing to do the right.[10] This traditional understanding of sloth is mildly suggestive that sin need not be character-ised by the potent, autonomous activism of pride; that, in the terms of the tradition, there are sins of omission as well as commission. Yet the con-strual of sin here remains axiological. For sloth refers traditionally to *acts* of omission arising out of a *wilful* indolence or indifference which is culpable because it involves a free choice: one could have done otherwise. But more than this, sloth is often after all construed as a form of overblown selfhood: one which is so turned in on and satisfied by itself that it cannot and will not stir itself to action as required by love of or joy in God and others. Tradi-tionally, then, sloth can represent a less active way of idolising the self, one that could be construed as another, less obvious, form of pride.[11] In any case, whereas sloth has the superficial appearance of immobility, it none-theless is traditionally regarded as inaction rooted in the autonomous freedom of the self to have done otherwise. Sloth is therefore a freely willed act and orientation for which, like pride, one is morally culpable.

If pride is used as the paradigm for sin, then it is assumed that we involve ourselves in sin out of our potent, fully autonomous, self-directed will and action. For that reason, the pride paradigm suggests a clear

10. See Richard Holloway, *Seven to Flee, Seven to Follow* (London: Mowbray, 1986); Kenneth Slack, *The Seven Deadly Sins: A Contemporary View* (London: SCM, 1985) for brief orientations; or Donald Capps' imaginative reconstruction in terms of Life-Cycle theory in *Deadly Sins and Saving Virtues* (Philadelphia: Fortress Press, 1987).

11. Hence, the term lends itself to a quite different recovery, interpretation and use than that which it achieves in theological feminism. See, e.g., Barth, *Church Dogmatics*, IV/2 (Edinburgh: T. & T. Clark, 1958), §65; Pannenberg, *Systematic Theology*, II, pp. 243ff., 250f., 260f.; *Anthropology in Theological Perspective*, pp. 88f.; S. Dennis Ford, *Sins of Omission: A Primer on Moral Indifference* (Minneapolis: Fortress Press, 1990).

demarcation between victims and perpetrators. Perpetrators are those in a particular situation or in respect of a particular action who personally exercise *causal* agency. Victims are those whose intentionality proves impotent, who exercise no effective personal power in the situation, whose willing is inoperative. From the perspective of the pride paradigm, only perpetrators sin. Sloth characterises one of the more paradoxical ways in which pride manifests itself through omission rather than commission. It is a sin committed, not so much by perpetrators as bystanders. But this is an insignificant distinction in this context, and certainly conveys no suggestion of sloth as victims' sin. The difference between perpetrators and bystanders is non-enduring, occurring only at the point of agency in a particular case, and marking no distinction in terms of social or personal power. Both belong to the same class, differentiated from that of victims in terms of their social and personal power. Bystanders possess all the freedom and potential for agency characteristic of perpetrators. The only difference is whether and how such potential is activated. Hence, as bystanders' culpable non-action, sloth is not something that could be committed by victims, since – on this view – they have lost the subjective conditions necessary to sin even by omission.

In feminist reinterpretation and use, however, sloth achieves a rather different meaning, indicating that it has been lifted out of the defining influence of the paradigm of pride. Feminist recovery of the image of sloth as precisely the sin of the victimised, then, challenges the entire network of assumptions centred on the paradigmatic status and interpretation traditionally given to pride.

Feminist use of the term 'sloth' conveys two analytically separable meanings. These meanings, as I shall show below, are intrinsically related and are always found together – although, on the face of it, they might appear incoherent. On the one hand, sloth indicates a mode or condition of selfhood, often termed in the literature a 'loss of self'. On the other, it denotes a mode of personal agency. Both meanings bring to expression the distinctive experience of oppression, as it is thematised under feminist analysis and critique. In articulating this experience, feminist theologians are addressing a number of pivotal questions concerning the nature and mode of the personal participation of victims in their own oppression and victimisation. Are women (and, indeed, all victims) merely the passive recipients of oppressive structures, processes and dynamics? Do oppressed people lose altogether the internal dynamics constitutive of personhood, or do they remain persons under conditions of oppression, still exercising the personal power of willing in some way? More importantly still, is there a way of speaking of oppressed *persons* that does not collude with the dynamics of oppression to blame the victims, which masks the ways in which 'loss of self' is attributable to oppressive relationships, ideology and practices? And is there a mode of recovery and protection of self that does not replicate the 'male' sin of pride?

Feminist reinterpretation of sloth represents just such an attempt to reclaim a personal and active dimension in the description of women's experience, *without denying the sense in which they are victims of an oppressive situation*. This explains the deliberate disavowal of the passive voice in rendering sloth. Instead, we find verbs with women as their unequivocal subjects. These verbs may be grouped into two related sets. By virtue of the fact that both sets of verbs have women as their grammatical subjects, both also render sloth as a mode of agency. Both, in other words, name a mode of personal participation in oppression exercised by victims, but they do so in relation to different grammatical objects: in the one case, selfhood; in the other, 'patriarchy'.

The first names the personal involvement of women in their diminution of selfhood, whilst also echoing the traditional sense of sloth as active inaction. Hence, we find verbs such as: *failing* (to integrate, actualise, constitute or individuate the self, to use her freedom to make choices, to take responsibility, or to rebel);[12] *hiding* (from),[13] *refusing*,[14] *abdicating*,[15] *abnegating*,[16] *denying*[17] or *fleeing*[18] (responsibility or freedom). A second series of verbs indicates rather more directly the mode of women's involvement in 'patriarchy', whilst repeating the echo of sloth as active inaction. Women are said to be *participating*,[19] *being complicit*[20] and *acquiescing in*,[21]

12. Plaskow, *Sex, Sin and Grace*, pp. 3, 35, 64f., 68, 85f., 90, 92, 114, 138; Hampson, 'Reinhold Niebuhr on Sin', p. 51.   13. Dunfee, 'The Sin of Hiding'.
14. Ruether, *Sexism and God-Talk*, p. 181.   15. Plaskow, *Sex, Sin and Grace*, pp. 3, 65, 67, 93.
16. Hampson, 'Reinhold Niebuhr on Sin', p. 49.
17. Plaskow, *Sex, Sin and Grace*, pp. 92, 118.   18. Ibid.
19. Mary Potter Engel, 'Evil, Sin, and Violation of the Vulnerable', in Susan Brooks Thistlethwaite and Mary Potter Engel, eds., *Lift Every Voice: Constructing Christian Theologies from the Underside* (San Francisco: Harper & Row, 1990), pp. 152–64, p. 156f.; Sharon D. Welch, *Communities of Resistance and Solidarity: A Feminist Theology of Liberation* (Maryknoll, NY: Orbis, 1985), p. 49.
20. Ruether, *Sexism and God-Talk*, pp. 180f.; Daly, *Beyond God the Father*, p. 52; Engel, 'Evil, Sin and Violation of the Vulnerable', pp. 155f., 180; Plaskow, *Sex, Sin and Grace*, pp. 64f.; Welch, *Communities of Resistance and Solidarity*, p. 49.
21. Engel, 'Evil, Sin and Violation of the Vulnerable', pp. 155f., 180; Ruether, *Sexism and God-Talk*, pp. 113f., 160–4, 180–3; Rosemary Radford Ruether, *Gaia and God: An Ecofeminist Theology of Earth Healing* (New York: HarperCollins, 1992), p. 141 (and cf. her understanding of confession in *Women-Church: Theology and Practice* (San Francisco: Harper & Row, 1985), pp. 131f.); Grey, *Redeeming the Dream*, pp. 15, 19, 27, 107f.; Mercadante, *Victims and Sinners*, p. 38.

accepting,[22] *consenting to*,[23] *complying*[24] and *cooperating with*[25] (their own oppression).

In the feminist reinterpretation of the sin of sloth, then, women are consistently presented as the grammatical subjects of these and parallel verbs. Whilst there is little extended analysis of the implication or conceptual content of these words, it is nonetheless clear in the literature that their use is both deliberate and significant. The express intention is to indicate that the experienced reality of oppression is one in which the victims are personally active as subjects, even whilst that subjectivity is significantly and adversely affected. What is being claimed here is that oppression has an internal aspect, and that this has a dual form. First, the condition and mode of subjectivity is affected. Second, there is a correspondence and conformity of subjective intentionality with the external realities of oppression. Women are not, then, the passive recipients of the effects of 'patriarchy'; rather, their oppression has a personal and voluntary aspect, in that will and other organs of intentionality are engaged. Women participate in their own oppression as subjects; that is, they do so personally. And yet sloth is also presented as a collapse in the conditions of subjective agency, as a 'loss of self'.

It is not altogether misleading to say that what is claimed is that women participate in their own 'loss of self'. Yet we should be wary of regarding 'loss of self' as a simple, linear consequence of women's agency, as though 'loss of self' were the effect caused by the hitherto unimpeded agency of an undiminished self. For it is clear that this 'loss of self' is presented neither as the end, nor the end result, of women's personal agency. 'Loss of self' is not to be read literally, as implying a total collapse in the conditions for personal life, where no personal energy is contributed in the direction of life. Rather than the result of a previously 'unfallen' or 'non-lost' mode of selfhood misusing and misdirecting its agency, 'loss of self' indicates the prevailing mode of women's subjectivity and agency in the situation of oppression. There is no antecedent, pre-fallen state, which is the cause of the present collapse. Indeed, the relation between sloth as subjective condition and as mode of personal participation is rather more dialectical than that between cause and effect.

How is this all to be unpacked and understood? It will help, I think, to begin by focusing on the mode of personal participation and leaving for a

---

22. Daly, *Beyond God the Father*, p. 50; Gudorf, *Victimization*, p. 2.
23. Daly, *Beyond God the Father*, p. 2.; Mercadante, *Victims and Sinners*, p. 41.
24. Ruether, *Sexism and God-Talk*, p. 186.
25. Ibid., pp. 180ff.; Mercadante, *Victims and Sinners*, p. 41.

moment the question of what is meant by 'loss of self' and how a lost self might yet be capable of such personal participation.

If read in moralistic terms, the claim that women's active intentionality is incorporated in the dynamics of oppression, that women exercise will (are, one might say, 'willing victims') in relation to their oppression, is liable to grave misunderstanding. The ubiquity of the influence of moral ('patriarchal'?) frameworks on our conventional intuitions concerning the nature, role and significance of willing is such that, indeed, misunderstanding is highly likely. In particular, we are likely to lend to personal agency a meaning unreflectively informed by conventional assumptions concerning the inalienable freedom of the will. Since sloth is here presented as an act of the person (therefore involving will and committed intentionality), it is prone to be construed as that kind of free act for which the agent is culpable. For it is a powerful, conventional assumption that willing necessarily involves free and culpable causal agency, a choice made from a position of neutrality and independence in relation to this and other objects of choice.

Sloth in feminist use, however, assumes and requires a quite different comprehension of personal participation and of the voluntary from that conventionally adopted under moral frames of reference. For theological feminism speaks here of the personal participation of victims in the context of entrapment, and this both invites and requires a radical reinterpretation of the nature of personal agency, of willing and autonomy.[26] It is true that this is rarely explicitly articulated or extensively

26. It is a sign of the extent of our saturation with conventional (and counter-feminist) assumptions concerning the nature of the subject, of the will and of its autonomy, that feminists themselves find it hard to avoid reading the implications of women's agency in conventional terms, even after having deployed a contrary understanding in the course of naming it. The need for a thoroughgoing reinterpretation of willing and agency is rarely in sharp enough focus for it to be carried through effectively. Hence, the conceptuality and terminology are rarely transformed by the analysis sufficiently for the writer to avoid confusion when drawing the conclusion that women contribute personal agency in their own oppression. The exercise of personal energy, agency or will is, after all, taken to connote freedom of choice and so threatens accusations of moral culpability. This explains what sometimes appears to be a confused backtracking on the claim of active, personal involvement which evaporates the claim (and so the analysis of women's situation) of its full force. It is also to miss the implication that the feminist analysis requires a transformation in the language and basic conceptuality of sin. Or else, it continues to prosecute the notion that there is, after all, some sphere of personal being sufficiently pure or neutral in relation to systemic situational pathologies for it to be possible to make deliberate choices *not* to fall prone to them. See, for example, Susan Nelson Dunfee, 'Soul-Loss and Sin: A Dance of Alienation', in Fenn and Capps, *On Losing the Soul*, pp. 99, 107 (but cf. the closing remarks on p. 115); Ruether, *Sexism and God-Talk*, pp. 181f.; *Gaia and God*, pp. 141f.; Plaskow, *Sex, Sin and Grace*, pp. 116, 151; Engel, 'Evil, Sin and Violation of the Vulnerable', pp. 155f.; Mary Grey, 'Falling Into Freedom: Searching for New Interpretations of Sin in a Secular Society', *Scottish Journal of Theology*, 47 (1994), 234f.; Mercadante, *Victims and Sinners*, pp. 142, 150ff.

developed in the course of naming women's personal participation. This naming, however, is carried on against two background assumptions, which provide the appropriate interpretive context for the use of these verbs, and which illumine the subtlety, force and significance of theological feminism's understanding of personal participation and of willing. Both show the substitution of an alternative register for the interpretation of personal participation rendered by 'acquiescence' and cognate terms, implying that personal participation may not mean culpability. That victims will, need not require us to blame them for their own oppression.

The 'nevertheless' of sloth

The first of these assumptions is embedded in the very search for a usable language to express women's personal participation in 'patriarchy'. For the search begins precisely at the point at which conventional assumptions concerning the potency and autonomy of agency, will and intentionality give out and prove to be unusable. It begins, that is, with an implied recognition of the descriptive inadequacies of what I term moral frameworks.[27] Feminist discussion of sloth proceeds from the critique of the pride paradigm's supposed descriptive omnicompetence. Its base assumption, then, is that women do not have the kind of self-centredness, autonomy and integrity in life-intentionality which moral frameworks would recognise as the mark of truly personal agency or participation. Hence, the discussion of sloth is always carried on in the context of an epistemologically prior 'nevertheless'. Women do not have the kind of autonomous agency in relation to 'patriarchy' that would render them liable to blame for causing or freely choosing their oppression; *nevertheless*, they participate in it personally, through the exercise of some other form of personal agency. If we read the acknowledgment of women's personal engagement in the context of this 'nevertheless', we may avoid assuming that any mention of personal engagement, involvement or agency implies the kind of autonomy associated with strong, 'proud' selves. We may also be able to read between the lines of the discussion of sloth to understand better what is meant by the personal engagement characterised by the various verbs used.

Whilst this 'nevertheless' is assumed as a background premiss and

27. In this regard, moral frameworks are roughly equivalent to what feminists refer to as 'patriarchal' assumptions concerning autonomy in agency and selfhood.

generally therefore left unspoken, there is an indirect intimation of it in the tension established by the apparently contradictory insistence that sloth involves a 'loss of self'. How may sloth be a mode of personal agency if it also involves a loss of the centredness and subjectivity that are prerequisite for such agency? Clearly, only if either or both are not conventionally defined.

'Patriarchy' as ideology

The second, background premiss of the characterisation of women's participation in oppression is the distinctive feminist analysis of women's situation which arises from the critique of 'patriarchy' as ideology.

Speaking very broadly, feminist theologians tend to adopt the secular feminist critique of 'patriarchy' as an all-pervasive and encompassing ideology,[28] which legitimates, institutionalises and normalises oppression of women by men.[29] The social, cultural, economic and material conditions of 'patriarchy' effect a fundamental and comprehensive distortion of every sphere of human life: the construction of personal and gendered identities; the relationships between men and women; the construction of meaning and of value; our relation to nature, including our own bodies. This ideology situates men and women (in gender-differentiated ways) in a pathologically distorted dynamic whilst masking its true nature. As ideology, therefore, 'patriarchy' presents itself as 'natural', as 'the way things are', as an unavoidable order of reality. Thus, it functions at once to legitimate (by 'naturalising') and to mask the relationships between beliefs, values and practices and the material relations and dynamics of social, political and economic power. Its distortions are so deeply embedded in the most basic means of our cultural, social and personal reproduction, communication and exchange that no-one may be free of its effects. In feminist ideological critique, 'patriarchy' is construed in dynamic rather than static terms, not so much as a set of structures, as a highly energised constellation of forces through which a systemic pathology is at once transmitted, intensified and reproduced. 'Patriarchy' is understood as operating by both distorting and sequestering the most fundamental processes of living and of reproducing human life (especially the means for symbolic representation and the codes for

---

28. For a highly readable orientation in the meaning of ideology, see Terry Eagleton, *Ideology: An Introduction* (London: Verso, 1991).

29. Cf., e.g., Kate Millett, *Sexual Politics* (New York: Doubleday, 1969) and Gerda Lerner, *The Creation of Patriarchy* (New York: Oxford University Press, 1986) with Mary Daly, *Beyond God the Father*; Nakashima Brock, *Journeys by Heart*, ch. 1.

communication).[30] It is construed, moreover, not simply as an external means of domination, but as a pathology that distorts our internal dynamics. As we are incorporated into its material and ideational practices, the pattern of our innermost life-intentionality (i.e., what we view to be good, right, true; how we intend ourselves and others; how we orient ourselves in relationships) internally confirms the 'patriarchal' ordering of reality. Particularly through its colonisation of the processes of social reproduction, through which we learn what it is to be a person, to be a self, it insinuates itself into the very seat of our personhood, in our basic structure of intentionality. As life-trajectories become disoriented in this way, we live out and repeatedly confirm a comprehensive confusion about reality – what is good, life-giving, true, responsible, etc. – which internalises distorted self-understandings and exports them to others through systematically distorted relationships. We breathe in this disorientation from infancy with every cultural breath we take, which leads us to confirm and add to the disorienting energy of 'patriarchy', to play our assigned roles. At the same time, we are ideologically conditioned to see these roles as natural, right, good and just – as necessary and unavoidable orders of life. So women learn, not only to be compliant in their own oppression, but to accept it as the natural, right, good and just basis for their own action. Living according to this 'reality' and 'truth', women internalise its oppressive meanings and confirm them in their own self-understanding, relationships and action.[31]

Feminist ideological critique makes it clear that women *situate themselves in* at the same time as *being situated by* 'patriarchy'. For 'patriarchy' draws the personal energy of committed intentionality into a corresponding and confirming orientation. It disaffects and disorients both the structure and direction of life-intentionality. Consequently, under 'patriarchy' women intend themselves (and the rest of reality) according to its systematic distortions, not only fulfilling the roles ascribed to them, but construing any departure from them as abnormal, irresponsible and blameworthy. Significantly, in the discussion of 'patriarchy' as ideology,

30. So, e.g., Ruether, *Sexism and God-Talk*, pp. 37, 164, 173; Rebecca S. Chopp, *The Power to Speak: Feminism, Language, God* (New York: Crossroad, 1991), 12ff., 25, 101–15; Sallie McFague, *Metaphorical Theology: Models of God in Religious Language* (London: SCM, 1982), pp. 145–52; Mary McClintock Fulkerson, *Changing the Subject: Women's Discourses and Feminist Theology* (Minneapolis: Fortress Press, 1994).

31. Daly speaks of this in terms of demonic possession (liberation is therefore exorcism) in *Beyond God the Father*, pp. 10, 33, 48–3, 49f., 122, 126. Nakashima Brock expresses this internalisation in terms of broken-heartedness in *Journeys By Heart*, pp. 7–17. Cf. Mary Daly, *Webster's First Intergalactic Wickedary of the English Language* (Boston: Beacon, 1987), p. 198; Mary Daly, *Pure Lust* (Boston: Beacon Press, 1984), p. 93; Plaskow, *Sex, Sin and Grace*, p. 115.

theological feminism finds it necessary to deploy terms also used to name the phenomenon of sloth ('acquiescence' and its cognates: the second set).[32] These are used to indicate the capture of women's will and active, committed intentionality by 'patriarchal' ideology as it is mediated through structures, institutions, relationships, social roles, habitual practices, social codes and language itself.

All this implies that the oppressive dynamics at the heart of 'patriarchy' do not obliterate life-intentionalities or self-directedness, so much as disorient them from within by means of internalisation. This is not a situation where there is no willing, no self-direction in life-intentionality. It is a situation where *self*-orientation and *self*-direction of life-intentionality (including willing) continues to operate, but subject to a profound disorientation. For 'patriarchy' has insinuated itself into the very structures and processes of subjective intentionality (first, through its colonisation of the processes through which they are socially acquired; then through its colonisation of the codes, institutions and processes of communication and action through which subsequent agency is repeatedly undertaken). This phenomenon of internalisation seems best expressed in terms of energy rather than substance: a pathological dynamic which *reorients* life-intentionality and the self-directedness of the person in all her relationships and action. Women's involvement in 'patriarchy' is personal, since it involves the active contribution and commitment of internal life-intentionalities and subjective agency. But all subjective agency is exercised, all living in the mode of active personhood is undertaken, under the influence of the field of force of 'patriarchal' structures of meaning, value and life, which has always already shaped the structure and orientation of subjective intentionality. Hence, what 'patriarchy' achieves, according to feminist analysis, is *the disorientation rather than the obliteration*[33] of women's subjectivity, as internal personal dynamics are influenced by the field of force of a 'body' with a greater social mass. In other words, sloth may now be interpreted as indicating a mode of *situated* personal agency; the asymmetrical interweaving of personal with pathological, situational dynamics.

Victims' willing and choosing
Thinking of the ideological function of 'patriarchy' in dynamic and situated terms helps us to understand the claim that 'sloth' denotes a mode of

---

32. See e.g., Engel, 'Evil, Sin and Violation of the Vulnerable', pp. 155f., 180; Ruether, *Sexism and God-Talk*, pp. 113f., 160–4, 180–3; *Gaia and God*, p. 141.

33. Cf. bell hooks, *Feminist Theory: From Margin to Center* (Boston: South End, 1984), p. 86.

personal participation that differs from that assessable under moral frameworks. When we read the characterisation of sloth in the context of the critique of 'patriarchy' as ideology, we are helped to see how there may be personal participation, involving the internal dynamics of intending, willing and desiring, without implying culpability. Culpability follows willing and all other marks of personal participation, only if it is accepted that willing, along with the internal conditions and processes of personal agency, is free and neutral in respect of situational influences. But here we have represented a quite different understanding of the person as profoundly situated. Here the active intentionality and self-directedness denoted by willing is neither disabled nor neutral nor free in relation to 'patriarchy'. Rather, intentionality is actively oriented under the gravitational attraction and pull of 'patriarchy'. Hence, to claim that women 'participate' personally in their oppression does mean that women will oppression and victimisation. Furthermore, the full engagement of their intentionalities does involve the commitment of personal energy in the making of choices. But this misleads unless we abandon any notion that willing means choosing in the sense of a free product of a neutral and asocial will (i.e., the arbitrary product of uncoerced self-decision, which could have been otherwise).[34] Feminist ideological critique suggests precisely that victims' will is not free in this sense. For, under the ideological colonisation of 'patriarchy', our life-intentionalities are not set in neutral, but set in movement under the influence of its attractive power – which operates from within as well as from without. Therefore, in using sloth to characterise victims' willing, feminist use effects a shift in meaning. Sloth no longer indicates a misuse of free will (in the sense of *liberum arbitrium indifferentiae*) in selecting an inappropriate object of choice ('patriarchy') through inertia or indifference, a choice which could have been made otherwise.

In feminist use, sloth indicates a much more radical and insidious pathology than the making of wrong choices in this conventional sense. For 'patriarchy' is not an external object of choice in relation to which will is neutral. It is already present within the internal dynamics of self-orientation and life-intentionality. Rather than presenting itself as one object of possible choice among others, 'patriarchy' functions as the *basis and foundation* of all choosing and acting, as the rules by which one makes choices, which are not themselves open to scrutiny or direct choice. Cer-

34. Cf. here Katie Cannon, 'Doing Womanist Ethics', *Women in a Changing World* (27 May 1987), 16.

tainly, 'patriarchal' ideology operates to impose external restrictions on the available (or at least socially sanctioned) choices that may be made by men or women. But its core ideological function is to shape and influence us, not just through external constraints, but through the *internal* shaping of cognition, desire and (therefore) will. 'Patriarchy' need not then be chosen explicitly or directly. It is 'chosen' implicitly in and with every choice that operationally assumes its base assumptions and meanings.

In feminist terms, then, sloth indicates neither an absence of willing, nor a loss of the power of choosing between available alternatives. Rather, it indicates three aspects of the embedded situatedness of persons, and therefore of their willing. It points first to the constriction in the field of possibility by narrowing the range of available choices in a gendered way. Second, it suggests that all choosing is caught up in the field of force exerted by the broader material, social and cultural dynamics of 'patriarchy'. Thus, in a situation of near total cultural colonisation, all lower-level choices assume and further embed the truth, reality and power of 'patriarchy'. Third, it indicates that the life-intentionality of the person (including will) is not only disoriented in external operation subsequent to and on the basis of the unsituated achievement of identity. Rather, it is disoriented *internally* by the pathological dynamics of 'patriarchy', which are present *already* in its basic constitution. For 'patriarchy' has colonised the processes and dynamics of social reproduction, through which we acquire the internal dynamics of subjectivity, life-intentionality and personhood. That is why 'patriarchy' is not simply an external object of choice, but a dynamic always *already* embedded in the most fundamental, internal dynamics of life-intentionality. Its *nomos* is always already insinuated into – indeed, is acquired with – the framework and organ of *auto*nomy. The sense of what is normal, good and right, and so the whole complex of motivation and desire and the criteria by which they work, are themselves constructed under its potent influence. Hence, it is indirectly willed in and with each act of willing (except, arguably, that of explicit resistance), since it is deeply embedded in the internal dynamics of willing. Sloth therefore names, not some accidental but potent act of the will, nor an explicit act of choosing, but the *active* incorporation of the whole of a person (their internality, as well as their externally directed communication and action) into the pathological dynamics of their situation. It names, in other words, the disorientation of intentionalities.

This intertwining of person with situation is, in fact, implied in a fairly straightforward reading of the second set of verbs which, in the light of the preceding comments, may now be seen to indicate 'second-order' choosing and willing. 'Acceptance', 'consent', 'compliance', etc. name involvement with a dynamic that is *already there*, rather than caused or created through women's will or agency. What is less obvious from the words themselves, but becomes clear when read in the context of the critique of ideology, is the sense in which this 'going along with' what is already there is a more dynamic interaction than is suggested by the traditional use of the term 'sloth'. The second set of verbs name a mode of personal agency dependent on and shaped by a prior set of social arrangements and processes with which the person is inextricably intertwined. Hence, the 'going along with' involves an internal predisposition or pre-orientation in willing and is not merely an act whereby one 'chooses' by omission.

Sloth as 'self-loss'

But what of the claim that women's sin of sloth involves a 'loss of self'? Is this not undercut by my interpretation of sloth as a disorientation and sequestration of the power of personal involvement, rather than a loss of its pre-condition, the internal structure of selfhood? Indeed, the notion of 'self-loss' could be read in this literal way. It might (though need not) then further be taken as implying that what women have lost and should find again is an unreconstructed 'patriarchal' self: women do not have the selfhood that men do. Is that what is bemoaned by feminists? Are women called by feminist theology to the mode of selfhood ('pride') stereotypical of men? The negative answers to these questions have already been anticipated in the preceding discussion. I hope in what follows to give more depth to them.

Indeed, the first set of verbs refers to this condition of 'self-loss', but it does so both indirectly and somewhat paradoxically. Women's sin is named as the activity of 'hiding from', 'refusing', 'denying' and 'failing to actualise' (etc.) selfhood. Sloth is not, then, the present consequence of previous agency, the resultant condition in which the potential for future personal life and interaction is lost. Neither do these verbs name sloth as a now past exercise of personal agency, the cause of the present condition of 'self-loss'. Sloth is rather named as a continuing mode of personal agency, which may yet itself be characterised in terms of 'self-loss': 'Woman is active, precisely in losing herself.'[35] Sloth and 'self-loss' are therefore to be construed as active and dynamic, not as static conditions. Consequently, 'self-loss' is better construed as a verb with a subject than a noun naming a resultant condition of verbal activity that renders women objects rather than subjects in interaction.

Again, we are helped if we read this set of verbs in the context of feminist ideological critique. Feminism is keenly aware of the ways in which the self is formed, not through a pure internal process, but within the dynamics of particular significant relationships, themselves set within the dynamics of a determinate social situation. We acquire a self by responding to the communicated expectations others have of us in interaction, the kind of responses and responsibilities we learn are expected of us as a person.[36] Indeed, self-formation could be described as a process in which we situate ourselves within, and are at the same time situated by, the broader dynamics of life within which we live. Evidently, this is a process through which the dynamics of our concrete situation may shape the internal dynamics of selfhood, becoming foundational to the self in its most basic orientations and intentionality. When these situational dynamics are pathological, the dynamics of self-formation are prone to shape selves with corresponding distortions. Feminist critique of ideology attempts to uncover the unjust power relations distorting broader social dynamics, which are inscribed into the gendered internal patterning of selfhood.[37] The sins of pride and of sloth name these gendered distortions of selfhood which, again, are best construed in dynamic rather than substantial terms.

According to feminist analysis, under 'patriarchy' men tend to be socialised in ways which encourage a strong centring of personal energies on ourselves.[38] Men are socialised into pride. Socialisation processes assume and energise a personal centre that is oriented towards sustaining and nourishing itself. Sense of identity would therefore be strong;

---

35. Plaskow, *Sex, Sin and Grace*, p. 23.

36. My own account of these dynamics may be found in *The Call to Personhood: A Christian Theory of the Individual in Relationships* (Cambridge: Cambridge University Press, 1990), ch. 3.

37. See, e.g., Annette Baier, *Postures of the Mind: Essays on Mind and Morals* (Minneapolis: University of Minnesota Press, 1985), especially p. 85 for her coining the term 'second persons'.

38. See, e.g., Nancy Chodorow, 'Gender, Relation, and Difference in Psychoanalytic Perspective', in Hester Eisenstein and Alice Jardine, eds., *The Future of Difference* (New Brunswick: Rutgers, 1985); Diana T. Meyers, *Self, Society, and Personal Choice* (New York: Columbia, 1989), pp. 141–71.

commitments to others in relationships, weak, since this would represent a dissipation of the energies through which we organise ourselves. This does not mean that external relationships would be avoided. But it does make it likely that the dynamic of self-orientation would operate in them. That signifies the attempted colonisation of both the dynamics of the relationship and the internal dynamics of others, influencing these energies into an orientation on us.

Women, on the other hand, tend to be socialised in ways that de-centre the orientation of their personal energies and dissipate them. Under the conditions of 'patriarchy', the nurturing self-giving and orientation on others expected of women easily turns pathological. The power to be genuinely oneself in relations is easily dissipated where such self-giving is systematically not reciprocated. Women, on this analysis, 'acquire' weak, dissipated and fragmented selves, giving and emptying themselves in relationships. Their possibilities for self-centring are de-energised through the dissipation in which their internal energies of life-intentionality are directed towards sustaining and nurturing others in relationships where there is no reciprocal orientation. Male selves tend to be oriented on themselves, and male identities constructed as exclusive of relation. Women's tend to be oriented externally and are inclusive of relation. But, in a situation where the broader dynamics of relation are also oriented away from women's selfhood, women receive no energising of self from external sources. Under 'patriarchy', women contribute their energy to a dynamic in which their own powers of full selfhood are neither nurtured, nourished nor intensified. They are not re-centred through the dynamics of relation; their energies are not refocused. They consequently experience a loss of the power of *genuine* selfhood in relation, which is the correlate and consequence of systematic distortion, disorder and loss of the possibility of genuine relation.

Sloth is construed by feminists as disorientation in life-intentionality in which the power to be a genuinely integrated self is, not so much lost, as dissipated. It is not that women become passive objects, having and expending no personal energy of their own. Women are rather the ones who are constantly 'at work', putting time and energy into one 'mundane' and 'insignificant' task after another in order to maintain relationships, nurture and meet the needs of others. Their life-intentionalities may become so fully oriented away from themselves, all their energies directed towards others, that they stereotypically have no time for themselves. With all personal energies directed externally, women easily become 'self-forgetful'. It is not just that they may have little time or energy left to look after their own integrity and identity. It is rather that the identity of the self loses its own integrity and collapses into relationships of nurture, service and care. All the energies of life-intentionality are thus sequestered in an orientation away from the self, so that the energy to maintain one's integrity, to be for oneself and for others as oneself, is dissipated. For as soon as it is marshalled it is spent elsewhere. It may never achieve sufficient concentration or duration in orientation on the self. Sloth is therefore equivalent to what feminists sometimes call loss of 'power in relation'.[39] It is a complementary disorientation in life-intentionality to pride, since both are produced by the systematic disorientation, disorder and distortion of relationships under 'patriarchy'.

'Self-loss' is a misleading term if 'self' is understood (as the idea that it may be 'lost' invites) in terms of substance, since it is clear that feminists do not mean by it a *loss* of subjectivity and personal agency. If, however, we regard the 'self' more as an activity than a substance, then it is possible to interpret 'self-loss' as a mode of performance of self. And when we read the discussion of sloth together with ideological critique, we are directed to understand 'self-loss' as the disoriented performance of self under systematically distorted conditions. Women, on this analysis, retain self as the activity of directing internal energies of life-intentionality. They remain personal centres in the sense of loci from whence energy is directed and expended. However, this centredness is weak, since its performance is not characterised by a re-energising orientation on itself. This is a centredness which does not centre itself, so to speak, but which 'spends' itself in externally directed orientations. And, since relational and situational dynamics are also disoriented from women's centring, no energy is directed back to these centres. Energies are dissipated, rather than centred.

This corresponds to the familiar feminist claim that, under 'patriarchy', women are not subjects *for themselves*; they cannot speak in their own voice, or recognise, pursue and act on their own interests or perception of the good in undistorted ways. Under the conditions of 'patriarchy', then, women's subjectivity is not simply overcome or opposed by an external field of force. Subjective life-intentionalities are rather actively disoriented and alienated. Women continue to act personally, to will, but they do so *as victims* – as those whose active intentionality internalises, embeds and redoubles the dynamics of their own oppression.

39. Carter Heyward, *The Redemption of God: A Theology of Mutual Relation* (Lanham, NY: University Press of America, 1982), passim.

Hence, sloth is a complex and situated form of agency in which personal power is directed according to a person's orientation in life-intentionality, which is itself caught up in the influence of broader situational dynamics. Sloth names the particular disorientation away from the self, which this often indirect contribution of personal to situational power effects. Simultaneously, it draws attention to the disorienting synergism between personal and situational energies. The addition of personal energy to the situational dynamics intensifies them, both in their hold on the person and in communication with and relation to others. Whilst pride superficially appears to be unsituated, potent agency, the product of an essentially unrelated, strong self, that is an ideological fiction masking the situational determinants of 'male' selfhood and agency. The only difference between pride and sloth lies in the direction of the disorientation of intentionality: in the one case, away from, in the other, towards, the self. Therefore, feminist theologies of sin, read in the context of ideological critique, bring to expression precisely that mode of agency that has emerged most pointedly from our engagement with concrete pathologies, where personal and supra-personal powers co-operate with synergistic and pathological effect. In the case of sloth, the co-option of the personal energy of willing into a more highly energised situational dynamic dissipates, disorients and de-centres. 'Self-loss' is therefore a dissipation and disorientation of the personal energies or power in life-intentionality that designate a mode of selfhood, of being a person in relation.

What is the self which is 'lost' and which feminism wishes women to find? It is tempting to work with simple dichotomies and to suppose that, if sloth is the opposite of pride, and sloth is 'self-loss', then the 'lost' and to-be-recovered self is the proud self. If sloth indicates disorientation away from the personal centre, is not the cure that orientation towards the centre characterised by pride? And if sloth is the incorporation of personal energies of life-intentionality into situational dynamics, is not the cure the proud isolation of the self from situational determination? Yet, pride is regarded by feminist theologians as a form of sin alongside that of sloth. Thus, pride – 'male' or 'patriarchal' selfhood – cannot function as the normative standard of reference for selfhood; sloth is not sin because it is not pride. Feminism must operate an alternative standard of normative reference, in relation to which, both pride and sloth may be deemed pathological.

Feminist standards

It is immediately obvious that what is *not* operating as a normative standard of reference for the good is the 'patriarchal' male. Women are not urged to adopt the self-orientation that is stereotypical of men under 'patriarchy' (pride): to save themselves from 'self-loss' through strategies of oppressive self-assertion or essential isolation from commitment in concrete relation. Indeed, feminism rejects the male as universal human norm and standard, and therefore as an appropriate model for women's genuine and full humanity.[40] If feminist rhetoric urges women, in their position of oppression, to have pride in themselves, this is not a call to that form of isolated self-centredness found so problematic in men. What is urged is resistance to an *inappropriate* diminution of themselves in their relationships and to adopt an *appropriate* form of (situated) self-assertion and protection. But if the latter is to be distinguished from excessive self-assertion, it can only be by a normative standard of reference that establishes what is appropriate and inappropriate to patterns, orders, structures, processes and dynamics of selfhood and relation. Such a standard must yield, in other words, a sense of the proper economy of self in relation; one which founds equally both the critique of men's stereotypical pride and that of women's stereotypical sloth. This standard of reference may be seen to be operating in the background of the critique of the sin of pride.

Complementing the tradition

Feminist theological critique often brings women's experience to expression by substituting alternative terms in place of traditional ones. In this instance, however, the problem with the tradition lies, not in the interpretation and designation of pride as sin, but in its over-extensive application. In regarding pride as the paradigm of all sin, the tradition suggests both that all sin is pride and that any form of pride is sin. This over-emphasis is addressed, not by the substitution of a new term, but by naming the corresponding dissipation of self as also sin. At first glance, this complementary naming hardly seems of radical consequence. Surely, this is a conservative strategy that names an additional set of circumstances as sin, but which leaves the traditional definition of pride otherwise untouched. Feminist

40. See, e.g., Catherine Keller, *From a Broken Web: Separation, Sexism and Self* (Boston: Beacon, 1986).

naming of the sin of sloth is, however, more significant than at first appears to be the case (and perhaps more significant even than feminist discussions often explicitly claim). Simply in naming a complement to what is traditionally claimed to be *universally* extensive and *omni*competent, feminist theology achieves a shift in the way that sin is being understood; a shift which is as radical as it is subtle. For naming sloth as sin fundamentally alters the normative frame of reference that underpins the identification of pride as what sin essentially is. Both the rationale for the identification of pride as sin (the good which pride disrupts) and the definition of sinful pride are fundamentally altered. The first and most obvious way in which this happens is in the suggestion that, if self-loss is sin, then not all forms of what we term pride in normal discourse are sinful. Pride itself therefore undergoes a reinterpretation once it is drawn into the orbit of the complementary sin of sloth, now referring to a more particularly defined and restricted range of self-assertions than traditionally. Self-assertion, self-protection, self-esteem are not sins in all forms or in all circumstances. Indeed, *failing* to assert, protect and esteem oneself might also prove sinful.

In the very act of naming sloth as complementary sin, feminist theologians effect a significant modification in the conventional construal of the sin of pride. It may no longer be interpreted as any assertion of self that rebels against self-obeisance and 'self-loss'. If both pride and its opposite are construed as sin, then, the very *sinfulness* of pride is significantly recast. What this actually indicates is a switch in the normative standard of reference underpinning the discernment of sin. The good which pride deprives one of has to be reconfigured when self-obeisance and 'self-loss' are no longer complementary *virtues* to the sin of pride, but represent instead *complementary aspects of the same pathology*. What this indicates is that feminist naming here operates by relating both pride and sloth to a more comprehensive standard of reference, which adjudicates the sinfulness of both: an understanding of the proper economy of self in relation. It is when the virtues of self-giving are unplugged from the nurturing dynamics of genuine love, that they take pathological form (sloth) and fail to be genuine forms of self-presence for and orientation towards others.[41]

The relational self

Underlying feminist critiques of the emphasis on pride and of 'patriarchy' as ideology is a quite different construal of self, subjectivity and

41. Ann Loades, 'Why Certain Forms of Holiness are Bad for You', in *Searching for Lost Coins: Explorations in Christianity and Feminism* (London: SPCK, 1987), p. 57.

autonomy in relational and situated terms.[42] In part, this represents the claim that the *achievement* of selfhood happens through relationships and is therefore dependent on the right relational conditions. This involves a critique of the dominant ('patriarchal') assumptions concerning the *origins* of selfhood and its autonomy. It does not in itself, however, substantively redefine either term. It offers an account of the relational *origins*, though not necessarily a relational *understanding*, of the self and its proper autonomy (though this is often subsequently developed). Nonetheless, the account of the relational origins of the self and its autonomy is of critical significance. It does just begin to hint at the possibility that personal and extra-personal dynamics may not always operate in oppositional terms, that the very processes of centring personal dynamics depend on our incorporation into those of the broader situation. Hence, it also cuts against the view that, since selves are asocial, 'loss of self' is an individual deficit unrelated to social conditions. If selfhood is, rather, a social acquisition, then one might wish to inspect the social dynamics that appear to inhibit the acquisition of selfhood and autonomy by some.

Just as the asocial understanding of the conditions for the achievement of selfhood and autonomy which predominates in our culture supports a particular account of their nature, so the feminist critique of the former is also sometimes used to support an alternative account of the latter. According to feminist analyses, 'patriarchy' construes the (male) subject to be independent, isolated and asocial – in its origin as well as essence: a product of internal processes by which it comes to possess and be itself. The 'patriarchal' self is founded on processes of self-relation, and is essentially unrelated, personal power being oppositional to extra-personal powers. Consequently, all relationships that are not modes of relation to the self appear 'external' and accidental. Identity and integrity are constituted and maintained through the internal dynamics of relation to oneself (deliberation, willing, choice, self-mastery, etc.). Relation to others might then be insignificant or incidental, not self-involving. Alternatively, because the integrity of each subject is established internally, independently of any relationships, relationships between subjects are between non-aligned fields of force (the internal dynamics proper to

42. For secular statements, see Sarah Hoagland, *Lesbian Ethics: Towards New Value* (Palo Alto: Institute for Lesbian Studies, 1988), pp. 144–7; Evelyn Fox Keller, *Reflections on Gender and Science* (New Haven: Yale University Press, 1985), pp. 97–113; Jennifer Nedelsky, 'Reconceiving Autonomy: Sources, Thoughts and Possibilities', *Yale Journal of Law and Feminism*, 1/1 (1989), 7–36; Lorraine Code, *What Can She Know? Feminist Theory and the Construction of Knowledge* (Ithaca: Cornell, 1991), pp. 73–108.

each). Hence, there is the danger (from the opposite vantage point, the opportunity) of one's internal dynamics being overpowered by the 'gravitational pull' of the other's. Consequently, integrity and autonomy are construed in terms of freedom *from* others in order to be truly for oneself.

Early versions of (liberal) feminism did critique the oppressive dynamics of 'patriarchal' society by claiming the right for women to be the kinds of autonomous selves that men were, no longer defined by their relationships.[43] More recently, feminist discourse has taken the risk of a much more subtle and radical approach. Women are not called to the form of individualised selfhood and autonomy characteristic, according to feminist analysis, of men under 'patriarchy'. Instead, non-liberal feminisms urge women to liberate themselves, not by becoming like 'patriarchal' men and escaping the bonds of relation, but by more radically construing and living out their fundamental relatedness. This emphasis on relatedness runs the risk of being misunderstood as advocating a flight into relationships *rather than* and *at the expense of* the integrity of particular personal identity or selfhood and the autonomy proper to them. Are feminists suggesting that women's liberation after all involves settling for relationships rather than autonomy? For dissipation rather than centring of the self?

Two comments need to be made here, both indicating that misinterpretation follows only if no account is made of the changed standard of normative reference deployed in feminist critique. That is to say, the risk of misunderstanding attends the emphasis on relationality only if it is read still against a 'patriarchal' standard of reference with an unchanged register of meanings.

First, the stated preference for relation as opposed to (what is actually only a fiction of) non-relation does not imply that any and all relationships are good.[44] That would hardly square with the criticism of the 'patriarchal' ordering of relationships criticised as oppressive of women.

---

43. See e.g., Jean Grimshaw, 'Autonomy and Identity in Feminist Thinking', in Morwenna Griffiths and Margaret Whitford, eds., *Feminist Perspectives in Philosophy* (Bloomington: Indiana University Press, 1988); Sharon Bishop Hill, 'Self-Determination and Autonomy', in Richard Wasserstrom, ed., *Today's Moral Problems* (New York: Macmillan, 1975).
44. It is the case, however, that the literature does sometimes speak of relation as though it were an undifferentiated reality in order to heighten the tension between metaphysics and ethics of relation and of (supposed) non-relation. Feminists are then tempted to speak as though all relation is good, then when reminded that some relationships are damaging backtrack (e.g., Grey, 'Falling into Freedom', pp. 231f.). Marylin Friedman's discussion of feminist philosophers' construals of autonomy is illuminating on this point. See 'Autonomy and Social Relationships: Rethinking the Feminist Critique', in Diana Tietjens Meyers, ed., *Feminists Rethink the Self* (Boulder, CO: Westview, 1997), pp. 55ff.

In other words, there are criteria in operation that make it possible to make qualitative distinctions between different forms of relation. In particular, these exclude relationships that are destructive of the personal integrity necessary to be a person-in-genuine-relation. So the very term 'relation' is in fact used as a cipher for a particular form of relation in which the integrity proper to persons is not systematically assaulted, oppressed and denied; the energies of life-intentionality, not disoriented. I have deliberately avoided saying that this is a form of relation in which autonomy is safeguarded. That is not an incorrect statement, but it may easily mislead if the meaning of 'autonomy' is not also interpreted in a manner informed by the change in the normative standard of reference. Terms such as 'person', 'self' and 'autonomy' are all redefined through the filter of feminist standards. Were autonomy to retain its 'patriarchal' definition, then 'right relation' would denote relations in which the essential unrelatedness of the partners, their freedom from one another, is safeguarded.

Thus, the second point that needs to be made here refers to the supposed opposition between autonomy and committed relatedness, between being-for-oneself and being-for-others-in-relation. Such an opposition appears only where autonomy is defined in terms of the fiction of the isolated, individual subject. Then being a centred self, being in one's own power, may be protected only by establishing forms of distance from (or overpowering) other personal centres, for fear of being pulled into their field of force and overpowered. Here, the power in and through which we achieve centredness and maintain integrity is incommensurable and unshareable, if not outright competitive.

What feminist theologians mean by 'right relation', by contrast, yields a much richer and more nuanced sense of what it means to be a person or a self and to have autonomy – all always 'in relation'. Despite beginning from a sharp and painful awareness of the ways in which the self may be overpowered and lost through its embeddedness in pathological relation, feminists do not fly from relationality into an extreme individualism. Instead, they maintain a full and rich understanding of the potentiality of genuine relationships to be empowering, which sets the standard by which relational pathologies are judged. The experience of 'patriarchal' oppression of the internal dynamics of selfhood could easily and understandably have led to a flight from relation into the fiction of an isolated self. That would mean reading the pathology to be escaped as *any* form of situatedness in which personal are influenced by supra-personal dynamics. Implicitly, however, feminism tends to operate with a painfully won awareness of the indelible significance of situational on the orientation of personal dynamics, for good as well as ill. Hence, feminists look for healing the pathologies of the self in part through situational dynamics. Rather than understanding liberation to be *from* relation, they look for liberation *in*, *through* and *for* 'right relation'. Although variously imaged in feminist theologies, this form of relationality always involves the deepest mutuality.[45] What is envisioned is a form of community in which the energies of personal life are mutually oriented and thereby focused in a highly energised dynamic which is mutually empowering of each partner's integrity and autonomy.

We may see this as the obverse of the situational dynamics of 'patriarchy'. In both, there is a synergistic co-operation between internal and supra-personal dynamics, the internal orientation of the person's life-intentionality being influenced by those of the situation, inviting the commitment of personal energy to intensify situational dynamics. There are obvious differences, however, between the dynamics of 'patriarchal' society and those of genuine community. In the latter, being a self, a subject, is not a self-bounded dynamic, but what might be termed an 'intersubjective' one, in which autonomy and personal integrity are not threatened, but actually empowered through relation. Here autonomy is conceived as 'power in relation' in a quite distinctive way, as the centredness required for differentiation of identity without separation,[46] for centredness that gains integrity from commitment in genuine relations. It is not the power unilaterally to define and maintain the integrity of one's self. It is rather the power to be for others in relation as oneself; to be empowered to find one's own integrity as identity is intensified through the dynamics and economy of 'right relation'. It is this power to be a self in genuine relation that is 'lost' in sloth, as in pride.

Where we are caught up in the dynamics of genuine community, our integrity and autonomy are not threatened in relation, but rather

45. See e.g., Daly, *Beyond God the Father*, pp. 32, 159, 172; Heyward, *The Redemption of* God; Carter Heyward, *Touching our Strength: The Erotic as the Power and Love of God* (San Francisco: HarperCollins, 1989), pp. 96f., 104f., 192f.; Carter Heyward, *Our Passion for Justice: Images of Power, Sexuality and Liberation* (New York: Pilgrim, 1984); Grey, *Redeeming the Dream*, pp. 106–8; Nakashima Brock, *Journeys by Heart*, ch. 2; Sharon D. Welch, *A Feminist Ethic of Risk* (Minneapolis: Fortress Press, 1990), p. 135; Letty M. Russell, *Human Liberation in a Feminist Perspective: A Theology* (Philadelphia: Westminster, 1974), pp. 107, 110, 121, 146, 152ff., 160, 163; Mary E. Hunt, *Fierce Tenderness: A Feminist Theology of Friendship* (New York: Crossroad, 1991); Mary Grey, *The Wisdom of Fools: Seeking Revelation for Today* (London: SPCK, 1993), ch. 4.
46. I owe this useful distinction to Miroslav Volf, *Exclusion and Embrace* (Nashville: Abingdon Press, 1996), pp. 64–8.

enriched, enlarged, intensified, empowered.[47] The reverse is also perceived to be the case, that loss of relation does not constitute but imperils genuine autonomy.[48] This explicitly achieves a redefinition of autonomy with intrinsic reference to relationships and situational dynamics. Autonomy is redefined in terms of committed intentionality, not individual freedom, since freedom itself is not defined in terms of withdrawal from relationships, but a quality of living within them, characterised by the giving and receiving of personal energy. Moreover, personal integrity is not construed in static, but in dynamic, terms. Identity is not, then, viewed as already set and determined *prior* to relation, neither may it be viewed therefore as something established in abstraction from the concrete embeddedness of a person in her relational history. It is rather something established through time as one is upheld by, and called to respond to, others. It is precisely through our concretely situated histories of responding to, and being responded to by, others that we may come to be genuinely for ourselves and for others (or the reverse). The orientation and centring on oneself characteristic of autonomy and selfhood arise here precisely through an orientation on others within the empowering mutuality of community and committed relation. The equilibrium of identity and its proper integrity is not static, then, but dynamic and open. It is not laid down once for all time as a given, asocial, inner essence, but found and discovered in the concretely situated interplay of persons in relation. Through committed relation, one may be drawn and invited into further abundance and intensification of identity and integrity. Significantly, committed relation cannot mean here: those relationships I choose to have on my terms out of my individually derived autonomy. For autonomy is not a sphere held apart from relation. Personal participation is not voluntary in the conventional sense, then, the capacity to stand apart from one's relationships, to choose to have a relationship or not. It rather involves committing personal energies (including willing) to those relationships in which I am already situated. Freedom and the bonds of relation are not antithetical; embeddedness in concrete relational situations is the field of personal responsibility redefined.[49] The power to be oneself, therefore, is here

---

47. E.g., Grey, *Redeeming the Dream*, pp. 87f.

48. A point made explicitly by the secular feminist philosopher, Susan J. Brison ('Outliving Oneself: Trauma, Memory and Personal Identity', in Tietjens Meyers, ed., *Feminists Rethink the Self*, pp. 28f.) in connection with the experience of rape survival.

49. See here Seyla Benhabib, *Situating the Self: Gender, Community and Postmodernism in Contemporary Ethics* (Cambridge: Polity Press, 1992), pp. 155–70.

derived from and intensified through genuine relation in which it is also shared with others. Consequently, a liberal notion of respect due to persons as they are, is supplanted by the dynamics of mutuality: mutual blessing, empowerment, enrichment and joy. Here human beings are envisioned as embraced by and properly oriented towards an immense plenitude and abundance that invites into an expansiveness and intensification of integrity and freedom in community.

What is sin?

This vision of 'right relation' is the standard against which 'patriarchy', pride and sloth are judged pathological in feminist theologies. Sin is that which constricts and restricts human beings from the abundance and plenitude of being-in-relation which is proper to them; that which dissipates, blocks, disorients or counters the dynamics of genuine and full mutuality.[50] 'Patriarchy' is pathological because it sets up a counter-dynamic that disorients, restricts and constricts the energies of mutuality through, for example, oppression, victimisation, inappropriate blame, abuse of trust or power, violence, or the systematic constriction of expectations.[51] Sin is that, therefore, which constricts and disorients from the possibilities of life in its proper and full abundance. This disorientation, feminist analysis shows, is internalised in a way which binds people to it from within, in their deepest intentionalities, and is transmitted through institutionalised structures and processes of interaction, through the generations. The systematically distorted processes of social reproduction, communication and exchange disorient our life-intentionalities, involving a deeply embedded confusion concerning the nature of reality and of the good, which informs and infects all our willing.

Willing (at least that of victims) therefore appears as the direction of personal energy, under the influence of (and adding itself to) supra-personal dynamics. The participation of victims in sin remains personal, then, since personal energy is centrally organised and directed. But the dynamics of life-intentionality are subject to an internalised disorientation away from the genuinely good and enriching. Sin is thus construed in terms of a co-operation between disoriented personal and supra-personal dynamics: an intensifying synergism.

50. See, e.g., Daly, *Beyond God the Father*, p. 158; Grey, *Redeeming the Dream*, pp. 103, 106; Grey, 'Falling into Freedom', pp. 231f.; Heyward, *The Redemption of God*, pp. 153–63.

51. Heyward, *The Redemption of God*, p. 2; Nakashima Brock, *Journeys by Heart*, pp. 7f., 19; Sallie McFague, *The Body of God: An Ecological Theology* (Minneapolis: Fortress Press, 1993), p. 114; Ruether, *Gaia and God*, pp. 141f.; Grey, *Redeeming the Dream*, pp. 17, 103–7, 130.

Engaging with feminist theologies of sin has both added to the cumulative case against the descriptive adequacy of moral frames of reference and given more specifiable content to the hypothesis of the bound will. In thinking through some of the implications regarding personal participation from the perspective of victims, feminist theologies of sin reject the view of the will as an internal, private organ of choosing, free in the sense of suspended in neutrality above all concrete choices. Rather, will is presented as situated and dynamic life-intentionality, influenced in its orientation by relational and situational dynamics. The pathological situational dynamics with which feminism is chiefly concerned at the same time invite participation through the engagement of willing, whilst actively disorienting life-intentionality through an internalised confusion concerning the nature of reality and the good. Hence, sin (at least the sin of women) is viewed, not in terms of arbitrary, free acts of the will, but in terms of the disorientation in life-intentionality (including the will). Feminist reinterpretation of sloth is to be read, I have suggested, in a way that meets the requirement that situational and personal pathologies be named together. For sloth may only be understood as a disorientation of life-intentionality effected by the energised internalisation of 'patriarchal' ideology. In other words, pathology is construed as internal to the will, not as an external object of possible choice.

In one significant respect, feminist theologies of sin go beyond the minimum requirements of descriptive adequacy in relation to our concrete situations. In its envisioning of the good, feminist theology articulates a normative standard of reference, which sets us before a fuller and richer conception of the potentialities of human life, rather than simply reversing the pathology. Because the pathology represented by 'patriarchy' is radical, its identification, interpretation and resistance require a trans-valuation of normative standards of reference: a reconception of the good, not merely the incorporation under its norm of those presently excluded from it. Furthermore, theological feminism, at least in its narration of the situation of women, is more interested in calling and energising towards a future-oriented responsibility in and for one's situation, than in a backward-looking nailing of causal responsibility. Even in this, it construes personal responsibility, and the reorientation of the energies of personal life-intentionality that this involves, to be related to the extrapersonal dynamics of a transformed and transforming community.

Feminist theology therefore does, I think, help to bring to more adequate expression aspects of pathology missed by moral frameworks, and to give substantial support to the hypothesis of bound willing. But does it do so through a specifically theological thematisation, language and conceptuality? True, its agenda and terminology are derived from the context of Christian tradition. Yet pride and sloth are not intrinsically theological terms. In themselves, they do not point to ways of relating to God. They have to be given this meaning through use. Otherwise, they function as ways of naming disorders of selfhood unplugged from the ecology of relation to God. It will doubtless have struck the reader that my presentation of feminist understanding of sin does not refer once to God. This reflects a reticence characteristic of feminist theologies of sin which, in fact, goes very much to the heart of feminist theology. Indeed, the discussion of sin reflects the problematisation of both the characterisation and the reality of God. For feminists are wary of importing 'patriarchal' constructions, which project on to God the characteristics of the supposedly asocial self. That wariness precisely reflects feminists' experience of human relationships when ordered in a way that secures the precedence of one partner over others. If God is almighty, transcendent, self-contained, sovereign, then His relations with creatures will be monological, hierarchical, dominating and generally alienating and expropriating of human autonomy. Indeed, this is the sort of God requiring self-obeisance; the sort of God before whom self-assertion would be counted the cardinal sin. It is hardly surprising, therefore, that feminist theologies of sin wish, in their critique of the pride paradigm, to avoid embedding the very theology which underpins it. Hence, they tend either to elide all reference to God or to make God so immanent to the dynamics of 'right relation' or selfhood that any meaningful distinction between them threatens to collapse.[52] Despite the reconception of power, autonomy and the voluntary in relational terms, feminist theologies are often wary of allowing that transcendent divine power might be reconceived as non-competitive, co-operating and empowering.[53] Hence, the standard

52. See especially the works of Daly, Hampson, Brock, Welch. In Heyward, God becomes a verb of which human beings are the subjects (*The Redemption of God*, pp. 153, 159; *Touching Our Strength*, pp. 188ff.). Russell is a notable exception.

53. So, e.g., Heyward, *The Redemption of God*, pp. 129ff., 158f.; Welch, *A Feminist Ethic of Risk*, pp. 111–21; Hampson, 'Reinhold Niebuhr on Sin', pp. 56ff.; Hampson, *Theology and Feminism*, pp. 151–5; Daphne Hampson, 'On Autonomy and Heteronomy', in Daphne Hampson, ed., *Swallowing a Fishbone? Feminist Theologians Debate Christianity* (London: SPCK, 1996), pp. 8f.; Carol Saussy, *God Images and Self-Esteem: Empowering Women in a Patriarchal Society* (Louisville: Westminster/John Knox, 1991). See further my 'Sins of Praise: The Assault on God's Freedom', in Colin E. Gunton, ed., *God and Freedom: Essays in Historical and Systematic Theology* (Edinburgh: T. & T. Clark, 1995), pp. 32–56.

whereby pathological orientations of life-intentionality are identified tends to be expressed in entirely immanent terms: the self in genuine human community, with God identified, if at all, only as the power energising mutuality (but not as the agential source from whence such power is directed). The orientation on self in community through which one genuinely wills to be oneself is not construed as in itself a matter of relation to a transcendent source of relational power: as, in other words, a mode of creatureliness.[54] I do not wish at this point to become bogged down in a consideration of the theological adequacy of feminist reconstructions of God. What is worthy of note here is the challenge posed by the feminist caution against affirming the transcendence and power of God. Can the sinfulness of pride and sloth be thematised in explicitly theological terms without reinforcing and legitimating the pathology? Can human beings be related to a transcendent and 'wholly other' God without their freedom, integrity and autonomy being de-energised and eroded, without their being called into pathologies of self-obeisance and self-surrender?

Concerning the agenda of this book, then, this discussion of feminist theologies of sin moves us on, but also leaves us with a problem. It has subjected the descriptive adequacy of moral frameworks to further testing. But it has made no positive contribution to testing the descriptive power of a specifically theological language and conceptuality. In its lack of clarity concerning the sense in which sloth and pride are sins against God and not just against self or 'right relation', one wonders whether sin is here a functioning theological language. Or is it retained only because of the communal location of this particular discussion, out of habit or for rhetorical flourish? Indeed, one is driven to ask again whether the language of sin holds any descriptive or explanatory power, or whether it might be translatable without remainder into the secular language and conceptuality of, say, social psychology. Is it accidental that the language and conceptuality of Christian tradition may be interpreted in ways that bring victims' willing to expression?

It may seem rather odd to turn from feminism to Augustine with these questions in mind. Perhaps it seems so odd as to whiff of a hidden agenda: let the male tradition have the last word over the women! Augustine is perceived by many feminist theologians as, in many respects, the father of

54. As it most certainly is in Kierkegaard, from whom much feminist conceptuality in this regard is drawn. See, e.g., *Sickness Unto Death*, pp. 14, 20, 49, 82, 131.

'patriarchal' theology; indeed, as the chief progenitor of the tradition's mistaken emphasis on pride and the main architect of the anathematical doctrine of original sin.[55] So, why turn to Augustine at this point?

First, I wish to read Augustine, not to squash dissonant voices with the weight of the tradition, but in order to subject the tradition to further concrete testing. In particular, I want to ask whether a specifically and explicitly theological standard of reference holds explanatory power in relation to concrete pathology, and whether it helps enrich, make yet more specific and make more sense of the hypothesis of the bound will. In asking this, I wish to read Augustine in the light of the understanding of willing which has emerged through the discussion of concrete pathologies and in the two subsequent chapters. Does this throw new and different light on Augustine's understanding of sin; can he, in turn, illuminate further the understanding of willing emerging through the discussion up to this point? Can his theology of sin hold descriptive or explanatory power? And can it do so, precisely as a functioning theological language? Augustine holds that pride is the paradigmatic sin. On the face of it, Augustine's view of sin looks unlikely to survive feminist theologians' concrete testing of the tradition against women's experience of oppression, which resonates so obviously with the discussion of concrete pathologies earlier in the book.

55. As examples of readings of Augustine inviting this generally negative judgment, see: Elaine Pagels, *Adam, Eve and the Serpent* (New York: Random House, 1988); Kim Power, *Veiled Desire: Augustine's Writing on Women* (London: Darton, Longman & Todd, 1996); Mary Grey, 'Augustine and the Legacy of Guilt', *New Blackfriars*, 70 (1989), 476–88; Heyward, *The Redemption of God*, pp. 116–30. But see West, *Deadly Innocence*, pp. 107–11, 144.

8

Augustine's will

Throughout the discussion so far, the phenomenon of willing in pathological situations has appeared both more complex and more extensive than is capable of description within a moral framework. In particular, the capacity of supra-personal and extra-personal pathological dynamics to sequester the personal dynamics of life-intentionality (including the will) is much more radical than may be allowed for by the supposed identity of willing and freedom (construed as the formal capacity to choose freely between competing options). In the face of the inadequacies and limitations of moral language for describing and interpreting concrete pathology, would a theological language fare any better? In order to test whether theological modes of interpretation, expression and discernment might prove more appropriate to these tasks, I turn to Augustine. Why Augustine? Is this merely the conventional move to engage with the dominant voice in Western Christianity? a theologian's reflex back into the familiar territory of the dominant strand of his own tradition, having charted a course until now through so much unfamiliar terrain? Augustine's understanding of sin is the conventional, and arguably even obligatory, point through which to engage the tradition on account of his unequalled role in shaping Western Christianity's understanding of sin, including its doctrine of original sin. Indeed, the debt that the Western tradition owes to Augustine in relation to its understanding of sin is measured by the fact that he could – indeed, often does – stand in for the tradition as a whole, whether to be attacked or venerated. I have chosen to engage Augustine in the task of concrete testing because he developed the doctrine of original sin as a counter to a position that anticipates characteristic modern assumptions concerning freedom and the modern translation of sin into moral categories.[1] In so doing, he developed an account of willing in a situation radically permeated by sin.[2] It is possible, therefore, that reading him in the light of the foregoing discussion might bring new illumination to his understanding of willing and of sin, more generally. At the same time, it is possible too that he might be an aid towards further *theological* specification of the nature of bound willing.

Pelagius on willing

The extended debate that led to the first systematic elaboration of the doctrine of original sin anticipates modern suspicions that the doctrine's traditional interpretation imperils the attribution of moral responsibility. (So, in what follows, we shall be moving back over some of the terrain sketched by chapter 2, with our attention drawn by subsequent chapters to a topographical feature which did not then seem quite so significant: willing.) We find, in other words, that the doctrine of original sin is not ambushed and taken by surprise by moral critique at some later stage on its journey down the road of doctrinal development. Rather, it emerged in initially self-conscious opposition to the supposed adequacy of moral categories to grasp the realities of the human situation before God, and therefore to the translation of sin into a moral language. And in order to capture the significance of Augustine's understanding of sin, and of its associated account of willing, it is first necessary to attend to that which he finds so dangerous.

For Pelagius, freedom in choosing and willing is an inalienable characteristic of the human creature. It belongs to our given *essence* as human beings to be free to choose between competing possibilities.[3] Pelagius understood will as a pure organ of free choice. Its freedom he construed in terms of a neutral suspension between different possibilities. Were will not neutral, then its choosing would not, so far as Pelagius was concerned, be a product of its own inherent freedom and self-movement. It

---

1. The characteristically Pelagian interpretation of free will in fact corresponds closely to Augustine's earlier position in books I and II of *On Free Will*. By book III, however (which preceded the Pelagian controversy), he is already moving towards his mature conception which incorporates at its heart an awareness of the weakness, insufficiency, fallenness and division of will.

2. Earlier intimations and formulations may be found in *To Simplicianus* and *Confessions*.

3. Pelagius, *Letter to Demetrias*, 8, 17, 24; Augustine, *On the Grace of Christ*, 43; *On Original Sin*, 14, 30; cf. Pelagius' follower Julian's *Unfinished Work*, iii. 82. Because this is an aspect of our creaturely nature, given by God, Pelagius regards it as (natural) grace. That affirmation allows him to declare any exercise of will for the good as a (passive) co-operation between God's (natural) grace and human freedom, rather than an unaided human achievement.

would then rather be moved by the power of attraction of a particular object of choice and so acting out of a kind of compulsion instead of innate freedom. So for Pelagius the will's freedom consists in its power to motivate itself out of its equal indifference towards one of a number of different possibilities of action. And because Pelagius held such freedom in willing to be inalienable, it follows that we are always in a situation of *possibility*: we may always will otherwise.

Pelagius did concede, however, that we could be *forced* to do things *against our will* (although he judged that genuine instances of coercion were much rarer than their use as an excuse for moral lapse). Even when coerced, however, he maintained that one's will remained free as a pure organ of choice, in that it may still wish for alternative possibilities – although without sufficient freedom and power in *action* to effect that choice. In that case, there is alienation between the subjective capacity of the will and the objective, practical possibilities of situated agency. Hence, the will retains its inalienable freedom as a *formal* property of the self to will, even if not to act, otherwise. Coercion represents a forcible *removal* of will from action through which one is forced to act *against* one's will. That signifies for Pelagius that coerced will plays no active part in what happens: will is present here only as inactive, formal capacity. And, because what happens can be explained without reference to the coerced will's activity, this is not, for Pelagius, a culpable act *of the person*.

Pelagius believed that the circumstances in which we are coerced and so genuinely victims are few and that these are marked by an absence of effective willing. Whilst people often speak of the *force* of habit or social convention in a way calculated to relieve them of responsibility for their actions, Pelagius was clear that habit and convention are not instances of coercion. He did allow, however, that will may be 'bent' in practice by their powerful attraction. Even so, he held that habit and custom do not internally bind the will. For they represent nothing more than the constellation of one's own and others' acts (in the form of social expectations and normative patterns of behaviour); they have no substantial reality.[4] And in relation to acts, even one's own acts, Pelagius believed the will to be external and to be related one-directionally. Will stands as the external cause of action, that self-movement which converts potential into kinetic energy, possibility into

---

4. Will, as an aspect of human nature, in Pelagius' metaphysics, was substance; acts were not. Hence the latter, having no substantial reality, could not affect the former. See Augustine, *On Nature and Grace*, 21.

actuality, but which itself is constituted in the sphere, not of action, but of pure possibility.[5] Acts and their consequences do not then rebound back on to will. Will remains suspended in perpetual neutrality and independence, a pure organ of choice, unaffected by any acts, whether good or bad, since will properly remains in the pure and neutral realm of possibility. There is no organic connection between a person's history of willing and acting and the present moment of decision – otherwise how could will ever be really free? Since Pelagius construes the will's freedom in terms of the capacity for self-motivation and movement in the moment of decision, he has to secure its independence and neutrality in relation, not only to everything external, but also to everything past – including its own past decisions and actions which are treated as effectively external to the self.[6] Consequently, the person is declared always to stand in a situation of free choice, of being able to will to do otherwise. And that applies, in Pelagius' view, even in situations where we so surrender our will to habit or convention that our action is unreflective and we are without consciousness of our freedom, of our will's transcendence of social and psychological conditioning factors. Hence, we *can* always will otherwise than our habits or social convention require. And because we can will otherwise, we are culpable for our failures so to do. Furthermore, since habit and convention are not regarded as forms of coercion, we can also always *do* otherwise and so are culpable also for failing to stand against their pressure towards sinful action.

5. Pelagius operated a threefold scheme of *posse* (natural, inalienable potentiality for alternative possibility), *velle* (will) and *esse* (actualisation). (See Augustine, *On the Grace of Christ*, 4, 5.) His affirmation of the goodness of the will relates to it as an organ of formal choice, of pure potentiality, equally disposed towards good and bad – so that our choice for either may be characterised as free, as our own. And so the will as such, this formal capacity, is always God's good gift. Active willing, however, he took to be a quite different matter, potentially either good or bad. Such a distinction between formal capacity and its actualisation is necessary if God (the gracious giver of the capacity) is not to be held accountable for the use to which the capacity is put. Even for Pelagius, freedom of the will is teleological, and so God shares responsibility for its good but not for its evil use. But it is so in intention only. God *intends* us to use this gift in an orientation towards the good. Yet such an orientation cannot be built into the structure of will without destroying its necessary freedom. So the freedom of the will for Pelagius remains a form of neutrality in relation to good as well as bad.

6. Hence, both individual sins and individual sinners are atomised by Pelagius. He saves the freedom of the will at the cost of being able to say that the will is in any sense *personal*. Salvation must consequently be worked out also at this atomic level – through individual illumination of the intellect by the scriptures and through imitation of Christ's good example, rather than through some organic healing of 'the human condition' which has fallen into distortion. That has too much of the ring of substance about it for Pelagius. On imitation as the means to salvation, see his *Commentaries* on Rom. 3:21, 5:16–19, 6:14, 8:10; Col. 2:6, 15; 1 Cor. 1:18ff. and Augustine, *On Original Sin*, 30; Augustine, *On the Grace of Christ*, 4, 5; 7f.; 39, 43.

It follows from his view of the will that Pelagius thought of sin exclusively in axiological terms. The will itself cannot be sinful, since it is a purely formal and neutral *capacity* to orient oneself in action through free choice.[7] It is only free *acts* of the will (or acts which one *could have* willed otherwise), and not the will itself which may be subject to moral evaluation. And since Pelagius' is a moralistic understanding of sin, it is only free acts which he termed sinful.[8] Moreover, his supposition that will is always free in relation to its history and situatedness renders it unintelligible to speak of the inheritance of either as sin; to speak, that is, of sin in terms of a *state* internally or externally pre-conditioning or binding will. On the contrary, the will is claimed to be always free to will and do otherwise, save in those instances where coercion has rendered it inoperative.

Put those two affirmations together and we find Pelagius affirming that it is always possible (though it may be extremely difficult) to avoid sinning; we are inherently capable of willing and doing the good and so are culpable for all failure so to do.[9] All that is needed to recall us from habitual sinning is a clear intimation and reminder of virtue. Once we know and see clearly what is right, we can freely choose and pursue it. Intellect and will remain unsullied in their capacity to discern, judge and motivate; their inherent capacity for recognition of the good remains intact. And once we have identified and willed the good, we are, according to Pelagius, intrinsically capable of doing it. Since, however, Pelagius wishes to maintain that all choices are made freely by a will neutral in relation to good and evil, he has also to maintain that we are intrinsically capable of rejecting the good. In practice, however, he believes that the will – as a rational faculty – always chooses the good when it sees it clearly (which begs many questions concerning the metaphysics of the good). Yet, he must maintain that the will holds the *capacity* to will counter-rationally if, in his terms, choosing the good is to be free. And so we can see that, in practice, the primary cause of sin will be a clouding of the intellect by habit and convention. That clouding represents an external impediment to

[Margin note: Socratic understanding of the will's relation to the Good]

---

7. Pelagius deems it good, but that is not, in fact, a moral judgment. For the will cannot, strictly, be morally good or bad. In his interpretation it is morally neutral, the precondition of free action – whether good or evil – and therefore the basis of acts which, because free, may be subjected to moral evaluation. When Pelagius acclaims will's goodness, he is making a theological affirmation of the inherent goodness of an aspect of God's creation, alongside a philosophical affirmation that the capacity for free (moral) action is good, although some free acts will prove to be morally bad.

8. Augustine, *On Nature and Grace*, 34.

9. Augustine, *On Man's Perfection in Righteousness*, 2.

active willing, not an internal incapacitation of the will as an organ of free choice (it is cloud not cataract). And because the will is untarnished, we retain culpability for adopting habitual and conventional modes of behaviour. For, were we sufficiently attentive to nature and revelation, we would see through the fog and should know, in any case, that – since will is always free – there is always choice. Hence we could, should – and therefore, in a sense, do – make a choice to walk in the established psychological and social furrows of custom or not. It is on account of an unused capacity to will the opposite that Pelagius deems all uncoerced action, whether good or bad, habitual or consciously willed, to be free.

So far as Pelagius was concerned, then, willing is co-extensive with the capacity to make choices that are free of any motivational compulsion (whether internal or external). Such freedom he considered inalienable, surviving as formal capacity even in situations of coercion. Coercion he holds applies to action, not to willing. Whilst we might be compelled to do something, we retain a capacity to *will* freely in relation to (against) whatever force we find ourselves powerless to *act* against. Pelagius assumes that, however potent a force may be in relation to our action, it is impotent in relation to willing. We carry on making choices, desiring and willing unfettered and uninfluenced by our coercion. Outward action may be compelled, but not the internal structures and dynamics of intentionality which lie behind it. For will, on Pelagius' account, always remains a pure, self-motivating organ of free choice. Consequently, we are always responsible for our willing. Willing implies moral culpability. Naturally, that culpability extends to all action in which will is embedded, where we could have willed *and acted* differently (i.e., all action with the exception of coercion). And it is these acts, and these acts alone, which are regarded by Pelagius as sin.

I think it immediately obvious that the Pelagian understanding of willing fares ill when tested against the concrete demands of the pathologies described earlier. Not only is there a Pelagian blind-spot regarding the reality and significance of victims' willing; perpetrators' willing cannot be reduced to the making of action-guiding, atomised decisions. The relation between action and will, as between internal and external more generally, is a deal more complex than Pelagius permits. In particular, the concrete pathologies suggest strongly that willing does not enjoy the kind of freedom Pelagius assumes, but is entwined with relational, social and structural processes and dynamics that have the power to shape identity, interiority and life-intentionality and to confuse the internal mechanisms and criteria by which decisions are made.

The bones of Augustine's contention

The most significant source of Augustine's contention with Pelagius' understanding of sin is its conflict with Paul's theology of grace (as interpreted by Augustine). Whilst it may be going too far to claim that Augustine's doctrine of sin is secondary, *derived* from his primary doctrine of grace, it is undoubtedly the case that grace is the context without which his understanding of sin (and, indeed, of willing) is unintelligible. Sin and grace are reciprocally interpreting co-ordinates in his theology. Hence, Augustine's criticisms of Pelagius for according too prominent and decisive a role to human agency in relation to sin may only be understood in the context of, and co-ordinated with, the role he assigns to it in relation to grace. Pelagius understood the freedom of the will as its capacity always to motivate itself to do otherwise; in particular, to counter and resist any external direction. In that way, Pelagius defends faith as a free act of the will. Augustine finds such a view unacceptable because it makes the faith through which we are saved a human act and achievement and does scant justice to the view of the human situation implied by the Christian proclamation of salvation. If our salvation is wrought through a radical self-sacrifice on God's part, then grace acts on the human condition from without (it is not then a natural property). In so acting, it does more than illuminate the good so we may subsequently, on our own resources, freely recognise and will it (or not). Augustine held that the means of our salvation imply a radical distortion in our being, not only in our acting, and that perfection also requires and entails something more than a self-modification in our acting: we cannot save ourselves.

This, for Augustine, was not merely a matter of abstract, systematic theological speculation. It was also the Christian's concrete *experience* of grace, conversion and resistance[10] which showed Pelagius' simple psychology of the will (supposing unity between knowing, willing, desiring and acting) to be inadequate to the existential realities of living humanly before an apprehension of the good and under the impact of grace. Augustine knew that willing, desiring and knowing were not always unified in practice. One could know the good, will it even, and yet find one's active willing still in the grip of alternative desires and attractions.[11]

---

10. Testified by Paul, recounted by Augustine in his *Confessions*, as well as a matter of his frequent pastoral observation.
11. This intimation lies behind Augustine's prayer asking God to 'give what you command and command what you will' (*Confessions*, X, xxix, 40 – cf. *On the Spirit and the Letter*, 22; *On the Merits and Forgiveness of Sins*, 5; *On the Baptism of Infants*, 5), which Pelagius explicitly abjured (Augustine, *On the Gift of Perseverance*, 53).

Pelagius' affirmation of the will's potency in relation to sin and evil was not primarily descriptive, but prescriptive: a call to take responsibility for one's own salvation instead of hiding behind the excuse that sin was unavoidable or relying on God's justification regardless of one's sins.[12] Since Augustine was sure that the will was impotent on its own to pursue the good, he was bound to consider that call dangerous – not because it threatened some speculative doctrinal system, but because it struck at the very core of the lived reality of a Christian life of confession, forgiveness and praise. In acting on the illusory assumption that sin has no real, conditioning power over us in reality, that we remain free in relation to it, we lend sin even more power and embed it all the more deeply. In a situation in which, Augustine is convinced, we cannot be our own help, Pelagius would have us enact a form of self-enclosure, leaving us solely reliant on our own impotent and distorted capacities. This false assumption of power in relation to sin and salvation actually serves to bend and direct all human energies back into the situation of sin, intensifying its pathological dynamic and its hold on people, whilst blocking us off from the real, transcendent energies and resources for transformation.[13] Trusting in the potentialities and capacities immanent to human beings, Augustine maintained, could only intensify the dynamic of self-enclosure and reliance that, for him, is a mark of sin.

In accounting for our lack of freedom regarding sin, Augustine puts forward an explanation of the relation between the will and action that diverges markedly from that offered by Pelagius. Significantly, this depends upon a distinction between the freedom of the will as an organ of choice and active and concrete willing. Such distinction allows for the phenomenon of the apparently divided or weak will.[14] As I have already

12. Augustine, *On Nature and Grace*, 1.
13. External illumination will prove entirely inadequate to break the power of sin and realise the active possibility of not sinning, since it does not remove the internal impediment disorienting the person's basic structure of intentionality. Therefore, Augustine insisted that external illumination cannot effect the necessary reorientation in our action because it does nothing to reshape or reorient the structure of intentionality. Indeed, revelation illuminates not only the good which is demanded from us, but our failure and inability to achieve it in our own power (see, e.g., *On Nature and Grace*, 13, *On the Proceedings of Pelagius*, 7–9). Consequently, as we shall see, Augustine finds that internal spiritual assistance from an external source of power is what is needed: an energising and reorienting communication of new potentiality, restructuring intentionality. Being dead to sin, we need assistance from an external energy source: the life-giving Spirit (*On Nature and Grace*, 25, 39, 62; *On the Baptism of Infants*, 5).
14. *Confessions*, VIII,v,10, VIII,ix,21, VIII,x,22; VIII,x,24. See further T. D. J. Chappell, *Aristotle and Augustine on Freedom: Two Theories of Freedom, Voluntary Action and Akrasia* (London: Macmillan, 1995).

suggested, Augustine's construal of will and willing as they relate to sin must be correlated with his discussion of their role in relation to grace. For it is his account of the role and place of human freedom in responding to grace which engendered his insight into their role and function in relation to sin.

The graced and the good will

On Pelagius' account, faith is a free act of the will because the will could choose not to be motivated by the good, which grace illuminates. That is to say, we appropriate grace by exercising a free choice from a position of neutrality outside the sphere of its influence. Our freedom consists therefore in the will's independent autonomy and neutrality in relation to God's movement towards us; its capacity to choose its own motives (in effect, to be self-motivating and moving) rather than be pulled into movement by the attraction of the good. Modern moralistic sympathies tend to be naturally attracted towards such a view of freedom as inalienable power to counter and to will arbitrarily. Indeed, there is a widespread assumption that human and divine freedom and power are competitive: either we are free to resist God or God is free to overcome our resistance.[15] And so modern sensibilities (tutored in the notion of freedom as indivisible, unshareable, absolute autonomy) tend to share Pelagian wariness when encountering Augustine's affirmation of God's sovereignty over creation, especially where that appears to include the power to counter the misuse of human freedom. When Augustine declares that faith is an act made possible only by God's active intervention in the self, that is taken by the wary as an indication that faith is considered by him to be, not so much an autonomous act of the person as an effect of God's coercive grace which suppresses human autonomy.

Augustine's preferred way of speaking of faith was as gift, since he was certain that its achievement lay beyond the unaided, natural powers of the will. Faith requires a prior conditionality, the *spirit* of faith, which is a consequence of the Spirit's working within individual structures of intentionality, revivifying and reorienting them.[16] That gift of grace enables all good works, including faith; without it, Augustine declares, it

---

15. On this point see further my 'Sins of Praise: The Assault on God's Freedom', in Colin E. Gunton, ed., *God and Freedom: Essays in Historical and Systematic Theology* (Edinburgh: T. & T. Clark, 1995), pp. 32–56.   16. See e.g., *On Grace and Free Will*, 43.

is impossible for us to will, much less to do, the good.[17] The Spirit does not illuminate the good so that we may then decide whether to pursue it from a position of neutrality; rather, the Spirit instils love of God and therefore of the good. This makes the will good.[18] That is to say, the will is reoriented *internally*; is internally motivated and attracted to pursue and choose the good. A good will cannot be neutral in relation to God and the good, but is drawn and draws itself towards them. It is unthinkable, so far as Augustine is concerned, that a good will should choose otherwise. A good will of necessity loves God and always chooses the good. But a will is not good in and of itself any more than it does the good exclusively in its own power; it is, rather, *made good* by the action of the Holy Spirit. That is to say, it is not good because, as it happens, it manages to draw and direct itself towards the good. It is first made good by the Spirit, by which Augustine means that the Spirit indwells and excites the will into a new orientation through which it may – no, must – draw and direct itself towards God. And yet Augustine maintains that this goodness which results from the Spirit's action really is the will's own goodness and the resultant action also belongs to the will as its own. Although will's independent and unaided power is insufficient to do and will the good, the action of the Spirit empowers and reorients the will so that subsequent willing and acting do not happen without the will's own (aided) power and active engagement. The power of an individual will is a necessary but insufficient condition for good willing and action.[19]

Free will saved, but the person dies

None of this makes much sense from a Pelagian perspective. Pelagius thought that the goodness of the will was inherent by virtue of being a gift of God in our creaturely nature, that aspect of our creatureliness

17. See *ibid.*, 1, 13; *On Nature and Grace*, 62; *On the Spirit and the Letter*, 52; *On the Baptism of Infants*, 28; *On Rebuke and Grace*, 2; drawing on the scriptural authority of, e.g., Rom. 8:26, 12:3; 14:23. Because the Pelagian critique of Augustine's theology of grace suggested that it was amoral, he is careful in his anti-Pelagian writings to be clear that faith has consequences for action, but clear also that the freedom of love distinguishes faith from legalism. Love is free in relation to the Law, both because it might sometimes have to refuse Law's obligations, but also because, where its obligations are met, they are so out of the free desire to do God's will, not out of fear of punishment. Furthermore, without the graced spirit of love, fulfilling the Law leads easily to self-righteousness and pride, in the belief that one acts in one's own unaided power. See, e.g., *On the Spirit and the Letter*, 36 and cf. with the freedom of love described in ibid., 5; *On Nature and Grace*, 67, 83, 84.
18. *On the Grace of Christ*, 19–22; *On the Spirit and the Letter*, 52; *On Grace and Free Will*, 1; *On the Baptism of Infants*, 28.   19. *On the Baptism of Infants*, 6; *On Grace and Free Will*, 7, 10.

which enabled freedom – defined as independent, autonomous, self-reliant action – and hence moral and spiritual life. Augustine appeared to make its goodness dependent on its good *use*. Does that not deny the *inherent* goodness of God's creation in a way that echoes Augustine's Manichee past?

Augustine would, in fact, concur with Pelagius' affirmation of the *ontological* goodness of the will. It is, however, will as *activity*, the phenomenon of *willing*, rather than will as bare, formal capacity, which principally occupies Augustine's attention. Evidently, the question of whether active willing is good cannot be answered by reference to the ontological goodness of the organ responsible for it. It is not an *ontological* but a *spiritual* question (since, as we shall see, it relates to the orientation of a person's spirit, which is a better category than, say, the moral). Augustine's concern in this matter with the ontological is derivative (it provides a way of accounting for the phenomenon of willing). Hence, it is the goodness or otherwise of *active* willing, not the possession of the gift of arbitrary choice, which shows whether or not a will is in fact good in any meaningful, concrete sense.[20]

The ontological and the active, spiritual goodness of the will are distinct issues. So far as Augustine was concerned, the Pelagian inability to honour that distinction rendered the active, conscious choosing of sin and evil by a supposedly free will unintelligible and descriptively incoherent (whilst it simultaneously excluded the concept of involuntary sin). But is that not the pot calling the kettle black? For Pelagius was himself convinced that it was Augustine who was incoherent in speaking (in his account of sin as well as that of faith) of necessity and freedom together. For where one is unable to choose otherwise, how can there be freedom; how, indeed, can Augustine speak of will?

In trying to sort out who might be pot and who kettle here, we are close to the conceptual heart of their disagreement. Augustine's holding together of will and necessity appears oxymoronic to Pelagius – obviously

> Pel. the incompat.
> Aug. the compat.

20. Because of his conflation of the ontological and the ethical, of the capacity to choose and actively choosing, Augustine maintains that Pelagius has insufficient basis to distinguish between the role of God's good grace in good and bad acts (as well as insufficient basis for establishing a distinction between them). For if God's gracious gift (the pure potentiality and potency of the will) is held to be the single root equally of good and evil action, how may Pelagius avoid blaming God for evil acts? (See *On the Grace of Christ*, 17; cf. *On the Proceedings of Pelagius*, 5.) Augustine proposes instead that the roots of good and evil action are two: attraction or orientation towards good and evil (*On the Grace of Christ*, 19; *Confessions*, X,iv,5), the one caused by God (*Confessions*, II,vii,15); the other originating from human causation – the sin of Adam reconfirmed in subsequent sinning (*On Grace and Free Will*, 6–9, 31f.; *On the Grace of Christ*, 21; *On Rebuke and Grace*, 3).

enough – because for him freedom approximates to absolute non-determination. But, as I have in fact already intimated, this implies a separation of the will from all other aspects of the person. If will is to be free to make neutral choices, then it must be unconstrained, undetermined and unmotivated by internal as well as external forces. It must supply its own, internal dynamic, not be 'excited' by dynamics lying outside the domain of will (whether they belong to other aspects of the person such as the mind, or to social context). Hence, any choice the will makes is free because it always stands outside of and apart from any external motivating factors. Pelagius suspends the will in perpetual neutrality in order to ensure that it may find and choose its own motives (to Pelagius, freedom) rather than be drawn into movement by forces of attraction greater than itself (to Pelagius, coercion). Hence he atomises will, separates it out from the person's structure of intentionality and motivational complex, as well as from determining aspects of her environment. Will, on this account, has no structure, no substance; it is pure, formal capacity. Consequently, it is incapable of being shaped in its operation by anything else. But then it is hard to see it as a specific person's will; hard therefore to understand its choices or its actions as in any way of the person. For every choice made in the will's absolute freedom is ultimately disconnected from any motive, desire or intention of the person whose will it is.[21] Will's freedom is attributed, in effect, to its arbitrariness, its incapacity to be reduced to anything to do with the person or her situation. And that is why Augustine was correct to deem this an account which renders willing unintelligible as an act of the person. For, in the end, a Pelagian account of willing saves the freedom of the will but loses the person. Any notion of rationality and continuity in the structure and history of personal identity is jettisoned. That is somewhat ironic. For Pelagians were, after all, attempting to establish the relationship between person and act against Augustine's apparent determinism by emphasising the agent's freedom of will in acting. Unfortunately, in the final analysis, free agency is attributed not to the person as such but to the atomic will, stripped quite bare of any aspect of personal identity which would restrict its freedom.

Does K's noumenal willing help us out at all?

21. Pelagius does allow that will may be informed by desire, but is adamant that it cannot be reducible to desire. For will preserves unto itself the capacity to choose contrarily. Hence, even where will chooses that which accords with desire, it acts on its own, independent 'motives' (which can really be nothing more than arbitrary choice). It is this independent, self-motivation of will which makes willing unintelligible as an act of the person – even to herself. This point is made well by James Wetzel, *Augustine and the Limits of Virtue* (Cambridge: Cambridge University Press, 1992), pp. 8, 231.

Integrated willing

It is from the perspective of the Pelagian account of the atomic will, disconnected from all else so that it stands in a neutral and external relationship to motivational factors and objects of choice, that will and necessity appear oxymoronic when conjoined. When Augustine puts them together, he is drawing on what might be termed an organic understanding of willing, one in which will is not a discrete organism. Rather, it subsists in integrated relationship with the orientation and disposition of the willing *agent*, the whole of a person's active intentionality. Whenever we make choices or act, Augustine maintained, we do so under some representation of the good. The good here stands for our basic decision, underlying and motivating other choices, concerning the ultimate values which we orient ourselves towards. That is to say, we will that which is congruent with what we value in our lives. Were we consciously to will that which opposes that representation of the good, then our action would be unintelligible because irrational. We may be mistaken about the good or may have a restricted conception of it. Augustine's point is that will is free when it accords with the motivation and desire to pursue this representation of the good. Although Augustine thought the capacity freely to choose inadequate as a total and defining conception of freedom, he also considered Pelagius to have misconstrued even this: our freedom to choose did not consist in our capacity to be arbitrary and unconstrained in willing and acting, but in the ability to act on desire.

For Augustine, will enjoys a neutrality of independence neither from the desires of the agent nor from the attractive power of the good; hence neither is it arbitrarily self-motivating and self-moving. It is always 'in gear', as it were, already oriented towards the good which forms the basis of a person's structure of intentionality and motivation. Will is organically connected to desire, to the affections.[22] It is not self-motivating, but drawn towards that identified as the good; or, rather, it is not only drawn by the attractive power of the represented good, but pushed towards it by the internal dynamic of intentionality in the mode of desire. In the case of faith, as we have seen, grace transforms the representation of the good, both internally and externally. God's grace both sets one before an appropriate[23] representation of that which is absolutely good – indeed, the

22. See, e.g., *On the Baptism of Infants*, 30.
23. I.e., the call is congruent with the person. See *On Nature and Grace*, 20, 36; *On Grace and Free Will*, 28, 31.

source of all other goods – and instils the corresponding internal motivation or desire – which Augustine identifies as the spirit of love.

If the person's internal orientation towards some good directs will, if will is inseparable from desire, then in what sense is the will engaged in choosing and in what sense might it be said to be free? If we simply act out our representation of the good, then does not will do little more than rubber-stamp desire? Is it meaningful to ascribe any role to will, or even to speak of will at all, if will cannot choose to act contrary to desire? What is willing if it is not the capacity freely and arbitrarily to choose? Moreover, with the loss of a conception of the will's freedom and potency in directing and deciding action, has Augustine not also lost the means to characterise action as genuinely *personal*, as involving the free decision of the self rather than the tug of nature – that which we cannot avoid desiring?

Compelled willing

Augustine, however, conceives of faith, not as a form of spiritual determinism, but as consent.[24] Faith is the act by which the will conforms itself to the good which knowledge of God sets before it, a love for this good being instilled by the Spirit. Under the impact of grace, the will acts under a kind of compulsion. Notwithstanding that, however, Augustine maintained that consent *is* a form of willing and therefore an act of the person, an exercise of personal power.[25] Faith is an act of will, is my act, even though the experience of being under grace compels my willing. How can that be? What underlies Augustine's entire conception of willing and acting is a redefinition of what it means for action to be voluntary, for a person to be acting under his own power. This moves away from the assumption that the power arbitrarily to choose or to counter is constitutive of personal power or of willing. It is this redefinition which permits Augustine to maintain that action may simultaneously be compelled and willed.

Alongside the redefinition of voluntary action, we find a precise definition of compulsion which helps us on our way to understanding what Augustine means by voluntary action. Augustine drew an explicit distinction between what he meant by compulsion and the interplay of forces between physical objects, for which he reserved the term 'force'.[26]

24. *On the Spirit and the Letter*, 31, 54.
25. Ibid., 34, 52; *On Grace and Free Will*, 1; *On the Baptism of Infants*, 28.
26. Where the significance of this distinction is missed, Augustine's insistence on the voluntary character of sin is sure to be taken to mean that he holds sin to be a moral category, dependent on free will by which one exercises power and control over oneself.

Therefore Augustine did not mean by the compulsion of grace (or, inde
of sin) something analogous to an irresistible, physical force meeting a
moveable object. There may well be circumstances in which action is
forced in that sense, in which the power of personal agency is entirely lost,
where the human being is no longer a person in interaction but a physical
object. But here it is *action* rather than *will* which is forced, and it is precisely the removal of the will from one's action which constitutes the act as
forced. Forced action, by this definition, is action *without will*.[27] All other
action, where the person is not reduced to a physical object in interaction,
Augustine deemed voluntary: action is voluntary whenever we act as
more than physical objects.[28] Voluntariness is not, then, coincident with
availability of choice.

Indeed, as Augustine pointed out, we are more used to working with a
sense of the possible coincidence of the voluntary and the necessary than
we might at first be ready to accept. We do so, in fact, whenever we speak
of a unitary orientation applying either to specific individuals or to
human beings as such. To take the latter case, it might be held that
seeking happiness (however defined) is a part of the human condition. By
this we would mean that we cannot but be motivated by that which we
deem to lead to what we define as happiness. Here there is no choice. Our
intentionality, it is claimed, is so oriented towards happiness that it
cannot be drawn towards anything else (which is not to say that we are
always successful in willing or competent in identifying our happiness).
We are so single-minded that unhappiness, for example, would not motivate us. That is because our will does not stand outside of, but inside, our
intentional orientation. Nevertheless, we would find it odd to hold that
we are *forced* to pursue happiness, that we pursue it without will, whilst
we accept that our natures compel us so to do. On the contrary, the total
disposition and orientation of all our desires, and so of all our personal
energy of willing, extend themselves to the pursuit of that which makes
us happy. Hence will is here engaged precisely where there is no choice. In
short, Augustine's claim is that we do not suppose there to be an absence
of willing to be happy when we suppose it to be a part of our human condition to be unable to will otherwise.[29]

It is significant in this regard that Augustine uses the language of love
to characterise the life of faith in response to grace. That too evokes a

See, e.g., William S. Babcock, 'Augustine on Sin and Moral Agency', *Journal of Religious Ethics*, 16 (1988), 32f., 37ff.   27. *On the Spirit and the Letter*, 31.
28. *On the Spirit and the Letter*, 31.   29. *On Nature and Grace*, 54.

worship

single-mindedness of devotion to its object which is at one and the same time an experience of the total engagement of will combined with absence of choice, of compulsion in which alternatives do not motivate. So will is here much more than the capacity to make choices. It is the addition of the personal energy of willing to the dynamic of life-intentionality. Here we begin to glimpse that this addition of personal energy which consents under the condition of compulsion might be more than an inconsequential moment wherein the will accepts its fate, that rubber stamp on desire which makes no difference because the power of choosing from outside the compelled motivation, the power to resist, is denied it. We begin to glimpse that willing might be characterised in terms of the addition of personal energy,[30] and so the intensification of the dynamic which compels willing. Willing is neither neutral nor inconsequential, even in its bondage.

There is another category of action which is characterised, according to Augustine, by a coincidence of will and compulsion, voluntariness and necessity: situations in which we may be said to act *un*willingly, where we are compelled to do that which we would not do. These situations provide further evidence for and help to clarify Augustine's understanding of the nature of willing, both in relation to faith and more generally.

Augustine contends that what we do unwillingly, we yet do voluntarily – that is, by means of willing. 'Unwilling' denotes to Augustine, not *absence* of will, as if it were a synonym for 'involuntary', but a *division* of will, a situation wherein we are compelled to will against our will.[31] A situation of compulsion is one in which the possible courses of action are constrained against our favour. But, Augustine argues, insofar as we act at all in such a situation, we exercise will and, insofar as that will effects an act, our willing is potent – constrained in its potency, but effective nonetheless.[32] Whenever we *do*, we will, we have personal power. And that holds true even though our power might be only sufficient to perform this one act and no other – where we have no choice as to action.

Here we see the genius of his distinction between force and compulsion. When we are forced to act, we are subjected to an external power, applied on us as objects. Force brushes will aside and renders it effectively inoperative. When a person much superior in physical strength holds a gun in another's hand, aims it and presses the latter's finger so that it squeezes the trigger and the gun fires, that is *forced* action. There is no

30. So is I think the clear implication of *Against Two Letters of the Pelagians*, I, 5.
31. *Confessions*, VIII,v,10f.   32. *On the Spirit and the Letter*, 31.

sense in which it is the forced person's act, since her will is not engaged but sidestepped or overcome by superior physical force.

Compulsion, on the other hand, does not overcome, but directs, constrains and utilises will. Far from rendering will inoperative, compulsion engages will. Here the power which compels operates internally as well as externally; it engages internal motivations and the structure of intentionality in willing whilst constricting the range of possible actions. Under compulsion, we find ourselves in a situation where none of the possible alternatives of action is what we would choose, were we free of situational constraints. None of them, in other words, conform to that representation of the good under which we would act. Although we do not have sufficient power to escape these constraints on action, we do stand before at least one possible course of action. To say that action is possible is to say that we are more than physical objects, is to say that we do possess *some* personal power.

An example parallel to that used to illustrate force might run thus: a person gives a gun to another whilst holding him and his family hostage. He is then told that, unless he shoots a third party, he and his family will be murdered. Let us assume that all alternative possibilities (such as shooting the hostage-taker) have been successfully countered by his foresight and planning in bringing several armed associates with him. The victim can take no course of action – even inaction – which will not result in the death of himself and his family, except the murder of the third party.

In such a situation, there is what might be characterised as a division of will – between, on the one hand, the desire to avoid murder (since it does not correspond well with the representation of the good under which he would act which normally excludes murder) and the desire to avoid his own death and that of his family. Compulsion, in other words, may initiate a conflict in the desires and orientation of the self, between the good which one would will and act upon in the absence of constraints such as murderous hostage-takers and the constrained good which is attainable by acting in a situation controlled by them. Strictly speaking, it is not the external power of the hostage-taker that compels the victim's will, but the hostage's desire to save the lives of those he loves. The criminal's power over the hostage is exerted through threat rather than direct force, and threats engage the victim's willing and intentionality even whilst denying them completely free play. Therefore, when he shoots the third party, he is acting on desire; he is willing unwillingly or against himself.

It is a voluntary action, compelled rather than forced, since it represents an enactment of his willing under these constraints which force a rearrangement or a realisation of the hierarchy of desires as a basis for possible action. 'Compelled action . . . counts as "voluntary" . . . because all forms of compulsion . . . originate from within. They may be occasioned externally by the threat of an outside power, but compulsions always have their immediate source in the conflicting desires of the agent.'[33] Thus can one find oneself compelled to do (acting voluntarily) what one would have avoided (whilst acting unwillingly); can find one's willing caught up in an orientation which one would not choose but to which one is compelled to add one's personal energies of willing.

Faith is unlike the above example only in that its compulsion is not unwilling but consensual (on account of the spirit of love instilled by the Holy Spirit). In place of the restriction of choice through circumstances, in faith choice is restricted in the will's single-minded devotion which disempowers the power of competing attractions to motivate. In faith, there is conformity between will and compelled desire. For there is no place outside of this orientation towards God and the good on which the will can stand to survey competing possibilities. In faith, the will is compelled but, claims Augustine, it is also free. Indeed, it is free precisely because it is compelled in movement towards God and the good. Freedom is here defined as freedom to do and will the good. Furthermore, since that freedom is enabled only by grace, that is to say that genuine freedom may not be defined apart from grace. We may not first develop an abstract and independent notion of freedom and then ask whether it may be correlated with grace. In faith, we find that freedom is not only actually but also epistemologically unavailable, and so unintelligible, without grace.[34]

True freedom

The supposed freedom to make choices in some neutral sphere outside that of God's saving grace, the freedom to withhold oneself from God if one chooses, is not true freedom of will. It is rather the will's bondage to sin, claims Augustine. How are we to understand this?

33. Wetzel, *Augustine and the Limits of Virtue*, p. 205, who helpfully illustrates this point with an Augustinian reading of Aristotle's conundrum concerning the captain of a ship facing a storm at sea in *Nicomachean Ethics*, 3.1.
34. So Wetzel, *Augustine and the Limits of Virtue*, p. 216.

First, let us consider someone choosing God and the good on the basis of an autonomous willing. Here the basis of the will's consent is its own, independent decision and judgment which could, at least in principle, be withdrawn in resistance. Augustine judges this confidence in the will's ability on its own resources to be able to discern the good, outside of God's grace, both ill-founded and dangerous. Far from an unreserved orientation towards God and that which is genuinely good, this represents a form of reservation in relation to God. The will is withheld so that it may make its own decision about God and what is good. But what informs the will's discernment of the good? Where can it obtain its standards and criteria of judgment in this position of neutrality and equilibrium? Only from itself. And so the Pelagian conception of free will has, in the end, to assert that appropriate standards of judgment as to the goodness of all possible objects of willing (including God) towards which it might orient itself are somehow resident in the will's equilibrial state, but without their motivating and exciting it into movement. Hence, this reservation over against God represents what for Augustine is the most dangerous form of sin, pride, with its concomitant optimism that sin has not effected a radical distortion in one's capacities for discerning and judging the good. For in the Pelagian view we hold ourselves to be capable of adequately representing the good and then both choosing and doing it out of our own unconstrained freedom.

In Augustine's view, the will's freedom consists, not in making autonomous choices (even when they may happen to coincide with the good), but in being so related to the source of goodness that one is motivated permanently, unavoidably and indivisibly in active devotion to it. Thus, he is able to proclaim it a great freedom, indeed, to be able to sin, yet an even greater one to be unable to sin (*non posse peccare*).[35] The Pelagian refusal to bind the will to the good in order to secure the will's freedom from any form of constraint, Augustine maintained, only succeeded in binding it to sin by requiring it to act under an inadequate representation of the good. It is not just that God would Godself be judged according to this independently derived and neutral criterion of goodness. Since God is the source of all goodness (i.e., things are good only in and through their relation to God), an independent representation of the good must perforce be misleading, inadequate and distorted. A genuine and full discernment of goodness cannot be derived independently of God. Even without the deleterious

---

35. *The City of God*, xxii, 30.

effects of original sin on intentionality, then, Augustine views the Pelagian conception of free will as a will freed from the good and so freed for sin – a will which is bound to act on an inadequate, partial and distorted representation of the good. And we cannot in any meaningful sense of the word be deemed to be free to will the good where our concrete willing is constantly misdirected by our misconstrual of what counts as good and why; where there is a mismatch between intention and achievement which we are not able to comprehend and correct from this perspective. Such a will cannot be free because it cannot bring about what it desires and, because it stands mistaken concerning the nature and identification of goodness, it cannot rationally motivate itself. In action, it suffers a disintegration of volition and desire because it ascribes value on a basis that does not correspond to the order and source of goodness in reality. Hence such desires must be deemed disordered and disintegrated, incoherent and unintelligible.

Conversely, a will which is compelled by its orientation towards God and thereby to that which is really good in the world enjoys the integration of volition and desire.[36] For the order of its willing is patterned by the true order of reality in its relation to God. A free will is hence also a rational one: one corresponding to the objective, rational order. A will disintegrated in respect both of subjective and objective order cannot be free.

The freedom enjoyed by the will compelled towards God is much more full and rich than may adequately be expressed in rational categories alone. Freedom, according to Augustine, is unlimited and unimaginable delight and joy in God – the fullness of life.[37] And it is precisely this freedom of joy in God, enabled – or, better, compelled – by grace, this fullness of life wherein desire and willing are drawn into conformity with the proper order of goodness, which is denied the will that maintains its supposed freedom in separate, independence from God. Hence such a will cannot be truly free, cannot sustain itself in the proper economy of goodness, because its motivations are not based on the true source of goodness. At best, it is sure to be disoriented in relation to the good. Even if it is not mistaken altogether about what is good it will, being mistaken as to the source of goodness, fail to co-ordinate it in a properly ordered way with all other goods, instead seeing these as good in themselves and to be desired without limit. Even when it seeks the good it finds itself oriented

---

36. Wetzel puts it this way in *Augustine and the Limits of Virtue*, p. 223.
37. *On Nature and Grace*, 67, 83, 84; *On the Spirit and the Letter*, 5, 41; *On Marriage and Concupiscence*, 33; *Against Two Letters of the Pelagians*, I, 5.

against it. That is to say, such a will finds itself adding its personal power of volition to the disorientation and disorderliness of sin: the binding of a will to sin adds to sin's power.

Sin

The foregoing exposition of grace-compelled willing affords a good deal of illumination on Augustine's understanding of sin, particularly the way in which the voluntary and the necessary may be held together. Sinning is, for Augustine, disorder and disorientation in active intentionality. All sins are acts of will. And in Augustine's framework this is an expansive category, including acts which are compelled either through the constraints operating within a situation or on account of a prior disorientation of willing (or, indeed, some co-operation of the two). Augustine's analysis of the compelled will in his discussion of grace shows how it is coherent to claim that willing and necessity may coincide, that unwilling action may yet involve willing. We can see immediately why Augustine does not find it incoherent also to claim that active sinning is a necessity under the conditions of inherited original sin and yet insists on naming such action as sin.

Whilst Augustine held that all sinful acts are willed (by virtue of belonging to the category 'act'), he did not hold them to be sinful *because* they involve will. Sin is coterminous for Augustine with neither act nor will. So far as he is concerned, sin is a category applicable equally to situations, states and conditions as to acts – as, indeed, his employment of the term 'original sin' itself implies.[38] (An occasion where one is forced to act sinfully may therefore be characterised *situationally* as sinful, for example.) Hence when Augustine goes to considerable lengths to show that we act by means of will even when we act by necessity, he is not interested in extending the classification of sins. Not act of will but opposition to God is his criterion of sin, and he is therefore able already to categorise compelled action as sin. His interest here lies in explanation rather than categorisation. Showing that compelled action involves willing, Augustine is able to

---

38. Inheritance of guilt, he maintained, was not an intellectual innovation of speculative doctrinal theology in the construction of a doctrine of original sin, but the received understanding of the Church evidenced by the long-formalised liturgical practice of infant baptism (Pelagius, on the other hand, maintained that infant baptism was for the dedication of children to Christ, not the remission of inherited sin in the form of guilt). Augustine, *On the Merits and Forgiveness of Sins*, 22–4, 35, 39, 55, 64–7; *Sermons*, 165,7; 174; 176,2; 294; *Confessions*, I,xi,18.

arrive at a description of the dynamics of sin that has real explanatory and descriptive power.

By abandoning the fiction that only acts originating within an autonomous and potent will constitute sin (indeed, by abandoning the fiction that the will is ever free in this sense), he shows that sin draws on the will's own, internal power. Even where sinful action originates from elsewhere, as in the case of unwilling sinful action, it compels the will to participate. Through such internal participation, the power of sin is internalised in a way that distorts the internal dynamics which structure intentionality and through which a person orients her life. Thus, for Augustine, an action which does not originate from the will (i.e., does not originate within the structure of intentionality and so does not represent the good towards which the person is internally oriented and drawn) is not one in relation to which the will is neutral and independent. For Augustine will, life-orientation and intentionality do not belong to a sphere independent of one's concretely lived existence. They are rather shaped through a concrete life, including those aspects of life in which one is an unwilling participant. That which originated outside of the will may enter it, altering the structure of intentionality, one's perception of the good and consequently one's internally directed life-orientation. The field of force constituted by the distorted dynamics of sin which surround one and in which one cannot avoid participating disrupts and distorts the internal energies by which one orients and directs one's life from within. So one's own originating action bears the marks of the distortion one was compelled to participate in. Because one becomes bound internally (as well as through future willing and action) to the dynamics of sin even in compelled action, Augustine refuses to speak of those dynamics as external to the self. That is one highly significant reason for his rejection of Pelagian moralism, which held the self to be accountable only for what it originates. Augustine, by contrast, maintained that one is accountable for and is to confess that which has originated externally.

Sin in the inheritance

Augustine shows how the will may be disaffected from the good as a consequence of its 'unwilling' participation in compelled sins. But he also spoke of an inherited corruption of the dynamics of willing: an inherited disorientation, disorder and weakness in willing which renders us incapable in our own power of discerning and pursuing the good unequivocally. This disorientation and distortion is not merely in the external situation, subsequently to be internalised through one's history of willing. It is always already within. In order to make it clear that this distortion is inescapable, always already there, the result of neither personal action nor socialisation, Augustine maintained that it is communicated biologically and received at conception. What we receive, argued Augustine, is the consequence of Adam's sin: separation from God. And if we lose God from our conscious perspective, then we can neither orient ourselves nor order our desires nor represent the good appropriately. Sinning is hence inevitable because all our desires suffer disorder when disconnected from active relation to God. And it is precisely this active relationship with God, inaccessible to our fallen nature, which is now possible to us only through God's active intervention.

We pass on and receive a distorted, disordered and weakened human nature through biological procreation (as well as through the means of social reproduction and interaction) because the sexual desire through which we procreate has the disordered character of lust – that is, desire, satisfaction of which has become its own ordering principle. Although Augustine sails pretty close to the view that sexual desire as we currently experience it is always sinful, that is not the essence of his meaning here. Rather, his point is that, under the conditions of the Fall, our sexual desires are not fully co-ordinated with our orientation on God: they are not rationally ordered. Thus, we create new human life through a sexuality which is itself disordered by sin, in which we relate to our bodiliness and that of our partner in ways which subvert the proper integrity of desire in the ecology and economy of the good, most clearly manifest in our inability to bring lust under rational control.[39] Through a metaphysics which remains somewhat opaque (to say the least),[40] Augustine maintained that children inherit the disorder of sin in their souls from the disordered intentionality through which they

---

39. On the Merits and Forgiveness of Sins, 20, 57; On the Baptism of Infants, 4; On Nature and Grace, 66, 67; Against Two Letters of the Pelagians, I, 34f.; On Original Sin, 38, 42f.; On Marriage and Concupiscence, 6f.

40. And, indeed, inconsistent. In On Marriage and Concupiscence, 11, 20 he implies a genetic distortion of human seed unrelated to concupiscence. In other places, however, we are incorporated into the sin and guilt of Adam on account of an organic, and possibly substantial, solidarity of the race, such that we were all present in Adam, so his sin is simultaneously our own (Against Two Letters of the Pelagians, IV, 7; On the Merits and Forgiveness of Sins, 11, 15–17, 19, 20). At other times, he locates the transmission in simple heredity (Against Two Letters of the Pelagians, IV, 7); at yet others, he speaks of a corruption of nature which now corrupts all those who share it (On Marriage and Concupiscence, 11, 57; On the City of God, xiv.1).

were conceived.[41] Hence, we are grafted into the dynamics of sin *biologically* before we are so socially; our solidarity in sin and its guilt is effected biologically before it is effected socially and personally. We do not enter the world in a state of innocence; the dynamics of our willing are from the outset already disoriented.[42]

Sin disempowered

The Fall weakened human nature in its capacity to perceive and then orient itself towards the good. That weakness is universally inherited and communicated. The inheritance of this congenital weakness – the effect, according to Augustine, of Adam's sin compounded by that of the generations since – represents a significant aspect of original sin. It achieves a particular significance in relation to concupiscence – the capacity of goods in the world to motivate desire independently of any relation to God. We have, in fact, already met with concupiscence in the form of lust – which Augustine uses as its paradigm case. In its weakened condition, human nature is not always strong enough to resist the temptation to act on desire in an unrestricted way, without rational co-ordination with a coherent representation of the good. Concupiscence refers, in effect, to the capacity of desire to overwhelm the rational determination of our willing. We consciously orient our will towards one thing, but find ourselves willing against ourselves in practice because we are yet in the grip of powerful desires to the contrary which we cannot bring fully under control.[43]

According to Augustine, even those for whom original sin has been disempowered through grace received in baptism are still subject to concupiscence. Whilst he maintained that, in faith, the will is compelled such that it cannot resist grace by deliberately sinning, he simultaneously claimed that the faithful will could nonetheless find itself resisting grace

41. *On Marriage and Concupiscence*, 21, 25, 27, 55; *On the Baptism of Infants*, 11; *On Original Sin*, 42; *Confessions*, I,vii,12. Jesus is the one exception – excepted, incidentally, not primarily because the virgin birth signifies the absence of the normal, sexual means of reproduction, nor simply by the absence of lust, but because Mary's belief of the Angel cancels Eve's corruption by desire (*On the Merits and Forgiveness of Sins*, 56–7).

42. Such a view is found prior to the anti-Pelagian correspondence in, e.g., *Confessions*, VIII,v,10.

43. Augustine's use of sexual lust as a paradigm and his retention of the Pauline existential dualism of spirit and flesh does not indicate a Manichaean, metaphysical dualism between body and spirit. 'Flesh' indicates a wrong kind of orientation towards the material and bodily, not an aversion to bodiliness. Concupiscence as disorientation in willing, whilst it might be expressed through the body, resides not in body, but soul. See *Against Julian*, VI,xiv,41.

'unwillingly'. 'Unwilling' resistance is not an act of supposed strength in which the will asserts itself in an act of defiance against God, but of weakness. For to sin by concupiscence is to fail to maintain one's own integrity of orientation, to find that fields of force opposing the good which one would orient oneself towards subject the dynamics of willing to interference. Concupiscence is the source of the phenomenon of the divided will which we have already encountered, in which the will is too weak consistently to resist altogether being drawn towards the attraction of alternative orientations. And that weakness is inherited from the biological and social means of human reproduction. We receive a nature already infirm. Hence our infirmity does not originate from ourselves, our own action, but is always already there. It is communicated to us in the origin of our biological being. But it is also communicated and reinforced by the social means of reproduction through which we become more than simply biological entities. The disorder of society and that of culture are also partly responsible for the disorder of desire.

The receipt of grace in the sacrament of baptism does not render one immune to sinning through concupiscence, according to Augustine. It has the effect of disempowering concupiscence rather than eliminating it. Under the internal reorientation of grace received in baptism, sins of concupiscence are committed *without consent*.[44] But does that not indicate that sin and concupiscence are more potent than grace? No, says Augustine. Grace is always effective, but the fullness of perfection that it sets before the person – the joy and blessing of eternal life with God – cannot by definition be realised in time. Grace is an eternal cause. Its effect in time is to reorient lives towards the future consummation.[45] Living towards a future of which it only has a foretaste, the life of faith is characterised by patient forbearance, struggle, failure, forgiveness, confession and hope. Whereas grace is an eternal cause which has effects in time, sin and concupiscence occupy a temporally bound nexus of cause and effect. Concupiscence experienced by those Augustine deemed elected towards eternity he regarded as little more than an epiphenomenon of their existence in a temporal world, the redemption of which had still to be completed within time (but is already completed in the eternity of God's decision and action).

The faith of the baptised reorients the structure of intentionality towards this future, but in a situation which is still in the grip of the

44. *On Marriage and Concupiscence*, 25, 28ff., 58; *Against Two Letters of the Pelagians*, I, 27; *Confessions*, X,xxx,41.
45. *On the Baptism of Infants*, 9f, 12; *On Man's Perfection in Righteousness*, 31.

distorted and disordered desire from which, in the perspective of God's eternal action, it has already been freed. It is not grace, but the will which is weak – and, indeed, which may be divided in practice as it experiences attractions which run counter to what is known to be good. Sins of concupiscence are consequently failures in willing actually to pursue that which one would; failures coherently and consistently to instantiate in practice the life-orientation consented to in faith. So far as Augustine is concerned, sins of concupiscence are irrational on two counts. First, they represent a self-alienation, a failure to co-ordinate knowledge of the good with action, a failure also in the rational integration of desires in orientation towards that which we deem to be the good. Under concupiscence, contrary desire proves itself stronger than our power rationally to direct our willing. We find ourselves not only doing but also willing (since for Augustine willing is a necessary corollary of all but forced action) something which we know is not good. Second, because in the case of the baptised who consent to grace in faith God is this represented good, acting on contrary desire must also run counter to the good which is rationally intelligible, which undergirds the whole of the created order of goodness.[46]

Baptism does not free one from the effects of sin in the general situation and in the human condition as it has been disordered and weakened – most significantly, in its capacities for achieving full rational control over desire. That the faithful will is divided when it sins by concupiscence indicates to Augustine that sin does not rule. For it has failed to pull the person back into a disordered life-orientation. Thus, Augustine does not consider the sins of concupiscence of the faithful to be sins of the self, deriving from an undivided attraction towards that which is not God. They are in a sense external to and alienated from the self.[47] For the structure of intentionality is yet oriented towards and desires God. It just remains weak within time, unable permanently to order and orient all desires appropriately.[48] Original sin corrupts and weakens the most basic conditions of our humanity, its power and effects being communicated both socially and biologically. The baptised live still in a social world disordered by sin, in which sin has been institutionalised in convention,

46. Hence, Augustine will have no truck with the Pelagian view that knowledge is itself saving – since we can know the good and still find ourselves unable to will and do it. See especially *Against Fortunatus*, 22.
47. This is Augustine's meaning in designating them sins of the flesh as opposed to the spirit – drawing on Gal. 5:17. See e.g., *On Nature and Grace*, 53.
48. *On the Spirit and the Letter*, 65; *On Man's Perfection in Righteousness*, 39.

structures and processes which 'naturally' draw people into a disordered orientation which may be both hard to resist and difficult to recognise. Similarly, one's personal history of sinning, in which one has acted on disordered desire, continues to influence present, post-baptismal volition through the sedimentation of habitual patterns of intention and action.[49] In convention and habit, the renewed orientation of faith encounters the resistance of inertia. For, through habit and convention, past desires continue to hold the power to attract the will, to carry it in the trail of past patterns of co-ordinating judgment and desire, long after they have ceased to represent the person's current life-orientation. In a sense, they threaten to throw willing back into the past, inhibiting grace. The baptised, Augustine says, are still subject to their previous habituation to sin in the form of the temptations of disordered desire but, in grace, they are empowered to resist.

Even those whose spirits have been reoriented through grace cannot shake off the reality of original sin, then. For grace does not break the fundamental solidarity of the human race and its temporal situation, but rather works in and through it. The inheritance of being communally 'in Adam' is shared even whilst one lives anew 'in Christ', energised towards the promised Kingdom. The mode of our social and biological embodiment entails our continuing to be affected and weakened by original sin.[50] Those who are elected towards the eternity of eschatological perfection must await the perfecting of the world, and of the means of embodiment in it, before they may be perfect.[51] An unredeemed situation cannot support perfection, even of the (proleptically) redeemed. That in which we are embodied cannot sustain yet the spiritual regeneration already eternally effected.

Even though it does not eliminate it, baptism, Augustine maintains, nonetheless disempowers such concupiscence. The receipt of grace is, in effect, for him the recontextualisation of the whole of one's life, its drawing into a newly ordered relationship with God, and thence to oneself, to others and to the whole of reality. Grace places one within a new 'field of force' which pulls a person's life-intentionality in a new direction, reshaping it. What it does not do – at least within time – is make one perfect. For this very reason, forgiveness and confession are the

---

49. *The Doctrine of Two Souls*, 13.19.
50. *On the Baptism of Infants*, 12; *On the Spirit and the Letter*, 65.
51. *On the Spirit and the Letter*, 65; *On Man's Perfection in Righteousness*, 39; *On Marriage and Concupiscence*, 20.

disciplines by which Christians must individually and communally live between-the-times. The Church is not, then, a community of the perfect (as both the Donatists and Pelagians thought) but a community of confession, of the forgiven and the forgiving.[52] Aside from the compulsion of willing towards the good, then, all one's life – good deeds as well as sins – are recontextualised in relation to God. The relation of the self towards the good that one has done is fundamentally altered, so that it is directed towards God in praise, no longer proud praise of oneself or a means for establishing a claim on God or others. The lapse into sin through concupiscence, the residual ruling of the old law of sin and death, is disempowered because it is always already taken up into, overpowered by, this primary orientation towards God and the eschatological Kingdom.[53] In this reorientation, the relation to eternity is in part mediated by confession and forgiveness. Forgiveness has already been received in the sacrament of baptism and so is in place prior to these subsequent sins of concupiscence and, because it represents a dimension of God's eternal decision and will, it is also more potent than any temporal and temporary state of affairs. Hence forgiveness is effective already, and those sins we fall into through the concupiscence which is unavoidable simply because we are between the times, are not imputed to us.[54] So, in a real sense, for Augustine the bondage of sin remains broken, its capacity to effect a total disaffection from God is rendered impotent, even in the commission of sins of concupiscence.

Sins of concupiscence do not, then, represent a new disorientation of will. Those whose lives have been reshaped and reoriented under the impact of compelling grace, who live towards a richer and more potent source of plenitude, do not sin with their wills when they find their willing still trapped in the old order. These sins do not arise from the internal dispositional structure of faith, hope and love. Consequently, they do not add personal power to the dynamic of sin in their situation, and neither does sin disempower their orientation towards God.

Testing the will (or the will in-test-state?)

In this chapter, I have offered a reading of Augustine through the lens afforded by willing in pathological situations. That has helped draw attention to and illuminate the nature and significance of willing in his

---

52. *On the Spirit and the Letter*, 65.   53. Ibid.
54. *On Marriage and Concupiscence*, 28f.; *On the Baptism of Infants*, 45f.

understanding of sin and grace. It has thereby reinforced the deductive connection between the doctrine of original sin and the hypothesis concerning the bondage of willing. Together with the discussion of feminist theologies in the previous chapter, it has also served to give that hypothesis further conceptual specification – which, at the same time, has helped draw out and re-express Augustine's understanding of willing in terms of the direction of personal energy. The theological superstructure associated with his understanding of bound willing is evident. But this requires some further constructive engagement to strengthen the case that *theological* interpretation of the bondage of the will has some comprehensive, explanatory and descriptive power in relation to concrete pathologies. Prior to that, it might prove helpful at this stage to review briefly the points at which Augustine's theology of sin may be correlated with the concrete pathologies.

Whilst the pathological dynamics that emerged from the engagements in chapters 4 to 6 differed markedly in their details, the accounts I gave of the holocaust and the sexual abuse of children nonetheless show a striking number of formal similarities. In each case, the pathological dynamic:

(a) cannot be construed in terms of the discrete acts of individuals, but rather appears as a supra-individual network of interrelations and interactions extended through time;

(b) habituates the whole life-intentionality (drives, desires, rationality, etc.) of victims, perpetrators and bystanders into disorientation by engaging their committed personal energies in material processes of consent, compliance, acquiescence and commission;

(c) effects a manifold confusion (in practice as well as in cognition) about reality – the limits, nature and possibilities of agency, the nature of causality, what is true and false, valuable and pathogenic, good and bad, right and wrong, and why;

(d) blocks access to transcendent criteria, frameworks and sources of meaning and value.

Augustine, like contemporary feminist theologians, understood sin primarily in dynamic terms – more as energy than substance. Sin is comprehensive turning away from God and the good (including, of course, one's own good), involving disorientation of life-trajectories and comprehensive confusion concerning reality. Augustine absolutely refuses to speak of this dynamic of disorientation in individualised or atomic terms. For it is all-encompassing, always already there, both internal and external to the self.

Hence, he speaks of sin as relational and situational (a). And yet Augustine's is absolutely not an impersonal construal of sin. Sin counts as personal for Augustine, not because we choose sin freely on the basis of an inner core at once uninfected by sin and neutral in relation to God and the good. Rather, we are personally incorporated – in fact, bound in the whole of our life-intentionality – into sin through our willing. Willing for Augustine is the internal energy through which one's life is directed, committed and oriented, through which a life-trajectory is established and lived personally. It is no longer the formal capacity for being self-directed through the autonomous making of choices. But this personal energy is not directed by the power of a pure, autonomous self. It is rather influenced in its directionality by fields of force within one's situation, communicated in highly charged ways through the dynamics of institutions, structures, processes and relationships (a). In this way, it is possible for Augustine to speak in the same breath of bondage and willing. For it is precisely through the contribution of personal energy in willing that the will (indeed, the whole of a person's life-intentionality) may be bound to sin. Through willing, one both contributes personal energy to the larger pathological dynamic and finds that, in so doing, the power of sin is internalised. The internal dynamic of life-intentionality (including will) is sequestered and captured by this larger dynamic; one finds one's internality 'possessed', consenting to, committed to, desiring and entrapped by a pathological orientation larger than the self (b). The echoes of this position to be heard in the substructure of contemporary feminist theologies of sin are immediately obvious. Significantly, feminist theologians arrive at the position quite independently of (if not in open antagonism towards) Augustine, and through an engagement with the concrete pathological dynamics operating on and in women.

Augustine broadens the concept of the voluntary more explicitly than does feminism, so that it includes all situations in which there is willing, even under conditions of coercion. Thereby he expands also the scope of what might be counted as *active* and *personal* engagement in a situation, to the extent that there appears little which we receive merely *passively* – that is, without some contribution of willing which internally embeds and commits us. The seriousness of the post-lapsarian situation lies, for Augustine, not in the misuse of our freedom of will, but in the inescapable misdirection and perversion of willing away from God and the good, so that our very use of and capacity for 'free' choice is already disoriented. Because will is not free of this disorientation but bound to participate in it, all willing further embeds the self in it (b). Up to this point, the resonances with the background understanding of feminist accounts of sin are clear. Where Augustine parts company from many feminist theologies, however, is in the way in which he follows through the implications of such an account in relation to the possibilities of healing. Since will and active intentionality are inescapably embedded in the pathological dynamics of the situation, they do not have sufficient potency or clarity about the good to free themselves. Moreover, the good is not available to us in pure form, without being tinged or clouded by sin. Therefore, healing may only come through a re-energising and reorienting grace from outside the situation; indeed, transcending all human situations and possibilities. This is a move that most feminist theologians are reluctant to make, since it appears to them to imply the continued disempowering and oppression of the victims of sin by setting aside their active agency.

For Augustine, however, the only important question in sin concerns the disorientation of people – in their acting, relating and in the very seat of their subjectivity – away from God and the good. This was a practical and spiritual, much more than it ever was an abstract, theological question for him. For it concerns nothing other than the orientation of the human spirit: the active, committed directionality and movement in practice of the whole person (and, indeed, society and the race as a whole), towards or away from God and the good (b). As we have seen, the proper question to ask, to Augustine's mind, is not whether we enjoy formal freedom, but whether we are oriented towards the one true source of our freedom or are in bondage to sin. Hence, the opposite of sin for Augustine is not the good act predicated on the potent freedom of the free (neutral) will, but faith (which issues, not in legal obedience, but a concrete spirit of love). Faith is, by contrast, predicated on the potency of the grace of God in instilling the spirit of faith. Yet faith remains for Augustine voluntary, since it requires the contribution of personal power through consensual willing. Willing, for Augustine, has the effect of both intensifying and internalising the dynamic of that which compels it (b). In the case of faith, that leads to joy, love and praise. (Critics, not least feminist critics, however, are unwilling to concede that this description of faith is genuinely a co-operation between human and divine energies.)

In sin, however, the life-trajectory of humanity has been disembedded from pursuit of God and the genuine good. This, for Augustine, both embeds and evidences a confusion concerning the nature of reality; a confusion both cognitive and practical, which in particular concerns the economy of goods and values (c). Since we habitually act under and orient ourselves towards a misrepresentation of the good, we practise a confusion concerning the proper economy of goods and of values: the location, source and nature of the goodness, worth and value of all aspects of reality (c). But more than this. Such confusion is so deeply embedded in our life-orientation that we do not have unequivocal access to criteria of truth, value and goodness, and so – on our own unaided resources – are unable accurately to discern the true character of our situation. For our very sense of what is good, right, true – and why – itself participates in and is distorted and disoriented by sin (c, d). That is why Augustine maintains the impotence of an independent, autonomous morality (even feminist community and praxis) either accurately to diagnose or appropriately to guide action in our situation. Moral discernment and action may themselves become vehicles and expressions of spiritual disorientation. In many ways, it was the Pelagians' inability to take account of this that alerted Augustine to the urgency and seriousness of countering their positions.

Many of the features of concrete pathology (given in the list above, p. 195) converge in the issue of the nature and function of willing. That was one reason why I used willing as my way in, when starting in chapter 6 to draw out the implications of the descriptions of concrete pathologies. The initial focus on willing also permitted an engagement with the dominant source of modern critique of sin-talk: the understanding of freedom as independence and separation, and its expression in moral frameworks. The description of both situations and the subsequent discussion in chapter 6 showed that people are incorporated and bound into the reality of sin in ways at once more subtle, more complex and more invidious than may be allowed for in such frameworks. In particular, certain core assumptions appear descriptively inadequate to these concrete situations. Whether they are cast more in the role of perpetrators or victims, people do not stand outside the situational pathologies already in place, in some uncommitted and neutral sphere from whence they may exercise free choices. Rather, the pathological dynamics of the situation exercise a disorienting influence on willing: in both situations, people are internally bound through their willing. Whilst people in these situations continue to enjoy the formal capacity for making choices, that very capacity appears to be sequestered and utilised by a more potent field of force.

Chapter 6 therefore showed the issue of willing to be decisive in testing the descriptive adequacy of a doctrine of sin. Consequently, I have read the accounts of sin given by feminist theologians and Augustine through the prism of willing. Moralistic frameworks of understanding fail this test of descriptive potency. Since Augustine (at least in his anti-Pelagian writings) was himself attacking such frameworks, it seemed a reasonable supposition that reading him with an emphasis on willing might not be distorting at all, but rather a way of bringing the whole of his understanding of sin into focus. It would also afford an opportunity for comparing the deep structure of Augustine's with feminist under-standings. I also think it incontestable that Augustine's understanding of sin shows a great deal of congruence with the dynamics which shape our two concrete situations and with the feminist understanding of sin. Without a doubt, he helps us bring aspects of the core dynamic to expres-sion. But does he do more than this? Does his understanding of sin have more than *expressive* power? Does it also have *explanatory* power – does it help us comprehensively to see and understand its concrete reality? And if so, is that power a function of Augustine's being a *theological* conception of pathology? One of the ways of getting at this set of interrelated questions is to ask after the criteria by which pathology is so judged and identified. That leads us back into the exposition of Augustine, to ask by what stan-dard is sin being identified and interpreted: what is counted as sin and why? That is to ask, in what does sin consist, on Augustine's account?

9

A question of standards: trinity, joy, worship and idolatry

Talking about the pathological necessarily involves some intuition of the good that is denied, destroyed or distorted by it. When we identify and discern what is bad, we do so according to some criterion or measure of the good. At least implicitly, we operate a normative standard of reference of what *should* be (the *logos*), against which its disorder, denial or disease (the *pathos*) may be identified. Every identification and description of pathology, then, carries an at least implicit characterisation of the good. Even where the pathological status of something like child abuse or the holocaust is so taken for granted that no explicit rationalisation is offered, the way in which it is described, the therapeutic interventions suggested, indicate an intuition of the good. It is very revealing, therefore, to ask of discussions of sexual abuse, the holocaust or sin, what standard of normative reference or criterion and definition of the good they operate with. What is abuse seen as abuse *of*? What is normal or right 'use' of and for human beings? In identifying the holocaust as gross *in*humanity, what conception of normal, right and good humanity is functioning?

What is the good for human beings, which pathology is taken to violate, and how is that to be construed appropriately? Many of the secular discussions of concrete pathology – and, indeed, many discussions of sin – in fact operate a fairly restricted notion of the good as their normative standard of reference, often reducible to maintenance of normal physiological, emotional or social functioning. Such restricted conceptions of the human good are severely problematic on two counts. Because they are not terribly rich conceptions of human flourishing, they fail to convey the full depths and significance of its denial and distortion. At the same time, they give those caught up in pathological dynamics a restricted sense of what they might properly hope for, and of what is naturally available to them. That leaves people with a restricted and restricting sense of their own good, which in many cases simply reinforces the damage caused through pathological dynamics, whilst minimising estimation of deviations from the good. Is all that is damaged, distorted or lost through abuse normal physiological, emotional or social functioning? And is all that may be hoped for through therapeutic measures the return of those functions to a normal state? Is the depth of its pathology adequately captured if the holocaust is judged wicked on the grounds that it denied to millions of human beings the right to maintain life and avoid harm?

Beyond this, I want to ask: is there a specifically theological conception of the good, which affords a rich comprehension of the nature of pathology and holds out an enriching apprehension of the good to people caught up in it? From the first, this largely unvoiced question has underlain the considerations of this book. I began by asking after the descriptive power and possibilities of sin as a specifically theological language. I noticed the temptation to translate sin into non-theological frames of reference in a culture that is blessed by powerful modes of secular analysis and explanation, and suggested that sin-talk was only worth maintaining if it could function as an explicitly theological language by referring the pathological to God. For sin-talk functions by incorporating the pathological into a distinctively theological frame; i.e., by operating specifically theological standards of reference and criteria for the identification and discernment of pathology. Indeed, to name human pathology as sin is to claim that its essential character is theological. It is to claim that what damages human beings, what makes something 'bad', is disruption of our proper relation to God. Of course, that formal statement is not, in itself, sufficient to produce a substantive characterisation of the good. Furthermore, as the disagreements between theological positions indicated in chapters 2, 7 and 8 evidence, agreement on the formal point will not necessarily yield substantive agreement as to the *way* in which right relation to God is to be construed. There is still room for serious disagreement, therefore, concerning the characterisation of the good, the criterion by which sin is identified and defined and in opposition to which the sinfulness of sin consists.

Not every theological conceptualisation, however, does equal justice to the concrete pathologies considered earlier in the book. The middle chapters of the book show, in particular, that an adequate construal of sin must be dynamic and relational. It must do justice to the disorienting and disordering of willing, in its innermost structure and dynamism, as it is caught up in situational pathology. By extension, an adequate conception of the good will be correspondingly dynamic and relational.[1]

Through the last several chapters, a cumulative case has been building in favour of the explanatory and descriptive power of the hypothesis that the will is bound to pathologies in which it is situated. The hypothesis gradually achieved more specific conceptual explication through the discussions of the previous three chapters. At the same time, focusing the expositions of feminist theologies and Augustine on willing proved to be fruitful in explicating a systematic account of their understandings of sin and clarifying what these implied concerning the mode of personal participation. In the last chapter, we encountered Augustine's specifically theological superstructure, in the context of which both his understanding of willing and the nature of sin are to be interpreted. I want, in this chapter, to extrapolate further from that in order to test whether specifically theological conceptions of the proper and pathological dynamics of willing further enrich the understanding achieved so far.

Augustine and feminism

Feminist theologies of sin proved to have a good deal of descriptive power in relation to abuse and the holocaust, partly because they tend to be dynamic. In particular, they operate with helpful constructions of the dynamics of will (though not always explicitly or consistently thematised). Significantly, feminist critique and reconstruction represent in essence a rejection of the normative standard of reference assumed operative in the tradition.[2] The traditional emphasis on pride is found problematic, partly because it appears to suggest that normative human good involves self-obeisance and abnegation. When set against the feminist

---

1. In one sense, all understandings of sin are relational, to the extent that they are functionally theological. Simply in deploying the language of sin, one invokes a relation between God and pathology (it is, say, rebellion, denial, disobedience, and is judged, forgiven, healed). But that relation (indeed, God) may be construed in static rather than dynamic terms. This tends to be so where, for example, sin is understood as the breaking of God-given laws and relation to God (and therefore the good) is taken to be mediated through regulative precepts. Right relation to God is then a matter of obedience to these codified norms of behaviour. God relates to human beings as the giver of laws; human beings to God as the keepers or breakers of them. Both God and God's relation to us are here construed as somewhat static. The mediation of fixed forms (codified regulations) easily substitutes for a more dynamic, living interaction and God can easily appear as a remote originator of laws, now at one step removed from the world.
2. See pp. 136, 155–65ff., above.

standard of 'right relation', both pride (in its traditional meaning) and self-abnegation may be judged to be complementary aspects of the same pathology, operationally redefined as the constriction or denial of the energies of genuine relation.[3] Feminist discussion of sin offers a rich conception of the good which holds a great deal of descriptive power in relation to the pathological dynamics discussed earlier in the book. However, 'right relation' is described as an interhuman possibility and process. God is either left out of the picture altogether, or else so entirely collapsed into the immanent dynamics of 'right relation' as to be indistinguishable from them. In either case, the feminist standard helps us to discern pathology as a denial of human fullness with and before one another, but rarely to see pathology in genuinely theological terms: as sin.

Augustine's understanding of sin, by contrast, is definitely theological, though subject to feminist suspicion concerning his theological standard of reference: can human good or pathology be related to God without that involving human subjection to God?

My interpretation of Augustine was illuminated by the journey undertaken through previous chapters of the book, including the engagement with feminism, which alerted me to conceptual issues and interpretive possibilities. Perhaps surprisingly, Augustine and original sin turn out to have a number of points of contact with feminist theologies of sin and to hold at least as much descriptive power in relation to the concrete pathologies under consideration. In particular, Augustine offers a subtle, dynamic account of willing, which does justice to the position of victims and perpetrators alike. When read in conjunction with the depiction of concrete pathologies, Augustine may be interpreted as construing willing as the personal energy through which one's life is directed, committed and oriented. But this personal energy is not directed by the power of a pure, autonomous self. Willing is rather situated and relational, influenced in its orientation by extra- and supra-personal fields of force within one's situation. Through willing, we incorporate ourselves into, internalise and redouble, dynamics which are generally supra-personal and not of our own making, whilst adding our own personal power to them. Thereby we achieve an internal integration in identity and orientation to match the external. Concerning human integrity and freedom, Augustine wants to know only whether willing is bound in an orientation to God. For true integrity (and genuine freedom founded on one's genuine

3. pp. 160ff.

being and goodness) may only be derived from the proper orientation of our life-trajectories as our willing conforms and consents to God's compelling. Thus freedom is redefined – which is to say, the standard of normative reference by which terms are defined has changed. Freedom no longer consists in the power arbitrarily to choose, but in our willing being pulled in an orientation towards what is genuinely good, and in relation to which one's own being and goodness are intensified and fulfilled, and our integrity has proper foundation. Alternative orientations involve instead dissolution of the proper conditions for personal integrity and relation.

The idea that personal integrity and autonomy might depend on relation represents a basic commitment of feminist theologies, and so is not, in itself, a point of issue between Augustine and feminism. For, against 'patriarchal' notions of selfhood (asocial, competitive and private), secular and theological feminists tend to articulate a highly relational view of the self and of 'autonomy' as amplified, deepened and enlarged through 'right relation' to other human beings. For Augustine, it is through the dynamics of relation to God that one's being is re-energised, revitalised and redoubled. For feminists, however, intensification of being and freedom is dependent on mutuality in the relation. The standard of reference in feminist theologies of sin is a *form* of relation that can pertain between human beings, which does not depend on the specific identities of the partners. 'Right relation' is marked, not so much by equality of power, as by a dynamic of mutual empowerment. Hence, a relation predicated on permanent inequality of power between the partners is suspected of supplanting such a dynamic with one bound to be abusive, coercive or oppressive of others' integrities, identities and good. When that is coupled with a general suspicion of identity being made dependent on any particular other or relation, feminist disavowal of Augustine is easily comprehensible.

For Augustine, the particular identity of the partner in relation is decisive. One could say that 'right relation' is also his standard of reference – though, for him, that can only mean right relation _to God_. The identity of God defines the form of relation, the proper ecology of which is the standard of reference for construing human pathology. From the perspective of feminist discourse, however, this is precisely the problem.[4] 'Right rela-

Anti-Climacus too!

---

4. For a recent example, see Daphne Hampson, 'On Autonomy and Heteronomy', in Daphne Hampson, ed., *Swallowing a Fishbone? Feminist Theologians Debate Christianity* (London: SPCK, 1996), pp. 8ff.

tion' is not thought possible with the God of Christian tradition. Why? Because the dynamics of relation with a transcendent and all-powerful partner must be asymmetrical. Shaped by divine precedence and super- iority, all energies will be directed towards God's sustenance at the expense of mutual empowerment; oriented, not towards building up the integrity and autonomy of human beings and their good, but towards God. Human energies will be drawn away from the locus of their auton- omy and integrity, oriented instead towards serving the locus of divine integrity, autonomy and sovereignty. That, after all, is why Augustine and the tradition condemn integrity and autonomy in relation to God as the paradigmatic sin of pride, and why he speaks of the Spirit's coercing the will: to subordinate humanity to divine heteronomy. Or is it? Are fem- inist suspicions correct in assuming that Augustine's standard of norma- tive reference involves the orientation of human energies so completely away from themselves that autonomy and integrity dissipate and disinte- grate?

The answer to this question hangs upon the identity of God.[5] What is this God like, which feminist critique assumes Augustine and the tradi- tion to have, and which it wishes to avoid? As I have already intimated,[6] the root of feminist concern about traditional understanding of God hinges on divine transcendence. With, it has to be said, a good deal of help from the tradition, transcendence is taken in much feminist theology to denote complete otherness, the lack of any intimate and intrinsic connec- tion with creation. If God's identity is totally other and located quite apart from creation, then relation with human beings will be monological, hierarchical, dominating and generally alienating and expropriating of our autonomy. Divine and human freedom, power, integrity and identity will be competitive and exclusive, such that an orientation of energies on one must perforce involve an orientation away from the other. Human movement towards God must then involve a disorientation and dissipa- tion of the energies of autonomy and integrity, whilst God's moving towards, presence in or action upon human beings involve an imposition of divine will which squashes or sequesters them. Augustine's insisting that we rely on an external source of energy for salvation, together with his contending that such grace is not a 'natural' human possession, is

---

5. This is itself highly significant in view of the discussion below, since the misidentification of God is a form of idolatry. Peter Scott develops such an account of idolatry, correlated with political ideology, and explores its significance for theology in *Theology, Idolology and Liberation: Towards a Liberative Theology* (Cambridge: Cambridge University Press, 1994), esp. pp. 78ff.; 169ff.   6. On pp. 164f.; cf. p. 175f.

taken as disabling and disorienting autonomous human energies and integrity. By the same token, human freedom must be defined as separation *from* the overpowering field of force of divine presence and activity in the world; maintenance of integrity becomes then a matter of drawing on what one is and has 'naturally'. Because of these assumptions concerning God's identity as transcendent, feminist theologians tend to operate with a different conception of power and freedom in this regard than when considering interhuman relations. In relation to God, being free means being free *from* external influences, and autonomy is non-relational. If transcendence is read in this way, there is a stark choice: either divine sovereignty or human autonomy. Augustine's support for divine sovereignty is read in this context as an assault on human freedom and integrity, whereas, given this choice, feminists are bound to place themselves on the other side, as defenders of humanity against the oppression of the projected, archetypal male.

Augustine could, admittedly, be both clearer and more consistent about the matter, and tradition does not always follow or develop him as accurately as it claims. But the truth is that his conception of God is much more profoundly and seriously trinitarian than this: not a static, simple, monolith, but dynamic trinity. Whilst Augustine tends not to make explicit links between his understanding of the trinity and sin, a dynamic construal of God's identity and relation with the world underlies and is required to make sense of what he says about both the proper and the pathological dynamics of willing. In particular, it is only within such a dynamic conception that one may grasp the significance of his use of overflow categories, such as joy. In his sense that joy is a basic constituent of the dynamics of right relation to the trinitarian dynamics of God, Augustine offers us a major lead to the discernment of the proper standard of normative reference for pathology. The clue he offers concerns the way in which the overflowing plenitude and abundance which is God, is repeated in the energy of reoriented life-intentionality called forth by God: faith.

Who is God? The plenitude and abundance of the triune God

Evidently, it lies far beyond the scope of this work to proffer a fully defended and elaborated doctrine of the trinity. I offer instead the following outline.

To say that God is trinity is to say that there is no divine being without relationship; or, better, that God's being is better construed in dynamic terms rather than as static substance. The dynamic by virtue of which God is God has a specific orientation, order and character, not given in some aseity of divine perfection, untouchable and untouched, but through interaction. That is true in respect both of God's internal and external relationships; better, it is true of the one as it is true and worked out in the other (the economic is the immanent trinity). God is Godself in the dynamic of God's life, and the character of that dynamic is love.

By love, I mean here a form of relationship founded on the particularity and integrity of the partners and at the same time on the indissolubility of their commitment and orientation one to another, which seeks the well-being and perfection of the other. We must avoid thinking here in terms which are individualistic and static. For the integrity of the partners, and so their well-being and perfection, are not withdrawn but inseparable from the dynamics of their interrelation. Love is not merely being open to the other as she is presently defined or defines herself. Love does not let the other 'be', but delights in the other with the desire to stretch one's own being in response to her, which in turn invites her to stretch her own being, and so on in an eternal dialectic of mutual delight, praise and joy. In the immanent trinity, we see a love which seeks the maximum expansiveness in the being of the other, of the relation and of oneself in relation. So to characterise the immanent trinity as love is to say that the energy of God's relational being is directed toward the perfection of the identity of the three Trinitarian Persons and of the triune relationship: perfecting perfection,[7] so to speak.

But even this is not yet a sufficiently relational and dynamic understanding of the trinitarian being of God. For the dynamic order of God, which seeks the fullest possible expression through relationality, cannot contain itself. The love that is God's being overflows in creative plenitude.

> What runs through all this relationality is a stirring ('the Spirit') which presses the activities not to some abstract perfection . . . but to the fullness of relationship with *this* one . . . So the relationality of God is one of energetic involvement and participation, moving toward fuller and fuller relationship. And this would not be complete until all the fullness of each one had enlarged the other. Even then it would not be

7. This phrase I have borrowed from Daniel W. Hardy's and David F. Ford's conception of praise in *Jubilate: Theology in Praise* (London: Darton, Longman & Todd, 1984), p. 6, also used in David F. Ford, *Self and Salvation: Being Transformed* (Cambridge: Cambridge University Press, 1999), p. 115.

complete, because the stirring would still continue in the vibrancy of the relationship . . .

Seen in such a way, it becomes clear that God is what . . . can be called an 'energy event' constituted by a concentration of well-being in relationship which is inseparable from the extending of this relationship with his people in the world, and from the expression of his well-being in that relationship. The world he has brought into being and maintained is therefore a relational one . . . His purpose is to move toward fuller and fuller relationship with it and all that comprises it, bringing it to its fullness by sharing his own fullness with it.[8]

Indeed, God is abundantly, as well as truly, Godself through the orientation to share such abundance with creation, to call it towards its own superabundance through relation with Godself, continually to resource and energise the possibilities of expanding towards further abundance of being in response. God's direction and movement in and towards creation in turn invites an 'answering' orientation in the dynamic ordering of creation at every level. As we shall see, joy in faith and worship represents a specially intensive 'answer' as creation in general and human beings in particular are thus caught up in the movement of God's trinitarian being. In this movement, creation is given its own proper integrity and directed and called towards its own fulfilment and perfection as it is caught up in the movement of God's own being in and towards creation.

This carries at least four immediate implications. First, the integral order of the world is dynamic and relational. Second, this relationality is an immediate consequence of the movement of God *in* and *through* the world as well as *towards* the world; which is to say, third, that the integrity of the world does not separate it from God. Rather, the world's very integrity as a dynamic system and order includes and is indeed founded on relation to and the presence of the *dynamics* of God. Finally, the relational and dynamic order of the world is directed and called towards its own perfection through this relationship with God.

If the world is this kind of dynamically ordered system, then its proper order, its goodness, may not satisfactorily be construed in terms either of initial or current conditions. The appropriate standard of reference against which we judge goodness is neither backward-looking nor static. We are not therefore to think of an already-established perfection to be

---

8. Daniel W. Hardy, 'The Foundation of Cognition and Ethics in Worship', in *God's Ways with the World* (Edinburgh: T. & T. Clark, 1996), pp. 28f.; cf. 'The Spirit of God in Creation and Reconciliation', in ibid., pp. 8of.

preserved, but one which we are called, directed and empowered towards as we are caught up in the movement of God towards the world. Indeed, this is a dynamic perfection. Being caught up in the movement of God, being filled with the abundance and plenitude of God, changes the understanding of perfection and of 'being filled'. The perfection of God presses towards yet more abundant realisation and expression, 'changes the meaning of "full" from implying completeness to an image of ceaseless overflow due to the dynamic abundance of God'.[9] (As we shall see, this qualifies the conception of joy appropriate to such abundance, in particular avoiding intimations of stasis carried by notions of being sated, satisfied, or saturated.)

Hence, creation may not adequately be construed in terms of a one-off act of origination. It is a time-laden relationship, one in which the dynamic relationality of God suffuses that of human beings and the world, continually inviting, energising and exciting their energies to be directed towards the development of their own dynamic order (having joy in God). Yet, since this history includes the blocking of, resistance to and distortion of the dynamics of creation's proper order and relationality (traditionally thematised in Christian theology under the heading of the Fall), this cannot be construed as a linear process whereby original perfection is gradually unfolded and intensified. The abundance of God positively lavished on the world must not be understood only in relation to what is made available to the world in its origination and consequently 'developed'. (For that reason also, sin is not primarily or exclusively to be construed from the vantage point of original, created goodness, as that which blocks, refuses and resists it.) That would suggest a deficiently dynamic understanding of God's being, relationality and goodness, and thence also of God's relationship with the world. We have to understand creation instead as a relationship between God's abundance and the world which God maintains even (in fact, especially intensively) when and where creation falls out of the equilibrium of original relation to God and therefore out of the equilibrium of its own internal order as well. Paradoxically, God's abundance is most lavished on the world precisely where it resists its proper ordering in relation to the dynamics of God. Closed off from the energies of God, the energies for free, dynamic order (life in full abundance) dissipate, so that the integrity and order of living structures and systems tend to stabilise and

9. Ford, *Self and Salvation*, p. 113, discussing Eph. 3:14–21.

rigidify, becoming resistant to transformation and transcendence; that is, non-dynamic. In response, God continually acts on, in and towards the world in ways which make available new energies for transformation and which may then become means for focusing naturally available energies for future transformation. Precisely at the point where those natural energies are most dissipated, God releases and directs energies that excite creaturely energies to resist the constriction of life from its proper plenitude and fullness and to allow themselves to be directed towards ever more abundant dynamic order, an intensification of creatures' own reality and goodness. This is not, then, restoring lost, original perfection as if the distortions and damage of creation's misrelation to God and itself had never happened. God does not set aside, but takes up, the contingencies of concrete pathological history into the dynamics of the life of God in order to pour out energies for increasing dynamic order precisely at those points where there is most resistance to it. This opens up new futures in situations which would otherwise have been closed to any future other than one which replicates the past and is overdetermined by it. This past is now taken up into the movement of God, energised and directed into a new future which is highly contingent on – although not overdetermined by – it.

Primarily, we see this release of energy for new dynamic order in the resurrection of Jesus (which gives Christians the main clue as to the dynamics of God). The resurrection was absolutely not a reconstitution of initial conditions in relation either to Jesus or to God's relationship with humanity, neither did it involve an escapist fantasy about the incapacity of particular, concrete events and relationships to effect serious damage. Jesus is not resuscitated to a life, which still has death before it; the killing of Jesus is taken absolutely seriously; not undone, but worked through. And the total collapse of humanity into sin is also taken absolutely seriously. It is met with a radical measure which, again, works through the reality and, instead of restoring initial conditions, pours out the possibility of and energises a more abundant life than was possible hitherto by concentrating and focusing the energies for an ever greater intensification of dynamic order in being and relationality.

It is the cross and resurrection of Jesus above all, which indicate the abundant goodness and plenitude of God, which are the source of joy in God and the standard of normative reference for talking about sin. Sin is that which counters the dynamics of God in creation and salvation. But, paradoxically, sin is known in the context of God's active countering of it, working through the damage and brokenness caused by sin, in order to reorient the world towards more abundant possibilities than were available hitherto. It is only in the perspective of this salvific orientation of God's movement towards us that we may achieve anything like an adequate intimation of the nature and depth of sin. The primary context for discernment and talk of sin, as opposition and resistance to the movement of God towards us, is that afforded by God's saving action in Christ. Sin may only be known in the context of the presence and action of God in the world, focused in the cross and resurrection of Jesus, healing, liberating and saving from sin. We know sin only in the context of God's resistance to our resistance to God. Yet, this formulation only partially does justice to the way in which the New Testament reconfigures sin as resistance to faith in Christ. For this includes also the sense in which sin is revealed as a continuing, residual resistance even to the event of God's resistance and opposition.

Not least of the ways in which this christological focus on the dynamics of God in the crucifixion and resurrection of Jesus is significant is in establishing a resistance to one possible misconstrual of my emphasis on joy and worship. Joy worthy of God has already gone through the cross. It must therefore be distinguished from those forms of professed Christian joy founded on the pretence that nothing is really pathological, damaging or painful. Joy in the crucified God is one that cannot be founded on the pretence that there are no crosses in the world, or that they are cancelled out by or even necessary to the abundance of salvation. Joy that has gone through the cross must allow the crosses of the world to stand, just as the resurrection allowed Jesus' cross to stand, worked through and with the pathological dynamics to reorient them and to draw the damage into relation to the abundance and fullness of God. God defines sin in the act of drawing it into the dynamics of salvation, by taking the damage of sin, including its resistance to healing, into Godself.

All this indicates that the teleological aspect of reality is much more appropriately conceived in the language of calling than preservation – calling into a future development of, an increase in, dynamic order by the appropriate concentration and orientation of energies, by drawing on the dynamic order of God in creation. This implies an increase in freedom, which, far from being a disaffection from or damage to creatures' own ordered particularity, is actually an intensification of it.

It is not possible to speak of this trinitarian God in terms of simple transcendence, as unequivocally other-than, apart-from or over-against creation. For this is a God who does not simply act *on* the world from outside, but who is present and active *within* the world – without corrupting, but rather fulfilling and intensifying its proper goodness and integrity, which is precisely given through proper relation to its creator. In trinitarian terms, immanence is not the opposite of transcendence. For Augustine to emphasise the need for grace, which is not a possession or property of human nature, but requires the active indwelling of God, does not therefore imply that what is 'internal' and proper to human integrity is laid aside or disoriented. Neither does it follow that, because grace comes from without, it comes as an alien imposition, finding no points of contact with what is internal. It does mean, however, that such points of contact are found and established by the workings of grace, and may not be domesticated as an independent property of humanity, considered apart from God's active relation. Nor yet does it follow, from holding that God and grace are not natural human *attributes*, that relation to God is not proper or is inimical to humanity. Augustine's whole theology is predicated on the assumption that the good integral to humanity demands relation to the God who created and calls us towards *our own* fulfilment, who is other than us but constituted by active being for us. Hence, Augustine can speak of the dynamic of God's movement towards and for us (grace) as at the same time coercing *and* co-operating with human willing by directing it towards its own, deepest fulfilment, in which it resonates with joy. The coercion of grace neither immobilises nor supplants the integrity of the internal dynamics of human willing. Grace rather excites and redirects willing from within, in a way that is not inimical to, but enlarges and intensifies, human integrity and identity towards joy.

Joy, faith and worship

Joy

What is the significance of joy in relation to the concern for autonomy and integrity? First, joy is intensely particularising – indeed, joy intensifies particularity.[10] Our joys characterise our personhood, our dynamic life-intentionality. It is our *life* which lives from our enjoyment; it is *our* life which is given shape by such joy: the things we most desire and enjoy

---

10. Levinas speaks of joy as 'the very pulsation of the I' and the 'ipseity of the I.' *Totality and Infinity: An Essay on Exteriority* (Pittsburgh: Duquesne University Press, 1969), pp. 113, 115; cf. pp. 147f.

become foundational for our being-in-the-world. We live from our joys, and what we most enjoy, we live from. The economy of our joys indicates our fundamental dynamic life-orientation, the way in which we live from and before others, the world and God. Joy invigorates and directs our concrete living.[11]

We most enjoy that which sustains us, that from which we live. We therefore need and depend upon the objects of our enjoyment. Yet, joy indicates a relationship to them, which goes beyond satisfaction of needs and desires, and which gives a character of freedom to our dependence on them. Joy relates us to realities other than ourselves non-instrumentally, in ways that go beyond what is strictly necessary to the physiological, psychological or any other dimension of life. Joy indicates the finding of abundance beyond what is strictly necessary or of direct, functional utility.[12] Joy is excessive; it is being-filled and being-overflowing. It represents desire, though desire so in touch with the overflowing plenitude of its object, and of living in relation to it, that it cannot properly be sated. In such desire and joy there is a responsibility towards that which is desired, to seek, celebrate, respond to and be stretched by its proper abundance and integrity. It is at the same time an orientation on oneself and on another. In a strong sense, one depends on what one most desires and has joy in. Curiously, *enjoyment* of our needs takes us beyond the physiological category of need and undercuts our usual notions of dependence. That I may have joy in that on which I depend indicates that I live my own life in relation to this reality; indeed, in relation to this dependence my joy marks out a kind of independence or, better, personal integrity of living. So, joy cuts across our usual ways of construing dependence and autonomy. It establishes the person's uniqueness and integrity apart from those others she enjoys. Yet, that independence is rooted in and dependent upon enjoyment of something other than herself, which intensifies the integrity of her lived personal identity. Hence, joy is a mode of relationship, both expressive of and constitutive for personal identity and integrity.[13]

Joy establishes, expresses and intensifies the integrity of a personal identity, being a relationship with an object of joy from the depths from which one lives. Clearly, relationships that are joyless are alienating and

11. Ibid., pp. 110f.

12. So, again, Levinas in ibid., p. 112: 'The bare fact of life is never bare . . . Life's relation to the very conditions of its life becomes the nourishment and content of that life. Life is *love of life* . . .' (italics in original); Eberhard Jüngel, *God as the Mystery of the World* (Grand Rapids: Eerdmans, 1983), pp. 192f.   13. See Levinas, *Totality and Infinity*, pp. 114f., 143, 147ff.

disintegrating. Yet it does not automatically follow that joy is an indicator of the absence of pathology. For, whilst joy is related to integrity, the question remains as to whether the actualised integrity of a personal identity, intensified through joy in relationship, is subject to distortion. Distortions in identity will be founded on and expressed in distorted forms of joy, or finding joy in an inappropriate object. Full and genuine joy is a relationship with another oriented on, not any possible integrity, but the fullest and most genuine integrity possible. So the object of one's fundamental joy is of decisive importance in determining whether, even in joy, one intensifies and resonates with dynamic integrity, expansive of who one truly is and can be, whilst oriented on the fullness of the other as he is and can be, beyond present definitions and self-understanding.

Faith

This is why it is inadequate to say that faith in God does not involve a dissolution or loss of the integrity; one must go on to say that it involves an expansion and deepening of the dynamic identity and integrity *proper to the person*. For the dynamic being of God is oriented towards filling and fulfilling ourselves with our own proper integrity in unimaginable abundance. The dynamics of human integrity are founded on their 'right relation' to the dynamics of God, and joy in God is thoroughly dynamic. Joy in God stretches one to respond to new, fuller and richer ways of being even more oneself in relation; it neither confers nor blesses a static integrity of identity.

This is precisely how Augustine understands the Spirit's instilling of the spirit of faith: as exciting willing into a new orientation upon God which, because God is not properly extrinsic to the person's proper order, is at the same time a renewed and properly reoriented orientation upon oneself. In faith, one internalises the dynamics of a God who is radically and genuinely for us. The spirit of faith is the excited and redirected energy (desire)[14] through which a person answers by orienting herself in the excess of joy, which repeats and redoubles as it internalises God's excessive movement *towards her*. In faith, one commits personal energy in consensual response to the dynamic in which God is for us, and finds oneself simultaneously filled with joy in God and oneself and others. Through the commitment of such personal energy, that dynamic is inter-

14. On his use and departure from Classical uses of desire and joy, see William S. Babcock, 'Augustine on Sin and Moral Agency', *Journal of Religious Ethics*, 16/1 (1988), 43f.

nalised and redoubled.[15] In the dynamic joy of faith, letting 'God be God' enables one to stretch towards being genuinely and fully oneself.

> Faith is that human attitude toward God which is called forth by God himself, in which man, completely without coercion and gladly, relates himself to God. The most original attitude of one ego to another, an attitude called forth by that other one, completely uncoerced and realised gladly, is *joy*. For that reason, one can say, 'joy in God' instead of 'faith'. For faith permits God to be that one who in and of himself *is for us* and *takes us unto himself* so that we do not *want to be* what we are without him. The self-definition for which man is determined in faith can thus only be the immediacy of a defined joy. Joy in God would then be the origin, the source, of the true thought of God, to the extent that joy is the 'existential' in which God is thinkable *for the sake of his own self*. For joy is always joy in something for its own sake.[16]

Worship

Faith is the energising spirit and worship the active form, in which human beings – excited, energised and directed by the Spirit – direct (better, stretch) all the energies of our own (situated) being towards the God whose own dynamic order is directed towards us and our world. Worship is that active, attentive response to the dynamic order of God, in which it becomes focused for us and the dynamics of human life become concentrated and focused, 'stretched', in responding orientation. In worship, our own dynamic order or relatedness is blessed, continually opened to and

15. Caution is required here, lest concern with the non-alienation of human integrity in faith misleads us into over-exaggeration back into assertions of the precedence of the interests of an independently constituted human integrity. Faith as joy in God excludes motivation and movement by self-interest – because it is somehow good for me. Indeed, genuine joy implies disinterest in outcomes altogether. It is simply captivated by wonder at God. There can be no instrumental or extrinsic rationale for joyful faith, since, in joy, nothing is withheld 'outside' of the relationship, there are no 'extrinsic' reasons, purposes, values or desires. All are captivated by the object of joy. Joy delights in its object for no other reason than pure delight in its being (Jüngel, *God as the Mystery of the World*, pp. 192f.). In the joy of faith, the overflowing plenitude of God is met with the excessive response of wonder and delight, which drives to worship. It is not true to say that this is selfless, since in joy one relates one*self* to God. And because God is in movement towards the self, active joy in God enlarges as it reorients. But it is not self-interested in the normal sense of the term.

16. Jüngel, *God as the Mystery of the World*, p. 192, emphasis in original; cf. 'My Theology; A Short Summary' in his *Theological Essays*, II (Edinburgh: T. & T. Clark, 1995), pp. 7ff. The disinclination to view faith as coerced represents an affirmation of it as a self-directed response, genuinely of the person, which at the same time is not 'coerced' by necessity but rather exceeds it as 'more than necessary' (pp. 192f.). Insofar as it appears to represent the usual modern understanding that heteronomy is avoided only by advocating a strict absence of determination, it sits somewhat awkwardly with the general thrust of Jüngel's work and cries out for Augustine's distinction between force and coercion.

incorporated in the dynamic order of God. Our own dynamic order is enriched through its incorporation and direction through worship into the dynamic order of God.[17] To speak of human beings as being constituted as and through dynamic order is to speak of being, identity and integrity as occurring through self-structuring in relationships. In worship, this dynamic ordering of self-structuring is incorporated into an overarching ecology. Relational dynamics between oneself and others, oneself and the material world, between oneself and the determinate social context (and so on) are all drawn into relation to the dynamic order of God. Consequently, they may now draw on and be excited towards the energies of a fuller dynamic order themselves, making possible higher-quality relationality and intensification of identity and integrity. Worship of the triune God intensifies and energises *being* as communion.

Joy in God is a way of living out and finding ever richer ways of being in communion with others, within the demands of concrete and changing situations and ecologies of relationship. It is surely joy in God, but it is also joy in oneself, in others, in the world. Joy as intensification of one's being-in-communion spills over into, and is experienced in, every relationship. It is the mode of participation in delight in the abundance of God for the world. This also explains why Augustine speaks of love as inseparable from faith: love of God, oneself and others is excited by the Spirit's activity. That is to say, there is a joy in God, oneself, others which seeks the richest, fullest being of each and relation with each. The mutuality, which is the mark of 'right relation' with God, is loving joy. This, the jubilant dynamics of worship, is Augustine's standard of normative reference. Here freedom is redefined as an intensification of the self through 'right relation' with and oriented towards the 'otherness' of God and other people in joy. Consequently, freedom and responsibility towards the full reality of God and others are indivisible. Freedom in joy is not founded on the separation of the isolated self, but is profoundly relational, oriented towards the genuine joy of God and others, and hence also oneself.

Worship as normative standard

Pride revisited

Without a sense of the way in which the trinitarian God functions as the controlling concept in discerning the nature of faith, sin and worship,

17. For the foregoing, see Hardy, 'The Foundation of Cognition and Ethics in Worship', pp. 13–17.

Augustine – no less than the rest of orthodox Christianity – is prone both to being misunderstood and misunderstanding himself.[18] More precisely, the normative standard of reference, which operates in the background of his discussion of sin, will be missed, leading to serious misunderstanding, not least in the interpretation of pride. It is only when pride is read in the context of the normative standard of reference of joyful worship that the sinfulness of pride may properly be construed. Whilst the way that he sometimes speaks of pride and the priority he lends it in his understanding of sin can suggest otherwise, it is the gift of faith, not self-obeisance, that is the opposite of pride for Augustine.

Why, then, is pride sin in this perspective, and in what does its sinfulness consist? Pride is misdirected worship: living within and from a false dynamic. Pride is sin, for Augustine, not because it is a refusal to be nothing and to allow God to be everything; rather, because it represents a stepping out of the ecology of relation to the dynamic order of God. Pride elevates oneself (or that with which one identifies oneself: class, race, sex, political movement) to the ultimate good, the arbiter and criterion of the worth of everything else, the good towards which all other goods (already defined in terms of their utility to the self) are to be dedicated. Pride is hence the attempt to live without reference to external realities as values, limits or claims, the active referral of all goods to the self. But it may also take the form of a falsely arrested dynamic, an attempt to stabilise identities apart from dynamic relationality. Since the proud self is found good in itself, it stabilises itself in a non-dynamic order of being or equilibrium, which must then be defended against relation with what is 'other'. Hence, it is unresponsive to external realities and values, confident in its own current and future worth without adaptation. In pride, human beings assert their unrelated identity, autonomy and potency in determining and doing the good. The sin of pride lies, not in finding human integrity and autonomy good, but in founding them in supposed separation from God.

Augustine does not emphasise the seriousness of pride, then, primarily as a means for protecting the sovereignty of God from the invalid incursions of human freedom. Rather, he does it as a means for drawing attention to the true nature of that freedom; not to disempower human beings, but to liberate us from the illusion that we have freedom, power

18. Cf. here the *theological* foundation of Kierkegaard's construction of selfhood, which is also frequently elided in feminist use of him (see *The Sickness unto Death* (Princeton: Princeton University Press, 1941), p. 49).

and integrity *apart from* the dynamic order of God. Pelagianism, in his view, invited people to live as if the power and integrity of their being were independent of God's active and dynamic relation to us in grace, mediated to us through the immanent dynamics of the Spirit (as well as independent of and unaffected by situational distortions). So, by pride, Augustine means the attempt to live from some form of primal self-relation. Pride is, for Augustine, a mistake about the conditions for human integrity and the nature of freedom, which supposes in part that we stand outside of relation to God and have criteria for evaluating anything and everything – including God – which are independently derived. Integrity and freedom are given and secured, not only apart from relation to God, but from an overstabilised order of being, a static equilibrium. Relation with the transcendent reality and claims of God or others threaten disturbance in its present identity structure and must be resisted, either by refusal of relation or by imposing one's own order on others through the patterning of oppressive relations.

The true life, by contrast, lives from relation to the abundance of God, finding the joy of that relation suffuses all others, including that to self. Faith directs one towards joy in love of others and the world, as one discovers that one is related to God, as the source of dynamic order, exciting into further abundance and joy, in and through these relationships too. Far from assuring human integrity and autonomy, pride leads to a disintegration and collapse of human being by unplugging it from the energising source of its life and integrity: its primal relation to God. It makes us incapable of praising God and of finding joy in ourselves, others and all aspects of reality through the dynamics of right relation to God.

Self-'loss' and worship

If the standard of reference is really right worship, then the emphasis on pride as the paradigmatic sin does seem misleading, if not misplaced. But once the emphasis shifts towards a definition of sin as misdirected worship, then self-'loss' is also immediately recognisable as sin, since love of self for and from God and before others are necessary constituents of worship.[19] In sloth, by contrast, the personal energies of life-intentionality are incorporated into dynamics which would be undermined were such energies to be *directed from* the dynamic integrity of a personal centre.

19. As Bernard of Clairvaux pointed out, the highest and most difficult stage of love of God is to love the self for God's sake (*The Love of God*, chs. 8–15). Cf. Paul Tillich's remarks concerning self-love in *The Shaking of the Foundations* (London: SCM, 1949), p. 158.

Personal energies are rather excited, directed and drawn away from such centring, and the energies necessary to sustain integrity in life-orientation and identity structure are dissipated and disoriented. With the energies of life-intentionality disoriented from central focusing, one loses the grounding for joy and love. Whereas pride involves over-expansive openness, sloth indicates an under-expansive or contracting openness. Pride focuses the energies of personal identity in a self-grounded and referring dynamic, thus blocking both transcendent orientation and the energies of a self-transcending dynamic order. Sloth blocks the energies of the dynamic order of God by exchanging them for a transcendent orientation which is self-dissipating, and which therefore counters the call to respond to God which intensifies dynamic integrity. Both represent disordered and disoriented desire.

Back to standards

Against the enclosed self-reference of pride, as against the constricting openness in relation of sloth, Augustine sets the permanent expansiveness of joyful, forgiving and confessing love. Love of God and praise of God invite, require and empower love of and joy in others and oneself. For the self-transforming reorientation of life towards God in worship is characterised by Augustine in terms of superabundance: joy in the Lord. This superabundance is set against the false overabundance of pride. In the joy of faith and worship, abundance is properly founded within the ecology and economy of God's transforming presence and action. Worship is not, then, a diminution of human selfhood and freedom, but their proper foundation – except that 'foundation' is far too static and thin a term for being caught up in the dynamic order of the triune God through the total life-orientation that is worship, christologically shaped and mediated as a being-for-God-and-others.

> Good worship resists any self-positing of the 'I'. The self is posited by God in community without that necessarily being a dominating heteronomy. Likewise, there is no 'shattered cogito' in fragmentation, but there can be a complex gathering of the self in diverse relationships ... before a God who is trusted as the gatherer of selves in blessing ... it summons the self into practices of joyful responsibility.[20]

> The 'I' has God intrinsic to its identity through worship: the one before whom it worships is the main clue to its selfhood.[21]

20. Ford, *Self and Salvation*, p. 99.   21. Ibid., p. 128.

Worship inspired through being loved and delighted in by God reconfigures the self-esteem of the worshipper. There is a radical affirmation of
self-worth through which intensified community goes with intensified
particularity.

Pride and sloth are modes of sin because they are ways of being a self-
in-relation which block the energies of dynamic order. In different ways,
they establish fixed and static structures of being-in-relation, resistant to
being excited by the Spirit into worship of God. This fixity is itself a sign
of their disorientation, that the dynamics of identity and integrity are
founded on and oriented towards some other 'good' than the triune God.
Some alternative dynamic becomes foundational to the commitment of
personal energies in life-intentionality. Some other relationship – to
oneself, others and the world – becomes basic to the self. Joy is misplaced
or displaced as its true conditions are lost and the person becomes disoriented at the level of their most basic intentionality and desire: joy.

Sin is thence resistance or opposition to the energies of God's dynamic
order, the disorientation of personal energies in an alternative dynamic, a
distortion or disruption of the conditions for genuine joy.

According to Augustine, faith is the consequence of the triune God's
exciting, enlarging and directing the will from within, without dominating it. The dynamism of the will is caught up in and incorporated into the
dynamic of the life of God, through the life of faith, the particular marks
of which are worship, joy and love. The will, faith and God are implicitly
understood, not as *things*, but in dynamic terms. This requires us to think
quite differently from the way we are habituated to do in our culture.
Faith is free. But its freedom does not consist in its being the uncoerced
choice of a neutral will (i.e., one standing apart from God), which it could
have made otherwise. Faith is free because it is joy in God, which enlarges
and intensifies who one really is and can be, in relation to the dynamics
through which God is who God is. Freedom is being freed for God
through the spirit of faith which drives to worship. In the joy of worship,
the will achieves its proper dynamic; is habituated within its proper
ecology and economy. What is primal is not the solitude of the will free
from all determining relationships, but our relation to – or, better, our
incorporation into – the dynamics through which God is God and God for
us. The overflowing abundance of joy and astonishment in this God, who
is not only for us but 'the inexhaustible mystery'[22] and foundation of our

---

22. Jüngel, 'My Theology; A Short Summary', p. 7.

being and of all being, is prior to and more basic than freedom as conventionally understood. Worshipping God is the context within which freedom, understood now as the correlate of joy, becomes possible. Since the dynamics of worship are not principally individual, but drive one towards joy in relationship with others, we might also say that relationality and situatedness are also prior to and conditioning of individuality, such that proper individuality is not principally a mode of separation and isolation but one of permanently expansive joy in relation.

Sin as disruption of genuine worship: idolatry

An understanding of sin (pathology) which formally matches this *logos* must be similarly dynamic and expressed in terms of worship and joy. Now sin appears in terms that re-echo the consideration of willing in previous chapters: as a conditioning disorientation of willing from within, which runs counter to the orientation of the spirit of faith. Sin is hence, not so much free choice, as spiritual disorientation of the whole person at the most fundamental level of life-intentionality and desire. Through our active willing, we internalise, perform and redouble the pathological dynamics in which we are incorporated. In this way, we are caught up in situational and relational dynamics through which the dynamics of God should and could be 'naturally' mediated to us, but which either distort or block them. The consequent disruption of the proper conditions of true praise may run in one of two directions. First, unplugged from the field of force exerted by the dynamics of God, one or other of the dynamics of human situatedness (material, physiological, social or psychological) exert their own independent power. Asserting themselves as universal and absolute frames of reference, rather than local mediations of the dynamics of God, they misdirect the intentionalities of those captivated by them. Here an alternative, ultimate orientation substitutes for that to God in genuine worship. Second, rather than mislocating God and misdirecting worship, situational dynamics may undermine the conditions for genuine worship of God by fostering an active misperception of the nature of God's being and identity, and so of the true dynamics of human beings in right relation to the dynamics of God. Typically, this form of idolatry operates with a less dynamic and much restricted sense of the fecundity and plenitude of possibility in God. Put far too simplistically, one might say that wrong worship either has the wrong object or the wrong dynamic. In either case, wrong worship is a dynamic disorientation of human lives away from the reality of God and consequently from others and from their own true fullness or being. Genuine worship involves that stretching towards fullness of being-in-communion in response to the abundance and plenitude of God which is joy. We should therefore expect the disorientation of being-in-relation through wrong worship to involve a corresponding constriction and restriction of the energies of being-in-relation, of the freedom associated with joy.

The construal of sin as disorientation or distortion of worship is familiar from both Bible and tradition, where it is named idolatry.[23] Whilst the word might conjure up images of people bowing down in ritualised acts of explicit worship before graven images, it has a much more nuanced connotation in its Biblical and traditional uses. It is neither restricted in its reference to explicit acts of worship, nor primarily concerned with the holding of false propositional beliefs. Both worship and therefore idolatry in the Bible are not primarily ideational realities, but pertain to the fundamental orientation of human lives in practice: whether or not they are oriented towards the blessing, glory and majesty of the true God.[24] Idolatry has to do primarily with active relationality, with behaviour; only secondarily with ideas. That is why, in the Old Testament, often what principally divides the faithful from idolaters is neither the form or substance of their theistic beliefs, nor 'the metaphysical picture of the world in itself, but the *method of relating* to it through worship'.[25]

Idolatry in the Bible concerns active orientation in relationship, the energised dynamics of the concrete practice of relationality. Here is an immediate contrast with our own cultural situation, where we have to remind ourselves that sin is a theological and therefore *relational* language.[26] Every verse of the Bible, however, is permeated by an undergirding consciousness of living in and through the great and dynamic drama of relation with God, which permeates all dimensions and aspects of life in such a way as to render problematic any firm distinction between sacred and profane.[27] Biblically speaking, no matter what other relationships might be being offended against, the category 'sin' is deployed to indicate that the real offence at the heart of any other pathology is against the dynamics of relation with God. Sin indicates the religious and theo-

---

23. Tertullian is the earliest example of a Christian thinker holding that all sin is at heart some form of idolatry in *De Idolatria* (Leiden: E. J. Brill, 1987), 1:1, 4f.   24. 1 Cor. 10:30.
25. Moshe Halbertal and Avishai Margalit, *Idolatry* (Cambridge, MA: Harvard University Press, 1992), pp. 3f.   26. See pp. 7ff., above.
27. In the Hebrew Scriptures, we find that indicated in words used to denote sin that are not intrinsically specifically religious, but which achieve specifically theological connotation in being thus used: e.g., Prov. 8:36; 19:2; Ps. 25:8.

logical dimension of all pathology, even those which it might be tempting to handle in secular or profane terms.[28] For the bonds of the covenant relation, which saturates Old and New Testaments alike, is the all-pervasive and ultimately determining context for human life. There is no outside to our relation to God; nothing in human affairs is unrelated to it, nor neutral in respect of it. However else it may be described or evaluated (in moral terms, say, as an offence against another), all human living enacts an orientation in relation to God, which constitutes its fundamental reality and the prime means for evaluation. In all our relationships, we live out an active relation or misrelation to God, we enter the dynamics of worshipping God or other forces and realities. Sin is therefore living out an active misrelation to God. Significantly, the words most commonly used for 'sin' in the Hebrew Scriptures are dynamic, conveying a sense of movement away from the proper orientation of life before and towards God.[29] Significantly, too, Jesus actively opposes sin by energising a counter-dynamic that reorients people in their relationships one with another and with God (love of God and neighbour as oneself). The gospels present him as actively drawing on a dynamic ecology of right relation with God, presented in terms which go way beyond what would be necessary for the restoration of lost relation. Instead, the Kingdom empowers people towards amazing abundance and plenitude in relation to God and others: the messianic feast. Since sin is energised disorientation in relationships, opposition to sin must take the form of a comprehensively energised reorientation towards the superabundance of life in, with, towards and from God, the bringing of a new covenant (indicated most clearly in the narration of the Last Supper) through the re-energising of superabundant life and relationality at the point at which they are most constricted in their opposition to God.

This is especially evident in the presentation of sin as idolatry, representing and rooted in breakdown from the human side of the covenant relationship. Israel was called into the dynamics of a relationship of reciprocated fidelity: to reciprocate the faithfulness Yahweh showed to them. That required ordering their life around an exclusive relationship to Him: having only Yahweh as their God and the community's living in and from the dynamics of a personal relationship with Him; by worshipping

---

28 See, e.g., Ps. 51:6; 2 Sam. 11; 12:13; Dan. 11:32.

29. This is true of *hata'*, *'iwwah* and *pasha'*. See the comment of Gottfried Quell in 'Sin in the Old Testament', in Gottfried Quell, *et al.*, *Sin* (London: Black, 1951), p. 16 (extracted from Kittel's *Theological Wordbook of the Old Testament*).

Him, and only Him, in the most expansive and pervasive sense that that word may convey. God was the only force in the world to be worshipped, and whatever may be ascribed to other forces, active relation to them was to be co-ordinated into the ecology of this ultimate and exclusive loyalty.[30] Again, it is necessary to emphasise the prominence of behaviour over explicitly formulated ideas or beliefs.[31] The communal *practices* of exclusive fidelity (including, significantly, the proscription of idolatry) preceded any explicit conceptualisation of monotheistic belief.[32] That followed the *practical* incorporation into the dynamics of an exclusive, personal relationship with Yahweh. The threat which idolatry is again and again taken by the prophets to represent precisely mirrors Israel's own experience of genuine worship. Incorporation into the practice of worship actively reorients the whole of life around a different set of values and beliefs. These operational beliefs embedded in the practice of a life-orientation may initially run directly counter to beliefs consciously held and affirmed, yet may (but do not necessarily) subsequently reconfigure *conscious* intentionality. Perceptions about what is true, good, right, valuable are reconfigured by the way in which we *live out* a relation to reality which makes a particular force, dynamic, relationship or reality the ground and criterion of active life-intentionality. All other desires and values are then co-ordinated and configured around it. This was precisely what happened to Israel's belief system when the relationship to Yahweh was reconfigured as exclusive of all other loyalties and the whole of the life of the cult was ordered around explicit and implicit acknowledgment of Him as their only God: as exclusive worship of Yahweh became foundational for all other relationships. Exclusive worship of Yahweh was not initially anchored in a set of monotheistic beliefs, but it did eventually reconfigure them completely, including changing the register of the term 'god'. Living from the dynamics of this exclusive relationship led to a comprehensive reconfiguring of reality (including, significantly, the soteriological reading of *world* history as under Yahweh's sovereignty). This God was more than Israel's tribal deity; this was the one, true God, creator

---

30. Halbertal and Margalit, *Idolatry*, pp. 4f.

31. This is more widely true of the OT's narration of sin, which is frequently concerned with behaviour regardless of intention. See, e.g., Lev. 15:1–32.

32. See the interesting and penetrating analysis of Halbertal and Margalit (*Idolatry*, pp. 1–3, 10f., 21f., 31, 36, 163f., 183f., 229, 237f.). They also make the point here that identification of the sin of idolatry depended on an anthropomorphic understanding of God and the corresponding construal of God's relationship to Israel as personal. Anthropomorphism is the condition necessary for the recognition of idolatry as sin; not, as is usually supposed, a primary form of that misrepresentation of God which is idolatry.

and Lord of the whole world. In the end, Yahweh was so differentiated from other candidates for deity that, whereas Israelites were prohibited from considering them 'gods' on account of their unworthiness (they were pronounced 'idols' instead), the use of that same word was proscribed in Yahweh's case on account of His holiness. Over against idols (as against idolatrous representation of God), the majesty, holiness, transcendence and constantly amazing abundance of life in God defeats any and all fixed or static representation.

The essence of sin consequently emerges as violation of the faithfulness constitutive of the dynamics of a committed personal relationship with God. Sin is idolatry, depicted as a counter-dynamic to fidelity to the one, true God (adultery, fornication, lust, whoredom[33]) by having other gods (substitution) or as concrete orientation which reduces God to an idol. In either case, the total disorientation of desire (the internal dynamics of life-intentionality) is embedded in idolatry, which runs counter to the dynamics of faith. That is particularly poignant when desire determines behaviour (active worship) contrary to consciously held beliefs (underlining that idolatry is not and need not involve any cognitive error).[34] Here the competition between satisfaction of specific desires and loyalty to God as God is obvious, in the unplugging of the force of such desire from the comprehensive ecology determined by an all-encompassing loyalty to God. A key feature of the substitutionary mode of idolatry is thus granting independence or ultimacy to other forces in the world, which has the effect of living out a different ordering of the world than that which accords with the sovereignty of God. The idol exerts a comprehensive and compelling field of force, which sequesters all other dynamics and forces (including God) into its own service. The worth of all else becomes a matter of its functional utility in relation to that which is worshipped, which functions as the criterion of truth and rightness as well as of value (goodness). Not only does the idol override all other claims, it bends the whole of life into its exclusive service.

Above all, then, sin is failure in orientation in the world to God as God: disruption of the proper conditions and practices of right worship. It is

33. Exod. 34:15f.; Hos. 1:2; 2:9–15; 3:1; Ezek. 16:15–34; Jer. 2:18ff. Halbertal and Margalit, *Idolatry*, ch.1. Tertullian (*De Idolatria*, 1:2) also employs the metaphor of adultery, but one step removed from the explicit idea of a personal relationship with a personal God, and with more of a philosophical than scriptural warrant. For him idolatry in this respect is adultery against the truth, which carries a taint such as that of fornication. Nonetheless, the scriptural context cannot be far away here.

34. Ezek. 16:15–34, giving a different twist to the terms of Hosea's narration in this respect (2:9–15).

through worship of the living God in the spirit of faith that people are incorporated into the joyful dynamics of life in abundance. Therefore, any distortion or substitution in life-orientation implies a constriction in living. Measured against the criterion of the abundant life of God, idols are dead.[35] Furthermore, their worship substitutes comprehensive dynamics of closure and rigidity in relational orientation (death) for the joyful, expansive, life-giving dynamism of true worship.[36] It binds the dynamism of our life-intentionalities into a comprehensive disorientation in all our relationships and in all dimensions of life. The Biblical language of demonic possession is an adequate representation of the way in which idols overpower and come to possess us.[37] They can only substitute for God by exerting demonic power over us, twisting our whole sense of reality and ecology of relatedness. Idolatrous dynamics colonise the whole of our life-intentionality as a false and falsifying dynamic supplants that of worship of the true God. In Biblical terminology, the heart is bound and hardens.[38] In genuine worship, people draw on and are stretched by the dynamics of God's abundance and plenitude; in idolatry, we are energised by, live from and towards, other forces which de-energise and disorient from the abundance, fullness and freedom of life with God. Chief among the marks of this constriction in life is the disruption of the bonds of human solidarity and community. Whereas true worship energises the loving dynamics of genuine community, idolatry undermines them (Babel). For only worship that draws on the dynamics of God, radically and genuinely *for all*, can energise and orient us towards genuine being and relation with all others which is universally extensive.

---

35. Rom. 1:23; cf. Wisd. 13:10.
36. So, e.g., the oppositions in Gal. 5:19–26 and 1 Pet. 4:1–6. See also Rom.6:23; Eph. 2:1.
37. Rom. 7:14–20. More generally, see further Paul Tillich, *Systematic Theology* (London: SCM, 1978) I, p. 134; III, p. 109.
38. The disorientation of the heart (active life-intentionality) is a recurring theme. See, e.g., Deut. 9:6, 13f.; Isa. 46:12; Ezek. 14:7f, 36:26.

10

Concrete idolatries

The previous chapter extrapolated out from the intimations in Augustine's construal of willing and of sin in order to characterise the necessarily theological construction he places on the dynamics of willing. This has given specifically theological content to the pathological dynamics of bound willing: in sin, the will is bound into the dynamics of idolatry. Thus, the bondage of the will hypothesis, which has proved its explanatory power through the course of the preceding deliberations, has now been given a specific, theological expression (in the course of which, the understanding of idolatry has itself been enriched). It is worth now returning to the concrete pathologies in order directly to test the explanatory and descriptive power of this theological identification of core pathology.

Does sin as idolatry hold descriptive and explanatory power in relation to concrete pathologies? Can the pathological dynamics of sexual abuse of children and the holocaust be re-expressed in terms of idolatry? if so, does that yield a richer comprehension of them? In answering these questions, what will we be looking for?

To worship is actively to orient and order one's life, whether more or less explicitly, around a reality as primary to and constitutive of meaning, worth, truth and value. In more dynamic terms, it is for one's personal energy (spirit) to be energised by and oriented towards this reality as the energising ground and criterion of active life-intentionality. Thus what is worshipped is an absolute, unconditional and therefore exclusive horizon of loyalty to which all else is related and in the service of which all is done.

> What makes something into an absolute is that it is both overriding and demanding. It claims to stand superior to any competing claim,

and unlike merely an overriding rule it is also something that provides a program and a cause, thereby demanding dedication and devotion.

Any nonabsolute value that is made absolute and demands to be the center of dedicated life is idolatry.[1]

To ask whether pathological dynamics are idolatrous is in the first place to ask whether they have these formal features of exclusive 'devotion'. (We must remember in asking it that this is primarily a question of *practice*, not of conscious beliefs.) That will tell us whether it may be analysed in terms of worship. What we then need to know is whether such worship is genuine or idolatrous – i.e., whether they may be analysed in terms of the dynamics of worship which substitute or misidentify God, thus disorienting from full and genuine relation to God. We will need to ask what people are committing their energy to, ultimately; what dynamics they are drawing on and being drawn into; what they most desire; what energises them and gives their lives direction. Above all, we will need to compare the dynamics of genuine worship with the pathological and to ask whether the latter establish a counter-dynamic to the former. More specifically, that will mean asking whether and how the conditions for joy and praise are blocked, distorted or disoriented.

Concrete dynamics of worship?

Notwithstanding the substantive differences between them, and the different ways in which they achieve such totalisation, the pathological dynamics of both concrete situations insinuate themselves into life-trajectories as absolute and exclusive.

Sexual abuse of children

In chapter 4, I portrayed the dynamics of sexual abuse as involving practices which isolate the child from other, transcendent frameworks of evaluation, whilst enclosing her in the comprehensive framework of meaning, truth, value and action offered by and through the abusive relationship.[2] By isolating the child, abusive dynamics may also raise themselves to primary significance as foundational to personal integrity, identity and life-trajectory. Abusive dynamics insinuate themselves into the internal structures of identity and communication as the sole frame-

---

1. Moshe Halbertal and Avishai Margalit, *Idolatry* (Cambridge, MA: Harvard University Press, 1992), pp. 245, 246. Cf. Paul Tillich, *Systematic Theology* (London: SCM, 1978), I, p. 13; Edward Farley, *Good and Evil: Interpreting a Human Condition* (Minneapolis: Fortress Press, 1990), p. 135.   2. See above, pp. 52–4, 59–62.

work for interpreting reality and as the sole criterion for evaluation and action.[3] That means that, in every relationship, the abusive meanings sedimented[4] into identity to enable survival are repeatedly enacted and confirmed. Because they function as the portable means for survival, which must be robust against any disconfirmation and communicated into every relation,[5] the structures of identity and relation harden and the power of the pathological dynamic is redoubled and ever more deeply embedded. Accommodation is too thin a term for this highly energetic process, through which abuse fosters an abused identity, framework of meaning and evaluation that shape the whole of a life-trajectory. All desires are ultimately directed towards the maintenance and strengthening of abused identity. Where abuse becomes foundational for the identity of the victim or survivor, personal energies are bent towards continual maintenance and nourishment of pathological dynamics in every interaction, and external energy sources will either be bent in their service too or else resisted altogether. All sources of energy, all other dynamics of life, they sequester, colonise, or resist.

This, I would contend, represents a clear, concrete manifestation of the dynamics pertaining to worship: the direction of all energies towards demands which do not only override, but exclude, all other loyalties and which are lived as foundational to identity, relation, meaning, worth and truth. Nothing transcends this locus of commitment, which energises and orients being-in-relation by establishing itself as a total enclosure of living. The dynamics of abuse therefore function in the life-orientation of many victims/survivors as the absolute boundary and horizon for all commitment, the norm for measuring goodness and value and for construing and acting in reality. Itself unconditioned, it functions as the fundamental condition for the worth of all else. Access to any transcendent reality, frames of reference, value, energy, potentiality is blocked as this absolute presents itself as the total framework of meaning, truth, value and action, shaping intentionality and desire as well as deliberation and active expression.

Holocaust

The pathological dynamics of the holocaust operated with some striking formal similarities. I described them in chapter 5 as colonising the social

---

3. Pp. 62f., above.
4. For fuller discussion of this term, see my *The Call to Personhood: A Christian Theory of the Individual in Social Relationships* (Cambridge: Cambridge University Press, 1990), pp. 40–2; 93–5; 116–18; 318.   5. See above, p. 75.

and material practices of a society. Whilst Nazi ideology obviously did achieve very explicit formulation in terms of beliefs, it is necessary to understand that conscious assent to the explicitly articulated ideas of the Nazi state was often secondary to people's being caught up in its material and social practices.[6] The latter shaped intentionality, both conscious and implicit, further radicalising the beliefs and practices of ideologues as well as securing the commitment of Party members. Furthermore, the dynamics operated in such a way as to secure the *practical* commitment of others (including bystanders and victims, but also many participants) without ever explicitly or obviously intruding into their set of con- sciously held beliefs. The dynamics for constructing a racial order became so powerful that they exerted a gravitational pull on all other dynamics in the situation (not least significant among them those of Christian faith and practice), drawing energy from as they redirected and redefined them. The practices of Nazism became the horizon for all commitments, action and intentionality, that to which almost all energies of public (and a good deal of private) life were ultimately committed in practice. Even where people held contrary beliefs, the orientation of actively committed intentionality and behaviour was in practice shaped by (and fed into) the dynamics of racial order. Everything except open rebellion led to *practical* participation in constructing a racial order, which had the further effect of normalising and radicalising both the practices and the construction of reality required and engendered through racially ordering dynamics. At the same time, the dynamics of racial ordering were energised and redou- bled as they colonised, sequestered and redirected other dynamics, even whilst masking the identity of that being worshipped (as in the way in which drawing on the dynamics of bureaucratic rationality radicalised action towards racial order).[7]

The Party's control of the institutions and processes of public life (including the means and framework through which the public good could be presented, celebrated and 'discussed'), the measures taken against non-conformity, coupled with fear of surveillance even in inti- mate contexts of life: all these were obvious and key components in the state's ability to secure commitment and dedication in practice. That was especially, but not exclusively, evident in the case of victims.[8] In addition, the significance should not be underestimated of presenting policy in terms of the quest for a just, right and true – indeed, perfect – order.[9] For

6. Pp. 80ff   7. Pp. 88ff   8. Pp. 98ff.   9. Pp. 82ff.

it was this that effectively collapsed eschatology into an historical project capable of attracting the dedication usually reserved for religious phenomena. In a sense, such pursuit creates a perpetual emergency, setting adherents on a permanent war-footing (intensified with the outcome of actual war) because the urgency of its demands are proportionate to the resistance of empirical reality to its claims – a resistance which must be cancelled out. In that context, action, which in normal circumstances would have been unacceptable, could be justified and excused as temporary 'emergency measures'. Facilitated partly by the appearance of temporary expediency, the creation of an emergency situation permitted the dynamics of racial order to operate as the criterion for the interpretation of reality (including, of course, the fact and character of an emergency situation), against which what is good, right and legitimate was discerned. The capacity of racially ordering dynamics to define and create an emergency situation was the point at which they not only became a self-legitimating criterion, norm and standard in public policy and practice, but at which they eliminated the claims of any competing, transcendent orientation and frame of reference.

In a different way, the effective sequestration of bureaucratic processes in formulating and administering policy further contributed towards this appearance of irresistible necessity. Nazi measures were justified on grounds of rational and therefore 'objective' analysis of the situation, governed by an 'objective' (purely instrumental) rationality of efficiency.[10] They could therefore commend themselves as what was objectively necessary, as quite independent of any particular ideological commitments and as value-free. In fact, bureaucratic rationality was not 'outside' the values and dynamics of racial order at all; it had already been drawn into their field of force and given an orientation towards their service. But its sequestration into the dynamics of racial order turned it into a vector carrying the pathogen of racial order, which enabled the latter to transmit and insinuate itself into other dimensions of public life in a covert way. Moral space was colonised by the criteria and standards of normative reference offered by technical-instrumental rationality. That incapacitated transcendent (supposedly non-objective) criteria of evaluation and left the regulation of moral space to the regulatory force of supposedly neutral, objective and value-free dynamics, in fact already sequestered by and oriented towards those of racial order.

10. Pp. 89ff.

We observe here the cumulative blocking of transcendence, together with the raising of the dynamics of racial order to the status of unconditioned, ultimate and absolute norm and horizon of committed intentionality in practice. Active life-intentionalities are enclosed in, energised by and exclusively oriented towards the dynamics of racial order.

True or false worship?

The dynamics of racial order in Nazi Germany, like those of childhood sexual abuse, correspond formally to those of worship. The question we must now ask is whether such worship is energised by, concentrates, participates in and 'answers' the dynamics of God's movement towards and for us, by virtue of which God is God. As I characterised them in the previous chapter, loving joy marks the dynamics of God. As the mark of genuine worship, this joy is therefore a point of discrimination between genuine and false forms. To ask whether the dynamics in these two concrete situations constitute genuine or idolatrous worship is therefore to ask whether they nourish, block or disorient genuine joy. For the blocking or disorientation of the dynamics of joy is the fundamental characteristic of idolatry and therefore of depth pathology from a theological point of view. What is damaged, abused, what people are disoriented from in pathological dynamics (which therapeutic measures should seek to regain), is not restricted to that which is strictly, functionally necessary. It is that which, in Jüngel's words, is 'more than necessary': a capacity for the super-abundance of joy in God, themselves and others; the energies of right worship.[11] This normative standard of reference resists that constriction of the full reality of persons often found in the heuristic tools used for guiding understanding and action in relation to pathological dynamics. Very rarely do the interpretive frameworks we most habitually deploy for this purpose encourage people to see themselves, or be seen and treated by others, as oriented towards and constituting a richer, deeper, more abundant and more particular reality than may be characterised in functional terms. Insofar as that is the case in practice, such frameworks repeat just that constriction of reality which people encounter in pathological dynamics, encouraging as well a much restricted conception of the energies of transformation available to people.

11. See my comments on pp. 200f.

Here we are able to glimpse what may be the nature of the theological task in relation to secular disciplines and the non-theological description of pathological dynamics. In exploring the potential for construing pathological dynamics in terms of the joy defined by the conditions of right worship of the triune God, I am not setting aside the non-theological descriptions worked out in conversation with secular disciplines in Part II. Potentially, however, applying the theological standard of normative reference (the dynamics of right worship), mediated through the notion of genuine joy, affords the possibility of indicating a greater underlying depth dimension to descriptions afforded through non-theological frames of interpretation.

Sexually abused children

In my description of the dynamics involved in sexual abuse of a child, I deliberately concentrated on the perspective of the child, not wishing to become distracted by questions as to abusers' motivations. I want now to remain true to my view that what the pathology is for the child, is independent of whatever it is the abuser is resolving for himself. Too much detail about the intentions and orientations of the abuser is therefore an unhelpful distraction. In particular, that means that I shall not discuss whether this is a distorted mode of sexual desire (and so sexual lust, 'joy' and 'enjoyment' directed towards an inappropriate 'object') or the means of satisfying other desires (resolving other pathological dynamics) through the medium of a sexualised relationship with a child. I want, if anything, to reinforce the point that such distinctions make no difference to what then goes on for the child. Furthermore, this means that I am not in a position to consider the existence or character of (the false and disoriented) joy in and for the abuser.

Notwithstanding that, however, what I can say is that the dynamics of abuse certainly do not intend and do not energise the genuine and full joy of the child. Joy which participates in and mediates the dynamics of God perfects and develops the dynamic order of persons-in-communion. In this joy, there is intensification of personal particularity in the dynamic ecology of joyful relation; whereas the intentionality of abuse reduces the child to a particular, perverse functionality or utility for the abuser. The child is not intended as having integrity in life-intentionality and identity apart from the abusive relationship: rather, these are to be structured around and energised by the dynamics of abuse as their prime determinant. Furthermore, the order of such intended identity will be non-dynamic, resistant to transcendence, development or transformation.

In other words, the abuser does not have genuine joy in and for the child.

Almost certainly, that will be read as an incredibly crass statement, one hardly credible as a response to the complexities and depths of the wickedness and damage of abuse – unless, that is, two things are recalled. First, that genuine joy concerns the deepest and fullest resonance of being-in-communion. Second, that the dynamics of abuse are frequently internalised and absolutised as the prime determinants shaping the development of identity and life-intentionality. Hence, abuse is more than the failure to recognise and respect the child as a locus of joy. That would be serious enough. But, since abusive dynamics are absolutist and internalised in the structures of identity and life-intentionality, the pathology is more severe still. Since abuse frequently colonises and sequesters the directionality of the child's own energies, her sense of reality, truth and goodness, we may say that what abuse is abuse of is the child's *own* capacity for, and orientation towards, joy. That is to say, it is abuse of her capacities for worship: an energised orientation towards the fullness of others, herself and God, which requires and facilitates the development and intensification of her own dynamic order.

Since abusive dynamics are not genuinely joyful, we have to say that abuse is not oriented on the child's particularity (or, for the sake of clarity, we had better say, *personal* particularity). They do not seek to engage or be engaged by, then intensify and develop, the dynamic order of her own particular identity in its (dynamic) integrity. Abusive relationships are not *personal*. The child is not sought as having that centredness characteristic of personhood and necessary for right worship. He is not therefore intended as having his own integrity as a locus of blessing and joy in himself and for others, establishing both limits and claims on others, from and towards which praise, blessing and joy may be directed. Yet, *in quite another sense,* we might also say that abuse *over*particularises in its overdetermination and overspecification of life-intentionality and identity. Identity is bound to one particular relation and dynamic, which energises, orients, directs and defines identity and life-intentionality into the future. The dynamics of abuse easily become absolutised in the construction and orientation of identity, repeated and redoubled through lived intentionality as the sole source of meaning, truth, and value. Access to transcendent sources of meaning, energy, truth and value are effectively blocked and, with it, the possibilities and energies of self-transformation, including the development of one's own dynamic order. One might say that idolatry reduces people to their determinacy and the determination of a closed totality.[12] But, since transcendence is an elemental condition of the human, this is a constriction and distortion of the very possibility of being human.

I have observed a number of times already that this entails the blocking of transcendence in several ways. What does this mean, more concretely? It means, in the first place, the construction of a rigid identity structure, robust against disconfirmation or transcendence. Abuse tends to press victims and survivors towards structures of identity which approximate to those indicated by the terms 'sloth' (depleted and passive sense of self, oriented towards further victimisation) or 'pride' (overbearing, dominating, apparently over-full sense of self, oriented towards abusive behaviour).[13] In both cases, the structure is non-dynamic. That is, it blocks and resists any intimation of transcendence, of the limitations of the absolutised dynamics which energise it and around which it is built. More concretely, such structures are closed against intimations of their own limitation, fragility or inadequacy, and so their own transformation or development. What is genuinely other must be ignored, resisted, opposed or domesticated. All relationships will be entered in pursuit or expectation of the reconfirmation of static identity. Why? Because absolute loyalty and devoted service is owed to idolatrous abusive dynamics, which have become foundational to meaningful and integrated life-intentionality. Anything 'other' will threaten to disturb the equilibrium of the only identity found viable to survive the trauma of being sexually abused as a child. Nothing else must therefore be permitted to become a potential informant of identity, for fear that chaos and disintegration would follow. Consequently, there can be no real freedom or openness in relations with others as other (i.e., as transcending norms and expectations derived from abusive dynamics and the sedimented abused identity), nor, therefore openness towards oneself as potentially other than what one is and has become through abuse.

From the perspective of joy in God, we may call this joyless. Where trauma is resolved in the direction of an identity vulnerable to further

---

12. See Farley, *Good and Evil*, pp. 69f., 159ff. for a discussion of idolatry in analogous terms.
13. See above, pp. 74–7.

victimisation, the energies for centring life in and on oneself, for ever-expansive joy in oneself and in others, are dissipated. Unable to value himself, this victim or survivor attaches himself to others in an overly dependent manner. Because this mode of identity expresses itself in high degrees of attachment to particular, significant others (usually one), one may think that it embodies some form of joy in this other. Yet, what we have learned from the defining perspective of joy in God is that joy in oneself and others are indivisible. Simply echoing the other, being nothing distinct for the other, is not joy. For it does not resonate from one's centre with, to and for another. It merely permits the colonisation of one by another, which leaves the other unaffected, unstretched and, perhaps ironically, uncelebrated in the tragic inability to bless the other with oneself. Real joy in the other seeks, not to mould oneself into what one supposes the other needs, wants, desires and will therefore respect, but to be present to and oriented towards his proper integrity in one's own proper and differentiated integrity. For the dynamics of genuine joy involve and require a constellation, concentration and centring of energies around the integrity of each person. It involves that centring of identity that comes with that joy in oneself, which is the correlate of joy in the other. It is the dissipation of the centring energies of joy in himself, and instead the unilateral expending of personal energies in an external direction, which makes the victim so vulnerable to future, repeated abuse. Indeed, the abusive and oppressive behaviour of others comes to be experienced as normal and right, even to be sought as confirming identity.

Similarly, resolving the trauma of abuse through the construction of an abusive identity also undercuts genuine joy in oneself, others and God. Most obviously, a domineering ('proud') self is oriented on mastery and manipulation, not celebration or fulfilment, of the other. Less obviously, since it appears to represent being full of oneself, such an orientation in identity structure undercuts the possibility of genuine fullness and over-flowing of oneself in true joy. Genuine joy in oneself does not constantly seek a repetition of present identity; rather, it involves a readiness to be stretched towards ever richer modes of identity and relationality in communion with others. The overabundance, power and freedom of the oppressive, abusive and proud self is only illusory. Were this a genuinely abundant identity, it would not have to defend itself so anxiously against the claims and limits of others as other, nor against self-transformation and development in response. It would be open towards the full reality of others and the abundance of God, and so open also to the possibilities of self-transformation, the development of its own dynamic order, through contact with such abundance.

Both modes of resolving the trauma of abuse do so through the construction of a non-dynamic equilibrium, which continues to bind identity to repeat, redouble and transmit abusive dynamics. By contrast, joy in God requires, empowers and develops dynamic equilibrium in identity structure and intensifies its proper integrity as a consequence. Dynamic order indicates the capacity of a system to reorder and restructure itself through interaction and relation with other systems and its environment: to change, to be open to a non-repetitive future, capable of refocusing its energies, of reorganising itself through disequilibrium. Having transacted the massive and traumatic disequilibrium of being abused, many children survive as persons by constructing an identity which cannot bear any further disequilibrium. Abused identity is pressed towards the construction of non-dynamic order, resistant to the temporary disequilibrium of relationships that mediate a different order of relationality, values or truth transcending abusive dynamics. Abuse all too easily dissipates the energies of dynamic order, of self-structuring in open relation, instead concentrating the energies of self-organisation into a static structure, stabilised against change, against otherness (transcendence) and futurity.

In theological terms, what is blocked are the dynamics of the triune God and the possibilities of non-distorted worship. God's love of the abused person is easily not trusted or is disbelieved. The direction of the movement of God towards her in blessing and joy, and so the sense of oneself as a locus of joy, is likely to be experienced as counter-factual. Or God becomes the projected means whereby the non-dynamic order of an abused identity is itself secured: abuse somehow serves this god's purposes (deserved punishment, teaching a valuable 'spiritual' lesson, etc.). Furthermore, a static equilibrium in identity structure will not only be resistant to being stretched through joy in God. It will also (if it expresses itself as a need for God at all) require both God's being and the demands of relation with God to be dependable by being static: codifiable into some non-dynamic fundament of belief or practice. God is reduced to what is 'necessary' (stripped back to bare functionality) for maintenance of this rigid identity. Genuine transcendence, and so the grounds for genuine joy, are blocked. In particular, the interplay of creaturely dependence and autonomy in joyful response will prove difficult to hold together, without unbalanced over-emphasis on one side or the other. (It is not insignificant that a number of empirical studies suggest an association between abuse and distortions in the images of God (accompanying those of self, others and world) and of spiritual orientation.[14])

What is damaged and distorted by sexual abuse is the child's relationship to the energies of dynamic order (which, through the creative activity and ordering presence of the triune God, are available 'naturally', as well as through God's explicit communication). Abuse threatens to distort her encounter with the enriching, empowering, energising, life-giving, transforming source of overflowing plenitude and abundance. It threatens to turn her face away from God and from those forms of relation with others which may be mediations of this dynamic, overflowing, abundant life. It threatens to block transcendence and joy in every way and at every level. So sexual abuse is a constriction of and resistance to the richness of life before God and others.

And so the energy of relating to the abundant resources for living humanly in relation to herself, others, the world and God are sequestered and her capacity for joyful encounter with herself, others and the world distorted. Abuse is abuse of the capacity for joy. Or, in theological terms, of worship – of the possibility of standing in the proper economy of thanks and praise of God, which requires dynamic self-affirmation and openness to others in loving joy.

Holocaust

Did the dynamics operating in the holocaust instantiate genuine joy? Again, that sounds an incredibly crass question, but it is one worth pursuing to see whether it might enrich our understanding of the nature and depths of their pathology.

In many ways, Nazi ideology and propaganda appealed explicitly to the motif of joy, most obviously in the slogan 'strength through joy' and by staging constant celebrations of the *Volk*'s blood, race, nation and soil and of the 'triumphs' and the leadership of the regime. More significant perhaps than the communication of positive *ideas*, was the incorporation

---

14. See E. L. Ducharme, 'Variations in God Concept as a Function of Depression and Incest', *Dissertation Abstracts International*, 49 (1988), 3434; D. Finkelhor, G. T. Hotaling, I. A. Lewis and C. Smith, 'Sexual Abuse and its Relationship with Later Sexual Satisfaction, Marital Status, Religion and Attitudes', *Journal of Interpersonal Violence*, 4 (1989), 379–99; Terese A. Hall, 'Spiritual Effects of Childhood Sexual Abuse in Adult Christian Women', *Journal of Psychology and Theology*, 23 (1995), 129–34; Donna Kane, Sharon E. Cheston and Joanne Greer, 'Perceptions of God by Survivors of Childhood Sexual Abuse: An Exploratory Study in an Underresearched Area', *Journal of Psychology and Theology*, 21 (1993), 228–37.

of people into the *practical performance* of explicit celebration, whereby they joined themselves (through their joy) to dynamics, the nature, significance, orientation or extensiveness of which could be masked.

Does such celebration bear the marks of genuine joy? That cannot be decided by a consideration of the object of joy alone. For there is a proper and appropriate place for joy in race, nation, culture, land, etc. in the ecology of joy in the movement of God towards us. God has joy in and blesses us in all our contingent particularities. It is not these particularities which are problematic, but the mode of orientation towards them. So this question has to be rephrased, to ask whether such joy is energised by and towards, or is unplugged from, the dynamics of the triune God. The major clue here, as in relation to abuse, concerns the way in which this joy is particular and particularises.

In the first place, the orientation towards the objects of joy (race, nation, blood, soil) absolutises them as the determinants of the value and truth of everything else, and it does so with claims to objectivity and universality. That is to say, the primacy of loyalty owed by Germans to their race is not relative to some more absolute value, neither is it understood to be contingent upon their being German. Rather, it reflects the believed, actual superiority (indeed, destiny) of one race over others. In other words, this is not a mode of patriotism one would expect to find, and would even affirm, in other races. It is not a particular example of a universal human phenomenon, such as love of country, through which all races and nations may allowedly order their affairs in the international community. And it is certainly not love of country as the most proximate locus for a life-orientation and the exercise of responsibilities transcending the closed boundaries of race: directed towards and established by the movement of God which establishes *universal* human solidarity. Rather, the primacy of the 'Aryan race' is the (material, and not merely formal) principle through which, not only were the loyalties of Germans to be ordered, but the world (or at least Europe) too. Hence, joy in blood, race, nation, soil is unplugged from the dynamics in which God is directed towards all races and nations – indeed, all humanity – and thus becomes an ultimate, non-contingent and non-relative value and commitment.

The dynamics of God are oriented towards all of humanity, the universal human community. Just as the dynamics of God in salvation and creation are unrestricted, unbounded and universally extensive, so the responsibility and commitment of human beings energised by these dynamics is similarly unrestricted: a universal solidarity in the dynamics of creation and salvation, and therefore also of sin. That the dynamics of God are unbounded in their direction for *us* does not undermine the claims of more local horizons of loyalty, but rather contextualises and gives an orientation to them. The particularities of concrete situatedness (such as interpersonal relationships, family, social institution, nation) may be local mediations of the dynamics of God and therefore local, penultimate horizons of joy, loyalty, commitment and responsibility. Hence, we may be called by God in and through these particularities, to have and give joy at more proximate levels (where interaction may usually be more *personal*) than universal humanity. Responding to the dynamics of God's orientation towards universal human community simultaneously involves the intensification of particularities (e.g., other races and nations), but does so by directing joy in and through them towards the (eschatological) reality of universal human community. Hence, proper and responsible joy in one's nation or race, for example, does not create an impermeable boundary around this particularity, so that it becomes a point of separation from and opposition to the good of other nations and races. Rather, it participates in and is directed towards their perfection and an intensification of their particularity. Joy, which participates in and mediates the dynamics of God, is itself oriented towards perfecting and developing the dynamic order of all human particularities in relation to one another. There is, in other words, a transcendent horizon of loyalty, which requires, legitimates and defines committed responsibility at these penultimate levels.

What does it mean for Jews as objects of German policy? Were they objects of joy? Legislation directed against the Jews in the regime's early years could appear to be a means for establishing and preserving Jewish particularity – indeed, it was so experienced by significant numbers of Zionists, who had their own reasons to oppose assimilation and to seek a separate Jewish homeland. However, and not only in the perspective of the eventual development of Nazi policy, such measures were not intended to celebrate, enhance and develop Jewish particularity as a partner in human community. Nazi policy was never oriented towards developing the dynamic order and particularity of 'Jewishness'. Indeed, it was not really oriented towards the particularity of Jews in a substantive sense. Nazi ideology and policy effectively reduced and denied Jewish particularity, notwithstanding its reference to the supposed behavioural characteristic of Jews in public life. Of course, the targeting of public policy against a group (especially when identified irrespective of subjective allegiances) involves a reduction of *personal* particularity, and this is one serious aspect of what I mean here: the reduction of people to one, determining and fixed, concrete (in this case, biological) particularity that removes them from that human community of interpersonal obligations. There was no serious interest in the characteristics of Jewish particularity, as Jews would define that themselves in various ways. For, despite all the anti-Semitic characterisations, in Nazi propaganda, the Jew was a cipher for all that threatened racial order as such, not so much a human or racial particular as a sub-human and racial pathogen.[15] Therefore, Nazi policy not only did not have joy in Jewish identity, it rather denied it had any particular integrity as a locus of joy and blessing. It represented nothing for itself, only a threat to national and international order based on the Darwinian struggle between the races. Jews were weeds or cancerous cells threatening the integrity of (racially ordered) social organisms, rather than social organism with its own, particular integrity.

Nazi policy towards and ideological representation of the Jews was a means for energising and securing German identity, and so tells us at least as much about German as it does about Jewish identity in Nazi intentionality. What we observe in its relentless pursuit of the fantasy of perfection and purity is immense structural rigidity. The intolerance of transcendence we observed in relation to abuse is evident here, but it is marked also by the structure's posture of defensiveness against all potential sources of ambiguity, dissonance or disequilibrium – the elimination of marks of transcendence from within. That the integrity of German identity required racial *purity*, that it was to be *perfect* in these terms, indicates a non-dynamic equilibrium. Its order was to be developed, not through interchange and relation with what is other, but through an artificial separation and distillation of the 'essence' of the Aryan as something in principle unrelated to anything other. Impure elements were to be eliminated, so as to clarify, concentrate and condense 'Aryan blood' and so true German identity, which could not be mixed with anything else without destroying its own proper order and 'degenerating' into a 'mongrel race'. The character and order of German identity was assumed to be known already. Future development could only involve its repristination, repetition or more intense expression, the focusing of all available energies on its reproduction. Yet this anxious repetition cannot signal a genuine joy in German identity, since it is closed off against the possibilities of any genuine self-transformation or

15. See above pp. 84f.

development of its own *dynamic* order, of reorganising itself adaptively when faced with the disequilibrium of, say, changes in the context of international history. It cannot be enriched through any other relationship than with its own (fictionalised) past. Failing to be open towards what is other or ambiguous, it closes itself in on itself, whilst blocking access to transcendent sources of energy and goodness – including its own. The energies of dynamic order are dissipated, concentrated instead into the organisation of a rigid structure, stabilised against ambiguity, otherness and open futurity. The energies of genuine joy in being German and joy in other races (and in God) are dissipated precisely through their separation, and the genuine richness of German identity undermined, along with the possibilities of true worship. (This is reflected in the regime's abuse of Christian symbols and language, its increasing Paganism, and in the *Deutsche Christen*'s rejection of the 'Jewish' elements of the scriptures and of faith, as well as in the general lack of timely theological or church resistance, except on issues of state interference with the churches.)

Significantly, at the *personal* level, the dynamics of Nazi polity and society could departicularise (i.e., depersonalise) identity. It did this in a number of ways, not least by relativising personal identity to that of the group (race, nation, State, Party, military unit): by raising the determining significance of group over personal identity. That could happen through ideological rhetoric, but also through the militarisation of vast numbers of men and the organisation of work and society in the service of national 'destiny', requiring the sacrifice of the centring of life-intentionality at the personal level. The context of struggle and war requires submersion of personal projects to service of the State and personal life-intentionality to be energised by and directed towards the State, Party and nation.

A similar departicularisation of the person occurred through participation in military service and in bureaucratic administration. In both situations, in somewhat different ways, personal particularity was exchanged for a mode of instrumentality. The character of and responsibility for action were depersonalised, shorn of personal particularity,[16] so displacing the possibilities of joy (requiring personal presence in all its particularity).

This departicularising and depersonalising effect of bureaucratic organisation on the *functionaries* of bureaucratic action extended also to

16. Pp. 95f; 118ff.

its targets. Already dehumanised in Nazi ideology (through incremental proscriptions on their behaviour and responsibilities and their removal from the processes, privileges and responsibilities of community), Jews were radically departicularised by Nazi policy. First targets of all-encompassing, bureaucratic administration of their lives (which swallowed all particularity into the designation, 'Jew'),[17] they were then often subjected to treatment designed to disorient and denigrate their humanity and particularity before these were obliterated completely in a death itself stripped of any vestige of particularity. Death, whether it was shooting in the woods or gassing in the camps, was not only the bringing to an end of a particular life, wresting away the organising principle which centres life around a particular, personal life-trajectory and returning its basic material to the non-particular: dust to dust. In mass death, and then in the industrial use of the 'waste product', it denied to this life any semblance of particularity that it might yet have succeeded in retaining.

This is of some significance in our understanding of the distortion and disorientation of Nazi and German joy. But its real significance lies in its effect on the Jews, the difficulties it posed for the retention, let alone the intensification, of Jews' own joy in their personal and Jewish particularity. I have already delineated the ways in which totalitarian Nazi dynamics disoriented and sequestered the active life-intentionalities of its victims. That is to say, the energies of Jews' life-intentionalities were, in practice, directed *away from* the intensification and celebration of personal, cultural and religious identities in their proper integrity and goodness. They were directed instead towards Nazi-defined goals and 'good', which included their own destruction. The massive constriction of human and personal life, which successive Nazi measures imposed on Jews, coupled with the totalitarian dynamics of the Nazi State, placed millions of Jews in circumstances so meagre that it too easily reduced their own integrity and worth as human beings and as Jews. The circumstances of the camps forcibly reduced the lives of many to an orientation confined to the strictly necessary, whilst the scarce and scant supply of necessities pitted them, in their need for basic sustenance, against others.[18] Instead of the excessiveness and abundance of 'more than necessary' joy in themselves, God and others, camp life was deliberately designed to constrict and constrain by reducing people to the needs of their own base, physiological survival. The camps were arranged to invite

17. P. 92.   18. See pp. 102f.

Jews to focus and direct their energies on that necessary to physiological survival: 'reduced to suffering and needs, forgetful of dignity and restraint'.[19] In such a situation, contact with the resources for intensification of the dynamic order of Jewish, personal and communal integrity and identity could understandably be experienced as blocked, and any glimmer of transcendence extinguished.

That blocking of transcendence and the dissipation and disorientation of the energies of dynamic order, of joy in self, others and God, would be serious for any human community, grouping or individual. But for Jews it holds a particular significance, since Jewish integrity is related directly to the vocation to worship, to order itself around and orient itself towards praise of God. 'Israel's vocation is to be a light to the nations: to teach them to worship Yahweh as the absolute, and not to worship the absolutized faculties of their own nations.'[20] Hence, the holocaust, as abuse of the capacity for joyful praise of God (and also therefore of joyful orientation on self and others), threatened the disorientation and dissipation of the energies of Jewish identity, integrity and community. It threatened to extinguish this joyous light of transcendence, both from the Jews themselves and from the rest of the world. It is not insignificant that the possibilities and character of Jewish worship after and in the light of the holocaust have preoccupied Jewish theological, ethical and philosophical responses to it.[21] And it is far more significant too that, even in the camps, there was not a total destruction of the integrity of Jewish vocation, identity and base humanity. Amazingly, each camp had its Lorenzo,[22] Primo

---

19. Primo Levi, *If This is a Man/The Truce* (London: Abacus, 1987), p. 33.

20. Walter Wink, *Unmasking the Powers: The Invisible Forces that Determine Human Existence* (Philadelphia: Fortress Press, 1986), p. 95. Wink goes on to quote from a 1942 article by Martin Buber ('The Gods of the Nations and God', in *Israel and the World* (New York: Schocken Books, 1948, p. 200): that it is because of Jewish negation of national idols that 'every nation is bound to desire to get rid of us at the time it is in the act of setting itself up as the absolute' (Wink's italics eliminated).

21. See, e.g., Richard L. Rubenstein, *After Auschwitz: History, Theology and Contemporary Judaism* (Baltimore: Johns Hopkins University Press, 1992); Richard L. Rubenstein and John K. Roth, *Approaches to Auschwitz: The Holocaust and its Legacy* (Atlanta: John Knox, 1986); Emil Fackenheim, *God's Presence in History* (New York: Harper & Row, 1972); Emil Fackenheim, *To Mend the World: Foundations of Future Jewish Thought* (New York: Schocken, 1982); Emil Fackenheim, *The Jewish Return to History: Reflections in the Age of Auschwitz and the New Jerusalem* (New York: Schocken, 1978); Eliezer Berkowits, *Faith after the Holocaust* (New York: KTAV, 1973); Eliezer Berkowits, *With God in Hell* (New York: Sanhedrin, 1979); Ignaz Maybaum, *The Face of God after Auschwitz* (Amsterdam: Polak & van Gennep, 1965); Arthur A. Cohen, *The Natural and the Supernatural Jew* (New York: Pantheon, 1962); Arthur A. Cohen, *The Tremendum* (New York: Crossroad, 1981); Marc H. Ellis, *Unholy Alliance: Religion and Atrocity in our Time* (London: SCM, 1997); Michael Wyschogrod, 'Faith and the Holocaust', *Judaism*, 20 (1971), 286–94; Irving J. Rosenbaum, *The Holocaust and Halakhah* (New York: KTAV, 1976).

22. Levi, *If This is a Man*, pp. 127f.

Levi and Leo Baeck who, individually or communally, maintained traditions and disciplines of worship, of orienting life towards God,[23] even in
explicit joy,[24] as energised and energising spiritual resistance to the
reduction to bare, physiological necessity: practising what was 'more
than necessary' for survival.

Hence, for the victims of genocide, as well as for perpetrators and
bystanders, being caught up in the dynamics of the holocaust meant
dynamics of life-intentionality being subjected to a powerful force,
pulling in a counter-orientation to their proper, dynamic order. It
meant, in other words, being subjected to a highly energised disorientation away from the abundance of life energised by the dynamics of God.
That entails a disorientation in relation to the abundance and fullness of
one's own identity and integrity. But, since joy is founded on relation to
the dynamics of God, being oriented towards one's own proper abundance is not a matter of enclosed self-reference. Transcendence is rather
foundational to it, it is profoundly and intrinsically relational and therefore thoroughly dynamic. Founding integrity and identity apart from or
in opposition to the dynamics of God, we place ourselves, not only in
some supposed neutrality or separation from God, but outside the movement of God towards the intensification of the being and goodness of all
human beings, of the dynamics and solidarities of universal human community.[25] We pit ourselves against the other, and so separate our good
from that of others, we part celebration of and joy in ourselves from joy
in them. Joy in the other is no longer foundational to our own integrity,
and so the intensification of their particularity can only be a threat to our
own. One of the main marks of pathology, when analysed in relation to
the joyful dynamics of God, is that integrity and identity are founded in

23. See, e.g., Bernard Maza, *With Fury Poured Out: The Power of the Powerless During the Holocaust*
(New York: Shapolsky, 1989), pp. 134–8; Eliezer Berkovits, 'Authenticity of Being', in Roger
Gottlieb, ed., *Thinking about the Unthinkable: Meanings of the Holocaust* (New York: Paulist,
1990), p. 211–16; Yechezhel Harfenes, *Slingshot of Hell* (Jerusalem: Targum, 1988), p. 147ff.;
Pearl Benisch, *To Vanquish the Dragon* (Jerusalem: Feldheim, 1991), pp. 325f.; Yaffa Elach,
Hasidic Tales of the Holocaust (New York: Oxford University Press, 1982); Azriel Eisenberg,
ed., *Witness to the Holocaust* (New York: Pilgrim, 1981), p. 299; Pesach Schindler, *Hasidic
Responses to the Holocaust in the Light of Hasidic Thought* (New York: KTAV, 1990); Bertha
Ferderber-Salz, *And the Sun Kept Shining* (New York: Holocaust Library, 1980), 93f.; Daniel
Landes, 'Spiritual Responses in the Camps', in Alex Grobman, ed., *Genocide: Critical Issues of
the Holocaust* (Los Angeles: Simon Wiesenthal Center, 1983), pp. 266–70; Sylvia Rothchild,
ed., *Voices from the Holocaust* (New York: New American Library, 1981), pp. 157f.; Jack
Kugelmass and Jonathan Boyarin, eds., *From a Ruined Garden: The Memorial Books of Polish
Jewry* (New York: Schocken, 1983), pp. 203–6.
24. Berkovits, 'Authenticity of Being', p. 221.
25. For this reason, solidarity with others is the test of idolatry for Karl Barth (*Church
Dogmatics*, IV/2 (Edinburgh: T. & T. Clark, 1958), pp. 442f.).

separation from, if not opposition to, others. When the bonds of dynamic relation with God are broken, so are the bonds of an, in principle, unlimited, dynamic solidarity with others. Joy is tragically constricted, constrained and reined in, whether to what is strictly 'necessary' to the maintenance of physiological, social or psychological functioning or to the replication or redoubling of a static identity. In the dynamics of God, one's own amplification in joy is indivisible from joy in the other (indeed, in all others). More than that, in the dynamics of God, joy in oneself is not only through, but for the other.

Conclusions and loose ends

I think the above discussion shows both the descriptive and the explanatory power of idolatry in relation to the holocaust and sexual abuse of children. It is evidently possible to re-express the previous descriptions of these pathologies in terms of idolatry, thus showing its descriptive power. But, when idolatry is specified in the terms that have emerged through the trajectory of this book, that is more than straightforward re-expression, translation or re-description which substitutes new terminology without significant alteration in meaning. For the meaning given to idolatry is not containable within the bounds of the frames of reference operating in phenomenological description. Instead, use of the term idolatry, given this theologically specified meaning, draws the non-theological terms, standards and frameworks of interpretation into a theological context, which deepens and enriches their register. Theological language after all holds explanatory power.

At the same time, the journey undertaken through the book, which has specified the meaning of idolatry in a non-conventional way by bringing sin into engagement with the realities of concrete pathologies, has enriched the understanding, not only of idolatry, but of sin as well. The concluding movement has brought the doctrine of sin into much more explicit relationship with the doctrine of the trinity, with worship and with joy than is conventionally the case. That has given a somewhat different twist to the conceptualisation of sin as pathology in relation to God. Sin now appears as energised resistance to the dynamics of God and, thereby, as constriction in the fullness of being-in-communion and of joy. Sin is thus construed primarily in dynamic terms, as highly energised, comprehensive disorientation in, through and of all relationships. Such energised disorientation is also communicable and, whilst the claim of biological transmission has not been amenable to testing in relation to these pathologies, it is clear that this disorientation is transmittable through the dynamics of social relationships. That includes those through which we construct our personhood, identity, life-intentionality (including desire) and sense of what is good, right and true. Sin therefore is not an object of possible choice, external to my will, but a dynamic disorientation already internalised in my will and redoubled with the addition of personal energy I provide through my own willing. All this suggests a working out of the doctrine of original sin in terms of communication, rather than causality.

The universality of sin and of accountability for it also achieves an interpretive shift once it is correlated with the dynamics of joy. Neither the universal solidarity of human beings in our (disoriented) relation to, nor our accountability before, God are created by us as the aggregate of our own, individual, free actualisation of ourselves as sinners. Universal solidarity is not something contingent in that sense on the empirical realisation of sin by *all* people; similarly, accountability for sin is not contingent on our free actualisation of sin and so does not follow lines of causation and moral culpability. The primary referent here is not the supposed freedom of human beings, but the dynamics of God. It depends instead on the direction of the movement of God towards *all* human beings in creation and salvation. It is therefore related primarily, not to the accidentally actualised extensiveness or free, individual realisation of sinning, but to God's determination to bless and have joy in the intensified particularity of all, to draw all together towards an even fuller realisation of joy in the universal solidarities of worshipping community.

From the perspective of the dynamics of God in creation and salvation, we are born into and for joy in a God who loves, blesses and has joy in us.[26] The movement of God is not merely universally extensive, blessing all in individualising joy, and calling us towards a joy in ourselves and God which separates both ourselves and God from the dynamics of God for others. Rather, the dynamics of God particularise rather than (individualistically) individualise. Joy in ourselves and God is at the same time joyous intensification of the particularity of others that knows no exclusions. Joy in ourselves is indivisible, not only from our joy in others, but from *their* joy in themselves, in us and in God. Universal human solidarity

---

26. Is it possible to read Luke's presentation of Jesus as born to a mother singing the Magnificat in these terms – Jesus born into joy in and praise of God? Is it then significant that the gospel closes with the apostles sharing in that blessing and joy? I am grateful to David Ford for pointing this out to me.

of joy in the triune God is something we are both born into and called towards. That is to say, it is also something we are *responsible* and accountable for. Being born and called towards joy that is for all and in all means being both dependent on and responsible for the joy of all others. It means being born therefore into indissoluble universal responsibility and obligation. I cannot be responsible for my own joy without at the same time being responsible for the joy of others. This solidarity of joyful obligation and responsibility is prior to my freedom. Or, rather, it is the dynamic that properly energises and directs my whole life-intentionality. It is authentic being-compelled, in relation to which, freedom must be redefined. No longer may freedom be construed as being constituted in my separation from others and God, but in terms of the intensifying particularisation of my being in relation to the superabundance of God, which intrinsically relates me to the abundant particularity of others. It is an ontology of relation, not separation.

It is in the context of this primal ontology of relation that we must interpret the doctrine of original sin. It is an expression of the *de facto* disorientation of and resistance to the dynamics of joy; that such joyful responsibility for others is never, in fact, fulfilled in situations constituted by dynamics constantly de-energising, disorienting and subverting it. So, original sin may now be read as *de facto* universal, original and radical lack of joy. It is 'original' because it is not a phenomenon of our freedom, but the situational dynamics into and through which our wills are born, formed, energised and directed. And yet it is *sin*, that for which we are held accountable. Guilt is responsibility for the joy of all before the Lord of all. The guilt that is communicated out of our situatedness in pathological dynamics does not, therefore, follow the lines of causality established by the exercise of freedom (in the sense of *liberum arbitrium indifferentiae*). It is more radically relational than that. I am not joined to others through my freedom, after all, but through the dynamics of God in creation and salvation. It is even more radical than the recognition that such distortion so permeates my situation that it is inescapable and I cannot be free from it. If, in the very heart of my 'self', I am born into radical and intrinsic relationality, *for* God and others, then one person's sin would be sufficient to disrupt the entire ecology of joy on which my very 'self' depends, for myself to be 'as another'.[27] If one sins, we are all inextricably involved in the very depths of our being.

27. Cf. Paul Ricoeur's analysis of selfhood in terms of substitution and radical responsibility for others in *Oneself as Another* (Chicago: University of Chicago Press, 1992).

Guilt as accountability before God therefore relates to the call and directionality of the dynamics of God. It means being called to take responsibility in and for our situation in its radical distortions. That is true to the predominant Biblical interest in guilt, not primarily concerned with locating blame, but in calling people to take responsibility for re-energising and reorienting their situation in relation to God (through, say, forgiveness, ritual acts of cleansing, healing, love, sacrifice, reordering the community's affairs). Such responsibility, however, cannot be taken in our own individualised power, since all creaturely dynamics are prone to this radical disorientation. Indeed, pathology is at its most dangerous when it invites us to think that we have such power over it, that we are uninfected by or freed from it in our independently derived capacity to forgive, be moral, love, etc. Sin can only responsibly be faced through grace and only responsibly brought to speech in a language, the predominant modality of which is confession conjoined with thanks and praise offering all back to God. Anything else finds that it is not empowered by grace (the dynamics of God) towards genuine worship and joy, but drawn into idolatrous dynamics that found responsibility on an ontology of separation. That results in constricting strategies of blame built on my supposed separation from the guilt-bearing distortions I am forgiving in others.[28] Instead, genuine responsibility for sin can only be taken in the context of a life-intentionality and orientation energised through worship that joins us to the dynamics of God. In Christian tradition, those dynamics are focused on the incarnation of joy and responsibility in one responsible for all others to the point of death. Or, better, who takes responsibility for others through death to make available anew the energies of a superabundant life of joy in God and all others, more fundamental than either the distortions of sin or creation itself.[29]

Original sin points us to the reality of sin in the context of the superabundance of a God of joy and calls us to meet the pathological disorientations in our situation with an equally radical accountability for them. Incorporation into the dynamics of God through worship does not free us from those distortions, but it does free us for radical responsibility in and through them, calling and energising us to draw its very distortions into the superabundance of life in the dynamics of universal salvation.

---

28. Cf Miroslav Volf, *Exclusion and Embrace: A Theological Exploration of Identity, Otherness, and Reconciliation* (Nashville: Abingdon, 1996), pp. 83ff.

29. Thus the traditions reading cross and resurrection back, through the infancy narratives, to a 'time before all time'.

Index of names

Index of subjects

look-up books/articles on ancient conceptions of freedom (+ Augustine)